Praise for *The Ta*

"*The Tameless Path* by Kamden Cornell is a heartfelt and intentional approach to magical herbalism when encountering invasive plants. This book is a great resource for those who are interested in invasive plants for food, medicine and magic. I really enjoyed the unique recipes,they were given with detailed instructions for use. The author focuses on not only magical applications, but wild foraging recipes for food and also helpful recommendations for medicinal purposes.

There is a significant section on astrological and planetary magic that is somewhat surprising,but adds to the plant work in some respects. The medicine making section is simple and easy to follow, setting the stage for working with the plants. Though not all plants may be in one's bioregion, the ideas and the approach to the applications, along with some of the ingredients, can be inspiration for other magical methods.

All in all, this is a unique book that is sure to bring practical help when 'getting ones hands dirty', which is such an important aspect of working with plants. For the harvesting, the processing and the utilizing of herbs and trees help us to remember the old ways in our day today lives."

—Corinne Boyer, author of *The Witch's Cabinet* and *Under the Bramble Arch*

"An eye-opening look into the world of 'invasive plants,' *The Tameless Path* brings much needed focus on plants that are typically regarded as unwanted and noxious "weeds." Cornell takes the time to get to know each of these resilient, powerful and healing allies on an individual basis sharing a trove of information regarding each plant's medicinal and magical properties. Incorporating green witchcraft, alchemy, and plant spirit work, this book provides the reader with tools for working with these plants—providing medicinal, culinary and occult formulas instilling in the reader that no plant is "bad" or "harmful" and that even the forgotten plants of the wayside have their own unique magic to share with us."

—Coby Michael, owner of The Poisoner's Apothecary and author of *The Poison Path: Occult Herbalism*

"Thoroughly researched and eloquently written, Cornell's new book on invasive plant magic is a paradigm shifting modern grimoire. Not only do we learn why we should work with invasive plants, we also take a deeper look at these so-called "weeds" from a magickal and alchemical point-of-view. The overview on alchemical elements, astrological timing and practical application methods Cornell offers in the book are helpful for both novice and seasoned practitioners; and the Materia Medica-Magica is a wonderful resource to get to know the"weeds" we often overlook or even loath. From *The Tameless Path*, I learned to view the weeds around me differently, even if they are not listed in the book. This is a must-read book for anyone who wants to develop a deeper relationship with Nature, and especially with their local Land."

—Eimi OstaraMoon, owner and founder of Poison and Bee

The Tameless Path

Unleashing the Power of Invasive Plants in Witchcraft

About the Author

An apothecarist and wortcunner, Kamden S. Cornell has an avid love for plants of all kinds. As a bioregional animist and folk witch, they specialize in using the plants around them for their herbal and magical craft. As a non-binary, gay, queer, the outsider perspective is important to them and they are deeply drawn to invasive species, which have been much maligned and persecuted. That working relationship spurred the creation of *The Tameless Path: Unleashing the Power of Invasive Plants in Witchcraft.*

Kamden also teaches classes on foraging, survival, and field herbalism in the Sandia Mountains east of Albuquerque, NM, as well as classes on tarot, alchemy, and witchcraft practices. They own a small, witch-craft-based business called Heart &Vine Apothecary that focuses on herbal remedies and ritual goods. They are the author of two self-published works- *Ars Granorum: The Six Seed Arts of Witchcraft* and *On Needles and Pins: A Witches' Book of Poppetry and Figure Magic.* They are also a regular columnist for *Noumenia News*, the periodical publication released by The Covenant of Hekate.

The Tameless Path

Unleashing the Power of Invasive Plants in Witchcraft

Kamden Cornell

Chicago, Illinois

Paperback ISBN: 978-1-959883-63-0
Hardcover ISBN: 978-1-959883-81-4
Library of Congress Control Number on file.

Cover design by Cho-hyun Kim.
Interior illustrations by Cho-hyun Kim.
Typesetting by Gianna Rini.
Editing by Cole Bowman.

Published by:
Crossed Crow Books, LLC
6934 N Glenwood Ave, Suite C
Chicago, IL 60626
www.crossedcrowbooks.com

Printed in the United States of America.
IBI

Other Titles by the Author

Ars Granorum: The Six Seed Arts of Witchcraft (Acorn Publishing, 2020)

On Needles and Pins: A Witch's Book of Poppetry and Figure Magic (Acorn Publishing, 2021)

Acknowledgments

One person does not make a book like this happen. Not only are there other authors and teachers to thank—all the people from the past who made this book possible—there are also the wonderful people who make the many currently moving parts in the publishing process move smoothly. Each one of them deserves to be honored as part of this process, and, as such, here is a list of the thanks I feel.

Firstly, thank you to my grandmothers on the Green Path, Bernadette Torres and Beverly McFarland. They have both been unbelievably radiant lights guiding me on this path, passing down their knowledge and their stories, and I cannot imagine the life I would have had if I had never met them. Bernadette is the first person who helped me see invasives as other spirits doing their job, which changed my whole viewpoint on herbalism and wortcunning. I feel like the luckiest person in the world for having been able to study with two such passionate herbalists. Thanks also to Sebastian Rose and Robin Moore of Dryland Wilds, the cutest cuties ever to walk the Earth. Their work with invasives and their philosophy on ecology, permaculture, and herbalism have been powerful resources in my own work, and I cherish them dearly.

Thanks are also due to Dara Saville, who is always an inspiration and who egged me on to make this book happen, and to Liz Gaylor, my dear friend and boss at Old Town Herbal, who let me work on this manuscript while I was on the clock. Thank you to my husband, Zachary Sears-Cornell, who supported and helped me as I worked on this project and who worked through the hard times with me.

Thank you to Blake and Wycke Malliway of Crossed Crow Books for seeing the benefit of this book and wanting to publish it. This wouldn't

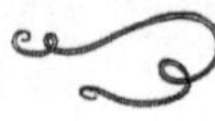

be possible without visionary people like them! Thank you to Cole Bowman, my editor, who made the potentially tedious editing process so fun and smooth. May any aspiring author have an editor like them! Thank you to Becca Fleming, the lead editor, who made the whole book meet and match the beautiful specifications that brought it to life. Thanks to Cho-Hyun, who drew such a gorgeous cover image and internal illustrations. I am gobsmacked by how lovely they all are! Thank you to Gabriella de la Hoya for getting the hardcover version of the book all set up and ready and for making sure I liked the design, and to Gianna Rini, whose work assured that I and other readers can benefit from the beauty that is the gorgeous layout for this book.. Thanks to Francesca Vitali, my publicist, who reached out and got an amazing forward written by the incomparable, fantastic, *stunning* Via Hedera. If you haven't read their book, *Folkloric American Witchcraft and the Multicultural Experience,* please go do so as soon as you can. It is a life-altering work.

I'm not sure of every name and every person who is part of this whole process, but thank you to the Crossed Crow team and the team at Red Wheel/Weiser, along with everyone who supports them in their lives and work. Because of all of you, my dream could float out into the world. I can't express how much I appreciate that and how grateful I will be for the rest of my life. Thank you!

CONTENTS

Chapter 5
MATERIA MEDICA-MAGICA • 83

Chapter 6
HONOR-HERBAL MENTIONS • 230

Spells and Recipes by Weed

Purple Loosestrife

Russian Olive

Siberian Elm

Foreword

In the shadows of the Cascade Mountains, here in the river valley where I make my home, our riverbanks are overrun with creeping bramble, our shores tangled with bittersweet nightshades entwined in poison hemlocks, our trees dangle with ivies, and our waysides are growing thicketed with pokeberry bushes. These herbs are considered somewhat invasive to our region and considered pests to the people, their mass-produced crops, and their manicured lawns. Pricking and poking, puncturing and poisoning. And, by contrast, binding and building, healing and giving, restructuring and reorganizing, feeding and teaching. They cannot be contained, they cannot be eradicated, and balance is careful to keep—especially in environments as fragile and delicate as old-growth forests and wetlands.

It is these same ruthless herbs that cause so much stress to our society that I find most valuable to my work as a practitioner of the old, woody, dirty arts of the land and the dead. These perseverant clingers to life, these reshapers of landscape and lore: they are the most overlooked and yet the readiest to be of service. They rebuke our struggle for control and conformity and rebel quietly, persistently, in protest against their oppressors. Here they stand, ready at hand! A poultice for a rash, a vine for binding a hex, a root for laying a trick—all around us, beckoning to the witch, *"Gather me!"* And so I do.

Like me, these plants are not from the Northwest but have eked out a home here and dug their roots deep into the soft, wet soil. The name, *Via Hedera,* translates roughly from Latin to mean "by way of ivy." Ivy, queen of invasives, has come to represent this particular practitioner's view of witchery as a gripping, binding, chaotic, and all-consuming force of nature. Like the ivy, a witch is a survivor and a spirit capable of both healing and harming virtues. I run my hands along the thorny ropes of bramble and carefully wade through the English ivy that coats the forest floor, and see a mirror of in the soul of witchery itself: the lack of conformity, the unwillingness to be silenced, the patience to weather whatever comes, the wildness to *dare.* Where others see exploitation, eradication, and a threat to resources, we, the wortcunning witches, see a cornucopia, a garden of possibilities. Where society sees a problem to be managed, we see a path to be taken with care and courage. It is a wild path and, by that very nature, a witch's path.

Unlike many sources that shy away from detailing the disturbing callousness with which our land management impacts our lives and futures, this book instead offers readers a glimpse into the cascading impact that our treatment of the land is having on our surroundings and on our spirits, and how we witches can mend this disconnect through reconnecting with our plant allies and all they have to give us, to test us, to teach us. To know that there are other practitioners, just like me, who have come to deeply love the unlovable and passed-over herbs of the green kingdom is of such comfort to me and instills a sense of community between us, an ecosystem being restored with medicine and magic.

I got my first taste of Kamden's flavor of work when I got my hands on a copy of *Ars Granorum,* which introduces readers to Kamden's green-handed ways and the inherent and intrinsic connection between witch and nature. *A Tameless Path* takes readers on a deeper journey into the cunning uses and natural attributes of our most undervalued and overlooked medicinal and magical herbs, their spirits, and their many virtues. This is not your average collection of well-known herbs and popular poisons; rather, this is a unique compendium of knowledge from the herbs you pass every day...the ones that have much to say yet speak so quietly.

Part exploration of spiritual ecology, part practicum in the wortcunning arts, this book approaches both our society's disruptive impact on our ecological balance, as well as the reframing of our perception of invasive plant species when it comes to everyday life—both magical and mundane. Kamden dares contemporary practitioners of witchery to embrace the interconnection between plant and practitioner, between common weed and common witch, as liminal forces, maligned and misunderstood, with so much to offer and so much mystery in store. I ended the final chapter asking myself, *"Do I truly appreciate the green world around me? Do I really know the riches that surround us? Am I grateful for what I have?"* In the end, I am reminded that witches, like so-called "weeds," are misunderstood, useful, fascinating creatures that will not be eradicated entirely.

It's hard to surprise me at this age, so the novel curiosity of being introduced to common plants that I'd hardly heard of nor seen and recipes I'd never tried had been of great cheer for me. As I look over to my herb storage, I grow more curious and glance back at these pages. What will I try next? Juniper arthritis oil for my creaking knees? Horseweed tzatziki for the sabbat potluck? Even as seasoned as I am in working with herbs on a magical and medicinal level, I found so much more information and insight in these pages: new methods I've never tried, connections I'd never thought to make.

As we explore the cosmic, elemental, and practical functions of the invasive ally with our magical guide, we come to see parallels between the witch and the wayside herb, underestimated and vastly powerful forces of nature that can hardly be contained, let alone controlled. These pages serve to instruct beginner and veteran herbalists in the use of our most accessible and easy-to-find herbs, particularly those we least appreciate.

What you read beyond this point is a declaration of rebellion from the expected and mundane—a break from the tired trendiness of our more famous and favored plant allies and a reintroduction to those familiar friends whom many have forgotten: the herbs of byway and highway and unexpected corners. From the wastes to the waysides, these witching herbs carve a green path for the witch to follow, where the ivy grows, where the mimosas sway, where spirits are undeterred, and the path taken is tameless.

—Via Hedera, author of *Folkloric American Witchcraft and the Multicultural Experience*

Atalanta fugiens emblem XLII

INTRODUCTION

What is a weed? A plant whose virtues have not yet been discovered.

—Ralph Waldo Emerson

A. A. MILNE ONCE SAID, "Weeds are flowers too, once you get to know them," a sentiment I wholeheartedly agree with. Though they have been labeled "noxious," "invasive," and even "dangerous," they are truly some of our most loyal kin. They live in the waste places, in the disturbed soils, in the tall grasses at the convergence of the crossroads, and I wish to point them out as a family of herbal allies, which has long been vilified, overlooked, and undervalued. Field bindweed, prickly wild lettuce, dandelion, saltcedar, Tree of Heaven, sweet clover, and plantain, among many others, are all powerfully medicinal and magical plants that have been waiting for us to see them. Their story is much like that of witches, who thrive at the edges of things, at the places where multiple worlds meet and make partnerships, but are hated due to misunderstandings, fear, and propaganda on the part of the powers that be. This book is meant to make introductions between weeds and witches, who I believe are the community who will value them as highly as I do.

My love for invasives began in 2014 when I started studying with my first herbalism mentor, a curandera local to my area. She said, "The medicine you need will grow close to you," which led me to look at the plants volunteering around my home. These were, in large part, what have been called "weeds." Plants like London rocket, Siberian elm, and horseweed, which were growing from the cracks in the sidewalk and on the margins of my garden, became my focus. I discovered that plants like those are good for digestion, anxiety, immunity, muscle soreness, and so much more than I ever thought them capable of…and were all available for free right outside my door.

What we call "weeds" have been used as remedies and food for thousands of years in the regions they were native to before being transplanted to our own soils. Many of them became useful to Native American populations in North America and, over the last few centuries, have developed lore here in the Americas. Though these "weeds" had already been adopted into local herbalism practices and naturalized into ecosystems, they were never spoken of in the herbalism and botany-related circles I found myself in. In fact, the mention of invasives was enough to start enormous debates and vitriolic exchanges about which of them were the worst and which ones needed to be eradicated the fastest. The mention of invasives in a positive light fomented even greater anger, often with myself becoming the focus of my peers' animosity.

Later, I met a couple running a local perfumery and botanical beauty business, Dryland Wilds, that relies on invasive plant species and trail trimmings left behind by the US Forest Service. We bonded over our love of marginalized plants, and they began to teach me more about the invasives that they work with, such as Russian olive and honey mesquite, musk thistle, and purple loosestrife. I fell even more deeply in love with the tenacity and potency of the plants so many others had deemed paradoxically valueless and dangerous.

Perhaps it was the image of them as dangerous that attracted me in the first place, that made them feel familiar. I soon found that they were the farthest thing from a danger to anyone, though, most of all to the environment. I found that, contrary to what "invasive biology" teaches, there is no enemy in Nature, particularly posed against Nature itself. There can be no true antagonism, no *threat*, between an ecosystem and a given plant, let alone a threat from a plant toward humanity, even if it is dandelion, garlic mustard, saltcedar, or kudzu. Rather, their naturalization into an environment relies on coming to a gradual understanding that leads to the betterment of all involved, which may take centuries or millennia. That is what ecosystems are: a long conversation. That is not to say that "invasives" do not require strict management, as all plants do, to create the fertile gardens we crave. It *is* to say that there is no such thing as a bad or evil plant—which is a dangerously false notion.

For the most part, invasive plant species are not spoken of in any detail, especially in works of magical herbalism. Weeds are considered just boring, dusty plants by the roadside, not really worthy of mentioning because… well, they're worthless. That just isn't true; it's just what we've been led to believe. Many authors prefer to write about the showy European plants found in grimoires or, more recently, the plants of the *via venenum,* the Poison Path—another of my favorite topics. Poisonous plants are enigmatic, powerful, seductive, and very exciting, making for an interesting subject matter, where the European herbs spoken of in the works of herbalists like John Gerard[1] and botanists such as Nicholas Culpeper,[2] along with the works of their peers, are attractive because of their long history in medicinal and magical practice. The same plants are cycled through book after book after book. Now, the weeds will get a bit of the spotlight.

What is a weed? A weed is a plant whose negative qualities we believe outweigh their positive ones, *if* they have any positive traits at all. Weeds grow where they are not wanted and compete with more desirable plants for light, nutrients, water, and attention. A weed is an *un*desirable thing and, therefore, an enemy, particularly when it comes to the cultivation of chosen plants or agriculture. That kind of thinking is even applied to certain plants in wild spaces, and it is said that they are greatly detrimental to the ecosystems in which they live, particularly if those plants are "alien" to the ecosystem in question (even if they've lived there for hundreds of years). In that case, they are not only weeds but "noxious" or "invasive," and we have decided that it is up to us to wage war against them to save Nature. Again, I want to make this clear: there is no such thing as a bad or worthless plant. The perceived hostility between Nature and weeds is entirely a human invention, for the Earth is just trying to do what it always *has* done.

Witches know that the Land speaks and that we can *trust* the voice of the Land. Invasive species are a sign that the Land is fighting back, trying to reach balance in the only way it can: through adaptation. The plants

---

1 John Gerard (1545–1642) published a mostly plagiarized work called the "Herball," an enormous tome of nearly 2,000 pages. It is complete with a great number of woodcut illustrations of plants.

2 Nicholas Culpeper (1616–1654) was a renowned botanist, herbalist, and medical astrologer whose work is integral to the art of planetary herbalism as presented in this book.

that have been labeled as "unwanted invasives" by some are here for a reason. They are the new inhabitants of the Land, filling ecological niches that have been vacated by plants that can no longer sustain themselves or that have been created by the incredible ferocity of human modifications. Invasive plants mostly occupy environments that can be described as "highly modified" by human presence, a description of almost every ecosystem on Earth. Due to climate shift and ecosystem degeneration, many native plants simply cannot survive where they have been for thousands of years.

The Land, the weather, the air, the water...all aspects of the ecological context in which plants evolved to become "native" are simply too altered for those same plants to survive as they have for centuries, meaning ecosystems must quickly adapt by bringing in new plants that *can* survive into an uncertain future. Invasives fulfill those roles. They provide food to pollinators and the small herbivores of the forest in otherwise barren areas, they remediate the soil and water polluted by human activity, and provide shade and shelter for insects, birds, and mammals of every kind. They are here to rewild the land and wrest control from human interest. They don't give a fig about profits or the bottom line, which is *why* they have been denigrated.

Witches see the reality of situations, and this is no different. Plants are called "invasive" or "harmful" not because they are harming the Land, but because they are a threat to the human economy. The "War on Weeds" is all about money, the ever-increasing production of which requires the total subjugation of the Land to human hubris and commercial agriculture. Soybeans, beef cattle, canola, and so many other crops are raised on US soil as a matter of course, though they are non-native. Enormous amounts of land are stripped of native flora and grasses, flattened, synthetically fertilized, and tilled to plant monocrops of non-native food plants, some for human consumption and others to feed astronomical numbers of farmed animals. The latter are housed in too-small spaces, filled with chemicals and antibiotics, fed poorly on crops they can't digest well, and finally harvested themselves. The land is torn apart, and the life on it is abused to *support* alien plants, which, if they were less profitable, would be called "invasives." Nothing we do agriculturally is for the benefit of life or the Land itself; it is *only* for profit.

The proof for this assertion is the fact that, even though we grow more than enough food to feed every human *and* all the animals we farm, there are still starving people. More food than we could ever use is produced from the Land, food that we end up wasting, food that just rots in unbelievable amounts. Still, we rip food from the Land, depleting and damaging it in the process so that more and more can be sold for greater and greater profit. Yet the blame for failing ecosystems and pollinator declines falls on invasive species, which are considered the second most dangerous thing to the health of the Land after wildfire.[3]

Further proof that health and life are not real concerns in agriculturally oriented invasive biology models is found in the methods of invasive species control. Along with manual and mechanical removal that rip apart ecosystems, these have a heavy reliance on the the herbicidal elimination of unwanted species. Glyphosate, 2,4-D, and imazapyr are three of the most frequently used active ingredients in herbicides, along with a slew of "inert" ingredients that are part of secret, proprietary blends, all of which are known toxins that damage the Land.[4] Herbicides are not meant to *protect* anything, only to poison and kill. I would rather have the weeds.

The point of this book is to shed some light on why and how invasive plants *are* desirable, particularly to magical practitioners. My specialty as an herbalist is in the use of invasive plants for remedial purposes, and because of that relationship, invasives have also become a specialty of mine when it comes to magic and charm work. I think they are some of the most potent plants a person can choose to work with. Invasives are strong and tenacious: they adapt quickly, and they can survive in conditions many plants find too harsh. In fact, they heal the Land so future plants *can* live in those harsher places and do a damn fine job of it. Because these plants are prolific in the areas they colonize, though, they are free to gather, and taking them does not cause detriment to the environment or damage a plant community. Gathering them actually helps the environment reach balance. Using invasives in our practices is a way of working *with* the Land rather than against it.

Let us, the witches, who have been called dangerous and evil, who have been the scapegoats for society's problems, who have been chased to the margins of the places and societies we call home, join the fight. Let us unite with our Green siblings and build not only a powerful relationship with them, but a new way of relating to the Land that

3 For more on this, see "Four Threats" at www.fs.usda.gov.

4 See Orion, pages 13–43, for more on herbicides.

creates unbreakable resiliency in a holistic community on the edge of things. We know that Nature does not believe in boundaries the way that humans do, that Nature flows and changes in its own way, and that Nature perpetuates patterns according to its own ancient knowledge. The beauty and diversity of wayside places and invasive herbs are proof enough of this. Let us break down the arbitrary and imaginary borders and boundaries between species. Let us at last become a family in the tall grass where the crossroads converge.

Each chapter in this book is meant to help the reader do just that. How better to get to know a plant than to spend time with it, to learn its history, ecology, and the ways we can help each other? The following will be filled with information not only on magic and witchcraft but also on the philosophical problem of invasives and invasive ecology, planetary magic and alchemy, herbal remedies made with invasives, ways we can forage from them to make food, the folklore of the invasive plants, and more. My hope is to help the reader become very well acquainted with these wonderful plants and to bring them wholly into relationship with each other so they can support, empower, and enrich one another as well as the environments they live in. I believe that is possible.

Kamden S. Cornell
Albuquerque, NM
November 2023

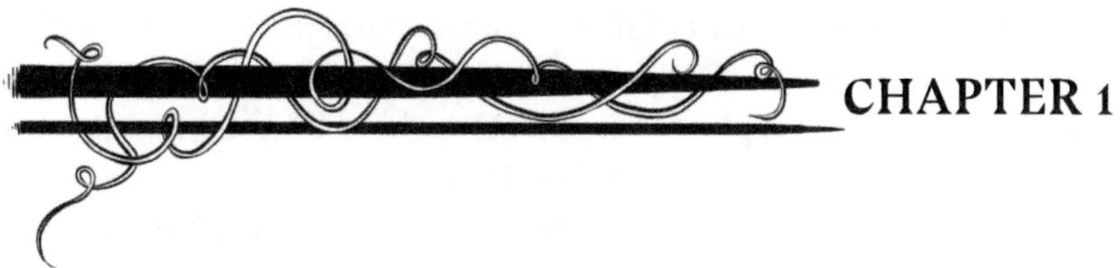

CHAPTER 1

The War on Weeds

I WANT TO PREFACE THIS CHAPTER with an idea that may act as a lens for the rest of the book, so keep in mind these first few lines. Ecosystems the world over are on the brink of collapse, and the hands on the Doomsday Clock tick closer to midnight than they ever have before as we stand on the cusp of the sixth great mass extinction. We cannot change that, but we may still have hope of mitigating the disasters that follow. To do so, we *must* shift our perspectives on land management and begin to see ecosystems as finely woven tapestries created by *all* species that live on the Land, especially when it comes to invasive plants.

Our ideas about these plants are backward and lead us toward greater ecological decay. The current methods to control them, such as ecosystem rehabilitation that focuses on eradication efforts, are myopic, short-term, money-centered, and ultimately detrimental to the health of the Land. A broader picture must come into focus, one where invasives are a *part* of the ecosystems they "invade" because they *aren't* going anywhere. If we can pull our vision back and see their place in the ecosystem, what they are doing, how they can be helpful, and how *we* can steward them into a more biodiverse future where they can serve all life on Earth... they will be the saviors of our future on this planet.

The importation and dissemination of different crops was once supported, facilitated, and encouraged by the US government for a long while. John Quincy Adams, the sixth president of the United States, in office from 1825–1829, even established a national policy of introducing plants "of whatever nature...for purposes connected with...any of the useful arts."[5] Various plant species have been introduced to the US for very practical, beneficial purposes, from halting soil erosion to providing new food crops to the enjoyment of their beautiful foliage, flowers, and fruits. In fact, most of the rampantly spreading invasive species that are now some of the most hated plants were first brought to US soil intentionally, such as kudzu, Russian olive, and Siberian elm.

Siberian elm was introduced to the US as early as the 1860s and was chosen by the United States Department of Agriculture (USDA) as the most suitable shelterbelt and windbreak tree to help remediate ecological disasters brought on by the Dust Bowl, itself a result of agricultural mismanagement. It was pushed in the 1950s, again by the USDA, as a replacement for privet species[6] for the creation of hedges. It has since spread into almost every state and ecosystem on the continent and is decried as one of the most invasive, least desirable trees, with some even saying it "does not deserve to be planted anywhere" and that it is "One of… the world's worst trees."[7] Can any plant be truly "bad"? I don't think so.

This notion of importing all sorts of plants without thorough research may have been somewhat misguided, but not any more so than the current philosophy of "eradicate at all costs" regarding invasive species generally. "The War on Weeds" has been raging since the 1970s with the Federal Noxious Weed Act of 1974,[8] though the philosophy of "plant pests" has been developing since the mid-1940s commensurate with the invention of herbicides as weapons of chemical warfare. These toxins were developed to be sprayed on the food crops of enemy nations for the express purpose of starving them into submission.[9] The known and unknown medical side effects of those poisons were just a bonus for the war machine. Now we spray them on our *own* crops and say it is to protect the people and the environment, which is, frankly, laughable.

The most common herbicides in the US are glyphosate and 2,4-D, which we will go over very briefly. The older of the two is 2,4-D, which

5 See Scott 9.

6 Privet is a family of small, evergreen trees native to Asia. Today, they are considered invasive and are spread throughout most continents.

7 See Dirr 1179.

8 A PDF of the Act can be found at www.govinfo.gov/app/details/STATUTE-88/STATUTE-88-Pg2148.

9 See Orion 13–15 for more on this topic.

stands for 2,4-dichlorophenoxyacetic acid, a chemical developed in 1945 by Dow Chemical for use in the biological weapon Agent Orange. What has become enormously clear over time is that Agent Orange and the chemicals that make it up cause cancer and neurological disorders in those exposed to them. Even so, we spray 2,4-D on our food crops as a broad-leafed plant killer, targeting things like plantain and dandelion. It acts to interrupt endocrine (hormonal) cascades, thus causing uncontrolled growth of certain cells within a plant, leading to defoliation and death, meaning it is *meant* to cause cancer.[10]

Even so, evidence is inconclusive, and 2,4-D cannot be blamed directly, as it was mixed with other possibly hazardous chemicals until the 1990s, such as dioxin, though it *has* been called "a possible human carcinogen" since 2015.[11] Because it is an endocrine pathway disruptor, multiple studies have shown a likely link between 2,4-D and hormonal disorders, particularly those involving androgens (testosterone), estrogens, and, most especially, thyroid hormones.[12] This means that it deals directly with reproductive and developmental disorders, of which there has been a marked increase every year, and that pregnant people, fetuses, and children are the most directly at risk. Yet, no studies have been done to determine the effects of the chemical on those populations.[13]

---

10 Everything in every living body is regulated and controlled by hormones, which are part of a biological chemical messaging system. They are the language of adaptation in the body, helping us to regulate ourselves to new phenomena as they occur, and are essential to processes controlling things from immunity, cell growth, body heat regulation, libido, and even outlook. They tend to be triggered by each other or by stimuli from the nervous system, which will then trigger another hormone to release, and then another, thus creating cascades of inter-regulatory commands that the body requires to function properly. When hormonal cascades are altered, so are the accurate workings of every bodily system and, in the case of something like 2, 4-D, leads to an overgrowth of cells and eventual death.

11 See Sedbrook (and also Orion 31-32) for more on the history of 2, 4-D.

12 See NPIC, 2, 4-D, and Orion pages 13-43 for more on how 2, 4-D affects the environment, how it persists, and how it spreads.

13 See Sedbrook for more on the effects of 2, 4-D in underrepresented populations.

Not only that, it has been linked to things like bladder cancer in dogs[14] and has been suspected of causing cancers in aquatic animals, as it persists not only in the ground but also in groundwater and drinking water, and it leaks into aquatic environments from inland farms. It can also spread through the air, as it is commonly dusted over crops with aircraft, and can be tracked into homes by humans and animals. Nevertheless, it is now even more prolifically used than it used to be, as it has been combined with the most used herbicidal chemical, glyphosate, in a product called Enlist Duo. This was patented by Dow Chemical Company and the Monsanto Company as a replacement for the Roundup Ready herbicides that are now less effective due to adaptation by the plants they kill. The chemical combo is contentious, even with the US Environmental Protection Agency, because of conflicting reports of toxicity, though it is still approved for use in thirty-four states.[15]

The other herbicide, glyphosate, acts on something called the shikimate pathway, a metabolic process that leads to the production of an enzyme called shikimic acid, interrupting the ability of plants to moderate their immunity, essentially giving them a sort of acquired immune deficiency.[16] Glyphosate is likely the best-known and most prolifically used herbicide as it is a broad spectrum, nonspecific plant killer, though it was originally patented as a metal chelator[17] and cleaner in 1964 by Swiss chemist Henry Martin. In 1970, it was developed independently by Monsanto while they were experimenting with derivatives of aminomethylphosphonic acid as possible water-softening agents. It was noticed that a couple of these had an herbicidal action, and Monsanto paid a chemist named John E. Franz to make them more potent. His third try rendered glyphosate, for which he earned several rewards, among them the 1987 National Medal of Technology and the 1990 Perkin Medal. Monsanto patented his glyphosate formula in 1974 under the name Roundup.[18]

---

14 See Knapp and also Orion 13-15 for more on 2, 4-D and canine bladder cancer.

15 See the 2015 article by Dan Charles on NPR about Enlist Duo and the controversies surrounding it.

16 See Orion 33-35 for more on glyphosate.

17 Chelation is a chemical process by which ligands are bonded together with singular metal ions, thus making certain minerals much easier to clean up with simple surfactants. The same process is used to chelate heavy metals from within the body during acute toxification.

18 See Dill for more on the history of glyphosate.

In the 1990s through to the present, Roundup has been paired with genetically modified seeds, which are called Roundup Ready,[19] meaning that glyphosate could be sprayed liberally on these crops, killing weeds but not endangering crop plants. It became wildly popular as the leading system in the US by 2007, and glyphosate has become the most marketed herbicide worldwide.[20] In 2016, Monsanto introduced Roundup Ready Xtend soy crops, which are also resistant to the herbicide dicamba.[21] At the time the seeds were introduced, Monsanto projected that cropland planted with the seed would be 50 million acres by 2020. Already, over 80% of crops (if not more) in the US are genetically modified to rely on glyphosate-based herbicides, almost 42% of the entirety of US land base.[22]

Study after study shows that glyphosate is only mildly toxic and only in high, undiluted doses,[23] but just because we *can* does not mean that we *should* be consuming *any*, especially *every* time we eat! Cumulative exposure *does* seem to have a connection to non-Hodgkin's lymphoma in humans and in cases of kidney and pancreatic cancer and hemangiosarcoma in lab animals, though many studies say there isn't *enough* evidence (though *any* evidence is enough for me, honestly).[24] Still, even with the IARC calling it "likely carcinogenic to humans," the official jury is out when it comes to glyphosate and its status as a carcinogen, so it has been sanctioned for use time after time. One further point: Because glyphosate is a metal chelator, it may also bind minerals in the soil, making them difficult for plants to uptake. Copper, zinc, magnesium, manganese, and other trace minerals are deficient in our crop foods in the US, at least in part due to our heavy dependence on this agrochemical, meaning we are growing plenty of food…it's just covered in chemicals and not very nutritious.[25]

---

19 These crops include soybean, corn, canola seed, sugar beet, cotton, and alfalfa, with wheat being in the process of becoming one.

20 See Costas-Ferreira for more on this and the effect of glyphosate on the nervous system.

21 A chemical very similar to 2,4-D and one that has links to an increased risk of developing non-Hodgkin's lymphoma, especially in testicle-having people.

22 View statistics at www.ers.usda.gov/data-products/adoption-of-genetically-engineered-crops-in-the-u-s/recent-trends-in-ge-adoption/.

23 See Berry for an opposing view to the ones presented in this book.

24 See Berry.

25 See Mertens, and also Orion 35, for more.

It isn't only the chemicals themselves that are dangerous in herbicides, either, as formulations are usually "adjuvant loaded," meaning they are mixed with surfactants and other chemicals meant to make them more effective. Many of these cocktails are undisclosed and proprietary, so they cannot be truly monitored, though they likely make their way first into soil and water and then into our bodies.[26] We also have very little to no idea of the effect herbicidal chemical cocktails have on microbial life in the soil, which is the very backbone of the food web. Not to mention that herbicides are also used in tandem with insecticides and fungicides, reducing mycorrhizal[27]and pollinator populations in huge swathes of Land. These chemicals seem far more dangerous to the health of humans, animals, and the Land than any invasive species could ever be, yet it is invasives that get the blame.

We may ask, "Why must we eradicate invasive plants and animals at any cost, even poisoning our own food supply? What makes them so dangerous?" The USDA lists them as the second most dangerous thing to the health of forests and wild spaces. Their website says of invasive species:[28]

> *These invaders cause massive disruptions in ecosystem function, reducing biodiversity, and degrade ecosystem health in our nation's forests, prairies, mountains, wetlands, rivers, and oceans. Invasive species affect the health of not only the nation's forests and rangelands, but also the health and survival of wildlife, livestock, fish, and humans.*

This perspective is entirely backward. If invasive species are flooding ecosystems at such an alarming rate that it seems there is a new, menacing species everywhere you look, that would mean there is a very great variety of species in a given area, even if they are not all native ones. And, if the Land were not already degraded via human activity, invasives would not be such a problem, meaning they are not the *cause* of the reduction in biodiversity or of ecosystem disruption, but opportunists doing their

---

26 See Orion 26–36.

27 The term "mycorrhizal" refers to the symbiotic relationship between fungi and the root systems of plants. These are extremely important to the health of both partners, each providing nutrients to the other and aiding in each other's immunity and ability to adapt to changes in the soil.

28 See more on the USDA website: www.fs.usda.gov/projects-policies/four-threats/.

job. If we look at it honestly, the greatest threat to biodiversity in every ecosystem is the development of the Land for human use, period. We destroy millions of acres of diverse ecosystems to build housing, strip malls, baseball parks, and parking lots and to plant monocrop fields of soy, corn, and wheat that stretch as far as the eye can see, all the while allowing our farmed animals to overgraze and trample through what grasslands are left. If there is an invasive threat to biodiversity, it isn't any of the species listed as such.

So, what qualifies as an invasive species when it comes down to it? The USDA defines an invasive species thusly:

> *As per Executive Order 13112 (Section 1. Definitions) an "invasive species" is a species that is: 1) non-native (or alien) to the ecosystem under consideration and, 2) whose introduction causes or is likely to cause economic or environmental harm or harm to human health.*[29]

According to the above definition, it is humans themselves that fit the bill most closely, but the USDA and other US government agencies don't see it that way. The Plant Protection Act of 2000 defines "noxious weeds" as

> *...any plant or plant product that can directly or indirectly injure or cause damage to crops (including nursery stock or plant products), livestock, poultry, or other interests of agriculture, irrigation, navigation, the natural resources of the United States, the public health, or the environment.*[30]

The PPA also states that, "(1) the detection, control, eradication, suppression, prevention, or retardation of the spread of plant pests or noxious weeds is necessary for the protection of the agriculture, environment, and economy of the United States."[31]

The semantics used by governmental agencies, such as the USDA and others that oversee legislation, are clearly telling. When the word "agriculture" is placed *before* "environment" and used as part of a sentence

---

29 See the USDA website: www.usda.gov/topics/invasive-species.

30 Plant Protections Act, Section 10.

31 Ibid. Section 1

also containing the word "economy," we can be sure that it is not the overall health of ecosystems that is of concern. Rather, the "health" of the Land as it pertains to the agricultural industry and the profit that the government derives therefrom is of primary concern. The US government has proven time and time again that the health of the Land is not as important as a healthy wallet, and it is that intense, short-sighted avarice that is the greatest problem facing us today.

Let's return to the USDA's list of ecological threats, as I think that may shed some light on what we are dealing with and clarify the skewed perspective with which we approach invasives. The first concern on their list is "fire and fuel," meaning overgrown forests and grasslands that have become tinderboxes. On the USDA website, the first sentence of their explanation for this making the list is,

> *Many of our fire-adapted forests have become overgrown and unhealthy. For example, historically ponderosa pine forests were extremely open, with a few dozen trees per acre. Today, we might have hundreds or even thousands of small trees crowded into the same area.*[32]

This is solely because of poor policy and ineffective, naïve land management that allows forests and grasslands to become "wilderness" because they are not arable.

In the book *Beyond the War on Invasive Species,* Tao Orion draws attention to the fact that for millennia, Native American peoples across the North American continent were actively stewarding the land before colonization occurred.[33] They took out the trees that were unnecessary, leaving large, open areas in forests that allowed other life to grow and were also importing food, dye, and utilitarian plants that were nursed into a good relationship to the Land. They were also managing the Land through low-intensity burning and conscious disturbance techniques that did not cause massive damage to forests and soil the way the raging wildfires of today can. Biodiversity flourished, food was abundant, water was clean, and the forests were healthy. The *entire continent* was a garden!

---

32 See the US Forestry Service website: www.fs.usda.gov/projects-policies/four-threats/.

33 Orion 139–145.

Early colonizers didn't see it that way, though. Because indigenous gardens weren't crop plots, the Land wasn't cut into pieces and parceled out into profitable agricultural units. They thought the indigenous people were unwise and unaware of how to use the Land "properly," that they were a rudimentary civilization living in the primitive chaos of uncultivated "wilderness," when, in fact, the colonizers were standing in a thriving, living, masterpiece garden that supported all the life that lived on it.[34] Now, we have for-profit monocrops that survive via millions of metric tons of herbicide, insecticide, and synthetic fertilizer, which is a very poor turn of events, in my estimation.

The concurrent problem that the first USDA bullet point about forest fire fails to make clear is that overcrowding of trees in forests not only leads to wildfire danger but also amplifies pest and disease infestation of trees. Things like bark beetles, fungi, viruses, borers, and all the rest of the parasites and pathogens that invade trees have a *much* easier time spreading in crowded, sickly forests. These forests also tend to have depleted soil because there are too many trees competing for resources, meaning they don't have what they need to maintain a good immune system to fight off these pests. Because of the too-dense canopy and overshading issues, there are also not enough companion and partner plants helping to remediate the soil, especially when we are purposefully eradicating some of the best plants for the job (i.e., the invasives). Eradication efforts are hard on the Land as well, further weakening the forest ecosystem and leading to further illness and decline. Though it may feel as if we are taking meaningful steps to turn the tide of ecological degradation when we go out to clear stand after stand of invasive plants, we are effectively hobbling ourselves and our environments with these misguided crusades against plants and furthering decline.

The USDA goes on to say that after an uncontrolled fire in an overcrowded forest, "The trees are dead, the watersheds that feed our municipal water systems are degraded, the soil is cooked of its nutrients, and the wildlife is killed or left homeless." This relates to the third item on their list, habitat loss, which they refer to as "open space."[35] Because of intense

---

34 See Orion 139–164 for more on the myth of "wilderness" and how colonization has affected the Land.

35 This is just another way of saying "wilderness, but accessible to humans." All of their language is anthropocentric and puts themselves in the light of right action.

and expansive commercial, domestic, and agricultural development, there are fewer and fewer spaces for animals and plants to live. The estimate, according to the USDA, is that four acres of the Land are lost to development *every minute.*[36] We have displaced animals and plants from their native homes and built on top of the wreckage, then blame them for the issues we see in the only places they have left to live.

We have accomplished this so thoroughly, in fact, that "wilderness" apart from developed areas became an idealized, romantic notion. The works of philosophers and poets like John Muir, Henry David Thoreau, and Aldo Leopold push forth this idea that the wilderness is a place that feeds the soul and needs to be kept safely apart from human interference and degradation. This led to some of the policies that left forests alone as "wilderness areas," ignored for their own good, an ecological form of Ferberization.[37] It was thought that by letting the forests be, we were helping them, though that was never the case. It was just a notion based on colonized misinformation. The beauty of the "wild" that Muir wrote about was the vestige of a well-managed and cared-for ecosystem left to its own devices for a few centuries because the Native stewards had been forcibly removed from them. They were far from "untouched."

The final thing on the USDA's list of ecological threats is "unmanaged recreation," which is the closest they get to admitting that thoughtless human activity is the core problem leading to ecological decline. It is also one of the places I agree with them. I am an animist, and my practice and philosophy reflect that. Everything down to the last speck of dust is a part of the spiritual community, everything has a consciousness and a voice, and everything *matters.* I think we should be mindful that the Land knows what it needs and has been taking care of itself for billions of years, but also that humans have acted as stewards of the Land, working in its service and to its benefit. Animism is far from the common consensus, it turns out, and most people tend to take the Land for granted, as just an inert *thing* we happen to live on instead of the sentient, conscious source of all life. Instead of honoring and loving the soil, we ride ATVs

---

36 You can find this statistic here: www.fs.usda.gov/science-technology/open-space-conservation.

37 *Ferberization* refers to Dr. Richard Ferber, the physician who, in 1985, advised parents to let their babies "cry it out" to learn how to put themselves to sleep. His work on sleep training has largely been criticized as negligent.

over it, pour our waste out onto it wherever we camp, rip branches from trees, tear up the flowers, muddy the waters, strew garbage and dog scat on our surroundings, and in a multitude of ways treat the Land like a free-for-all rage room that we go to for relaxation.

The main problem facing every ecosystem on Earth is human activity because so many of our relationships with the Land and its resources are extractive and built around how we can best capitalize off those resources in the short term. Corporate farming is an enormous issue, as it farms money, not food, and it creates a separation of people from the Land, which is a destructive thing. We need to change our perspectives and pull our vision back to see the larger picture of what is happening, and invasives are here to help us do so. They are little red flags that say, "This ecosystem is damaged, and we need to start the process of remediation."[38]

The soil is not the only thing being affected by the way we treat the Land, either, because the waters are becoming more and more polluted the world over. Our fertilizer use, chemical fracking, and mining practices, as well as the waste produced from factories, the runoff created by roadways, and *so* many other factors lead to high levels of various chemicals, heavy metals, nitrogen, and salt in the waterways. Invasives are some of the only plants that can withstand these conditions and help to purify the waters over time, including invasives like tamarisk, knotweed, and purple loosestrife, though the most toxified waters need a bit more help.

One of my favorite invasive plant stories is about a place called the Berkely Pit,[39] an open-pit copper mine located in Butte, Montana, established in 1955 and abandoned in 1982. This single, mile-long, half-mile-wide pit is an ecological timebomb because approximately 900 feet of its 1,780-foot depth is filled with water that is about as acidic as stomach acid and has been leeching toxic minerals, such as arsenic, cadmium, zinc, copper, and sulfur, from the surrounding rock. The toxic water has risen to within 150 feet of the water table that feeds Butte's drinking water. In 2003, a nineteen-million-dollar water treatment plant

38 The term "remediate" does not actually refer to stopping or reversing ecological damage, but remedying it. It takes into account that there is no "going back," but acknowledges that steps can be taken to prepare the soil for greater biodiversity over time.

39 For an interesting article on the Berkeley Pit, see Dobb.

was established, which is meant to clean up the water from the pit and slow the rate at which the water rises, but it cannot stop it.[40]

Since the 90s, the pit has killed thousands of migratory birds, such as geese, which spurred an interesting development when a colony of *Euglena* that was possibly carried in their feces moved into the pit.[41] *Euglena* is a flagellate protozoan that colonizes the surface of water and forms algae-like mats, turning the surface a slimy, greenish blue. The colony in the Berkely Pit, *Euglena mutabilis,* is a novel species that has adapted to the toxic environment and has begun producing novel, toxic compounds (berkelydione, berkelytrione, and berkelic acid, now being studied for their use against cancer cells). The compounds are created as the *Euglena* feeds on the toxic minerals in the water, thus cleansing and purifying it! The heavy metals they eat end up isolated in the bodies of these microorganisms and sift to the bottom of the pit when they die.

Euglena are intermediate between animal- and plant-like organisms, both photosynthesizing *and* searching for food. As they feed from the Berkely Pit waters, they oxygenate it and precipitate iron, which provides stability for other species to grow amidst, meaning these little organisms are helping to manufacture a novel ecosystem. Over forty species of microorganisms, including several other novel species, have been discovered in the Berkeley Pit since the initial invasion by *Euglena*. In fact, species like them are the only reason life exists on Earth today, as they provided remediation for primordial water and soil and created oxygen at levels that can support life.[42]

Another interesting point to note about these organisms: studies show that the organelles of *Euglena* species have different DNA than their nuclei, meaning their ancestors were likely single-celled organisms that came to coexist as one multicellular organism through symbiogenesis.[43] This same process is evident in the bodies of all eukaryotic species as the

40 Orion 87–89.

41 Ibid 87.

42 Ibid 88.

43 Symbiogenesis is the currently accepted model for the evolution of eukaryotic cells (i.e., cells with a membrane-bound nucleus). The theory states that ancient prokaryotic (non-nucleic) cells may have absorbed or "eaten" one another, inadvertently creating a symbiotic relationship that allowed the separate organisms to survive better as a singular one. This would lead to the evolution of complex cells and to multi-cellular organisms.

mitochondria of the cell has DNA different than that of the nucleus, showing that if continual competition had been the basis of ecosystem dynamics rather than symbiogenisis, life would not exist. Biologist Lynn Margulis, who developed the philosophy of symbiogenisis in her work, states, "Life did not take over the globe by combat, but by networking."[44] Herbalist Michael Moore, considered the father of modern herbalism, had the idea of "Mother Ocean," which posits that the cells of our bodies, since they first started their networking in the primordial waters, figured out a way to carry it with them as internal salt water, bodily fluids, and blood.[45] Our own bodies and *Euglena* are proof that species come together in novel ways to create new life. They create environments that are better for themselves but also support other organisms as they become established in the new ecosystem, which is the very cycle that invasive species perpetuate when they are allowed to.

This brings us to ecological successional cycles. There are five basic stages of ecological succession, which are nudation, invasion, co-regulation, reaction, and climax. Nudation refers to the disruptive event that leads to bare spots and denuded areas within an ecosystem, a place where nothing is growing. This can happen naturally (and should) as part of an evolving ecosystem, but it happens more often and more rapidly today because of detrimental mechanical intrusion by humans.

Invasion refers to the propagation of the denuded area by what is termed first-stage successional plants, or what we might call "weeds." They are often the only things that *can* grow in these barren places, which is why nothing else does. They often have deep tap roots and wide lateral roots, seed widely and quickly, and create thick stands of themselves across the denuded area. This is their job. They are meant to cover the soil and draw nutrients up into it, bring moisture, and shade it from the sun so microbes and mycorrhizae can build colonies beneath the surface. They are an essential part of succession, and many native

---

44 Lynn Margulis and Dorion Sagan, *Microcosmos: Four Billion Years of Evolution from Our Microbial Ancestors* (University of California Press, 1997) 29.

45 I was handed down stories about this idea by my mentors, but it can be found in Michael Moore's *Medicinal Plants of the Desert and Canyon West* 79. There is also a lovely article by Elaine Sheff about this topic and its relation to lymphatic herbs, which can be found at www.greenpathherbschool.com/greenpathblog/tending-mother-ocean-herbs-for-the-lymph.

first-stage successional plants can no longer perform the job because the ecosystems can no longer support them, not because of invasive species but because of climate shift, ozone degradation, and human-led decline.

The third stage of succession is where first-stage and second-stage successional plants coregulate, so invasive plants find a more moderate balance within the developing ecosystem and give way to later, larger plants like shrubs and small trees. They have an active conversation, which, as we know, is what ecosystems *are*. Eventually, usually over centuries, they reach an accord and come to an internal balance. In the process, they nutrify and enliven the soil and the environment reacts to the conversation, adding its own voice, and thus, the ecosystem is established. The climax period is when the third-stage successional plants—or the hardwood trees, the deep-rooted prairie grasses, and the other hallmark species of an ecosystem—become established. These are the long-lived members of the environment working in tandem with the cycle of succession as it happens around them, repeatedly and eternally. This is the ideal.

The cycle of succession, however, is continually interrupted by human activity, and it stays stuck in the invasion and co-regulation steps, which means that as invasives continue to proliferate, nothing changes, and the ecosystem degrades to the point of collapse. It is nearly impossible for the ecosystem to have a balanced conversation over the cacophony of noise that surrounds the human species and its condition because we live in such a disruptive, unregulated manner that nothing around us can rest. We must learn to become quieter and much, much better listeners than we have been over the last several hundred years. Our species is only about 200,000 years old, if not slightly older, and we have only recently become bad actors. We can learn to change and learn to move forward in equilibrium with the Land, but we must first remember we are part of it, not its master.

This, I think, is where witches come in. I see the pursuit of witchcraft as an environmental adaptation and magic as a tool for an ecosystem out of balance. It is a calling from Nature itself. The practices in which witches engage, the overall philosophy that many of us share…it indicates a distinct connection between us and the Land and a desire to really hear its song. It shows that we can sing in harmony with the song of the Land as well and that we can come into union with it and its power. In many cases, that is where the power we wield finds its root—with the spirits of the Land and our relationships with them, which are demonstrative of the relationship we need to have with the Land itself. If we are to get what we want, we must empower *each other*. Invasives are here to prep the Land for the next stage of succession, and witches and those who wield magic are here to prep our cultures for it. We are part of Nature and its rewilding.

Instead of waging war against them, we need to begin to dream *with* invasive species and bring them into our future ecological designs and stewardship plans. They can be enormously helpful when we look at them on their own terms and let them teach us about how they operate to heal the Land. They can be sources of food, fiber, construction material, forage and fodder, medicine, art, magic, and so much more. They also clean the soil and water of heavy metals, radioactive toxins, and other pollutants, remove salt and chemicals, and remove harmful molecules like sulfur dioxide and CO_2 from the air, which diminishes the effects of greenhouse gasses.

Invasives can be powerful allies if they are well-managed. I am not advocating for spreading invasives around or planting them in your garden, nor am I saying they are problem-free. They *can* be more problematic than helpful in ecosystems, such as with cheatgrass and American ivy, but even plants like these can be managed to benefit the overall environment with a bit of creative problem-solving. It takes work, dedication, and a willingness to overcome challenges, but overhauling our collective perspective to one of holistic ecology where *all* species may play a helpful part and shepherding the Land toward its future health is the most important thing we can be doing today. So, let's stop the war on weeds and instead begin to creatively collaborate with them.

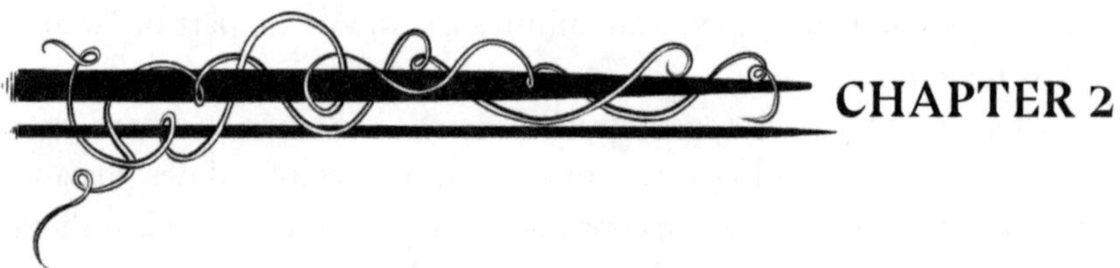

CHAPTER 2

Ex Uno Plures, E Plurbus Unum

Why choose that phrase as a chapter header? It translates as: "Out of one, many. Out of many, one." This is just about as alchemical a phrase as a person can make, for it speaks directly to the Chain of Being, the architecture of all existence. For the medieval philosophers and alchemists, the Chain was decreed by God, and it is dependent on Him as the apical figure and anchor of creation. The reason for the development of natural philosophy, alchemy, and much of the occult, at least in parts of Europe, was to figure out the secrets of the Chain of Being so that the magician could understand the Will of God and the methods by which His Will is done. Thereby, the magician could have some manner of control over the world if they could somehow approximate or manipulate that method. So, the studious minds of many philosophers went into trying to crack this primordial code and to a fair extent, they succeeded. Their work is the progenitor from which came all the works of science and philosophy that today provide us with a world filled with wonders.

Though the alchemists and natural philosophers were monotheistic and Jewish, Christian, or Muslim, *you* do not need to be in order to utilize their work. In my own practice, I have developed a system that is Hellenic polytheist that works with these philosophical structures. Nyx is at the top, Hekate is woven throughout, and the other gods play their parts as intermediaries and rulers over the various elements, planets, and powers. The work of the old occultists is a wonder, really, a cohesive whole, but that whole is made of parts represented by the names of God, angels, demons, and all the rest. The parts can be renamed, reimagined, and brought into your practice.

For our discussion here, we need to focus on just some of the building blocks those early thinkers parsed apart from the universal source code. We don't need to review every constituent of every plant, every element from the periodic table, every formula of physics. These are the "many from one," the great panoply of possibilities descended from the upper parts of the divine order. All we need to do is discuss the uppermost parts to understand their role in working with plants in a magical way.

ALCHEMY AND ITS ELEMENTS IN BRIEF

Alchemists were (and are) obsessed with purity, not in a purely mundane or merely spiritual sense, for alchemy is essentially a spiritual materialism. They were obsessed with purifying materials to get as close to the original material, the *prima materia,* as they could. The *prima materia* is the basic, perfected, unified substance that stands outside of time and space, from which all things are created.

Because this substance exists beyond time and space and, therefore, the place where creation is possible, it underwent the *premium mobile,* the first motion toward creation, which caused *prima materia* to separate into two distinct parts. These two parts are born from an intermediary, an avatar of the *prima materia,* called *prima mater,* the first mother. This is akin to the idea of quintessence and is related to the philosophies concerning the *anima mundi,* or World Soul, which, for me, links alchemy directly to Hekate. She is called *Soteira* in the Chaldean Oracles, which is understood to be the *anima mundi,* so I consider Hekate to be the *prima mater,* the mother of all things, and I believe that all alchemical works are derived through Her, meaning they are inherently magical. Practicing alchemy is a way to get to know Her better, to work in the liminal way that She works. This is not the accepted philosophy, of course, but rather my own take on it.

As mentioned earlier, the *prima mater* gives birth to two parts, which are the extreme opposites of creation called Celestial Salt (order, magnetism) and Celestial Niter (chaos, electricity). These are the twin torches of Hekate, the very roots of the power we tap into as witches, and the forces that cause the Wheel of Fate to spin and weave its tapestry. They can also be understood as the celestial pair, Helios and Selene, or the twin gods, Artemis and Apollo. These two primary siblings, through the motion of their own magnetic and electric energies, create the fifth element, which is the progenitor of creation and the force we work with when performing magic. Franz Bardon, among other magicians, called this "electromagnetic fluid," "aether," or "Astral light." This "aether" is then itself subdivided, almost like white light through a prism, into the four Aristotelian elements of creation: Air, Earth, Fire, and Water.

Celestial Salt is the mother of elemental Earth and Water, both fixed elements, and Celestial Niter is the mother of elemental Air and Fire, which are both volatile. These create the generational oppositions that lead to the creation of all things by virtue of their interwoven and opposing constitutions, which are described as cold, warm, moist, and dry. Earth is dry and cold, Water is cold and moist, Air is moist and warm, and Fire is warm and dry. These constitutions were the basis for the philosophy upon which early medicine was built, including the humoral theory.

THE ELEMENTS

Each element relates to plants differently and creates in them certain morphological traits and herbal actions that we can learn to interpret. They also inform the general *personality* of a plant so we can learn more about which elements each plant harbors within it in the greatest preponderance. The elemental structure of plants is complex, and understanding how they are attributed can be difficult, but there are a few guidelines we can follow that are helpful.

Certain parts of a plant's anatomy are associated with one of the elements, or the element is represented in a plant by those parts—however you'd like to see it. With Fire, it is the flowers; with Air, it is the leaves; with Water, it is the stem and twigs; and with Earth, it is the root system. Aether is represented in the seeds, which are both the end and the beginning of a plant, its death and its dream of a future life, and therefore, they are magically very potent.

Every plant harbors all of the elements, just as do we. Everything is a mixture of them because everything is a mixture of their precipitates: Salt, Mercury, and Sulphur. Some species may harbor more of one element than another—or perhaps more of two or three, and so they may express admixtures of various traits. An example of this is the plant yerba de la negrita (*Sphaeralcea spp.*), which is mucilaginous and has physical traits that speak to the Water element, but it also works on the respiratory system, meaning it harbors some Air elemental qualities. Another example is the rose, as its showy flowers with their fleshy petals and demulcent qualities indicate the Water element, but it is also covered in thorns, which is a Fiery trait.

Do not feel boxed in to a certain way of thinking or a certain attribution, either, as an individual plant may harbor more or less of an element than is typical for the species. Plants are unique individuals and aren't exactly the same across the board, just as we aren't. Speak to each plant as a new friend and let it guide you in the way it wants to work with you.

Earth

The power of the Earth element draws the leaves of plants downward toward the ground, spreads their leaves out wide, and makes them rough as stones. They may also have thick, sturdy root systems that dig deep into the ground. Earth plants can tolerate drier soils but prefer shade and coolness.

Earth element plants benefit the bones, the densest organs, and the joints and cartilage, as they tend to be mineral accumulators. They have an array of flavors that speak to their power but are mainly either sweet and moistening or bitter and drying or astringent. This is the case because these two flavors stimulate the digestive system to begin functioning as a cohesive unit. The stomach is one of the organs related to the Earth, as it is the organ that nourishes the body.

Sweet flavors stimulate the production of saliva and the function of the pancreas, the primary producer of digestive enzymes in the body, which in turn stimulates the stomach to begin producing fluids for the breakdown of food. Bitter flavors stimulate the liver to produce bile and get the eliminatory organs ready to make room for a new meal. Both flavors produce downward and inward energy in the body as food goes into the mouth, down the alimentary canal to be broken down into basic nutrients, and then disperses into the cells.

As the densest of the elements, Earth is often associated with the material world we live in, with acquiring resources, and the mundane workings of daily living. As such, Earth is the element that most relates to the cycles of life and nature. Its lighter side is represented in the verdancy of fields, swamps, and forests, in the budding of flowers and their scent on the breeze, and in the sounds of newly born animals and the flow of milk from the teat. But Earth is also the element of the Underworld and the dead. Its darker side is the cradle of the grave, the caves and caverns that served as our first temples, the deepest parts of the planet where the eyeless beasts skitter across slick stones, and the places that have never seen the light of the Sun and never will.

Being one of the two fixed elements, Earth is one of stability. Earth element plants bring energy down and in, holding it, making them good vessels for spirits and caches for power. They are good for grounding and balancing, strengthening the spirit, lending steady courage, and increasing prosperity in the home or business.

Earth element plants can also be used in hexes for binding, imprisoning, and for drawing an enemy down into the mire of their own darkness. Plants that harbor this element are also excellent binding agents for other ingredients, as they can hold each energy in your formula separately but still bring them together cohesively. Earth plants also help to build boundaries, making them good additions to preparations meant to guard and ward. Alchemically, it represents the Salt, the body that the alchemist works upon.

Water

Plants that harbor the Water element tend to grow near or in water. They have sprays or cascades of flowers and grow in trailing groupings or in patches that look like pools. They tend to be graceful and luscious, flowing in long tendrils, like periwinkle, or they are leafy with thick mid-veins, like many lettuces. The flowers of Water plants can be of any color, but they tend toward white, purple, blue, and orange.

They can taste sweet, salty, or sour, which are all flavors that increase salivation or cause the body to retain more water. Sour foods have also been shown to increase sexual desire, memory, and appetite, all of which have resonance with this element. An overabundance of water in the body, however, can lead to toxicity and accumulated waste, damaged circulatory vessels, and stress on the heart, which can be alleviated by Earth plants that soak up the water or Fire plants that dry it out. Water plants are often aphrodisiacs, lymphagogues, demulcents, emollients, and diuretics. Being the more active of the two fixed elements, the energy of these plants has a downward and *outward* motion, bringing life to the otherwise inert Earth element.

Plants with this element in preponderance are used magically to get things to flow, to wash things away, and generally to cleanse. Water plants also make good additions to spells meant to bring things *toward* you, for spells of obtainment, especially things that may be difficult to get. They are also often used for love magic and other spells meant to influence emotions, dreams, and visions. They can be used in preparations meant to increase self-confidence and alleviate shame, guilt, and long-held resentments. Conversely, if you want to erode an enemy's will, Water plants help to break them down completely and sweep them away in a flood of shame and doubt.

Water is the element most often associated with emotions, which can be light, warm, and kind, or brutal and deadly. Emotions are shifting and changeable, moving from superficial and shimmering to crushingly deep from second to second, so they truly do embody the essential character of elemental Water. It is the gentle flow of creeks and streams, the variety of tidal pools, and the flash of iridescence on a pearl. It is the water of the womb in which we first gestate and the primordial waters our most ancient ancestors evolved in. It is the blood flowing through our bodies and the sweat of our brows, the water that sustains our lives and is vital to every being on the planet. It is also the deep, dark, mysterious places of the ocean where the great leviathans sleep, places which we will likely never lay eyes on. It is the rip tide that takes us under, the mighty current that washes away towns, the hurricane flood, and the tsunami. It is also the heart of Nature, the element that connects the body of Nature (Earth) to the mind of Nature (Air), and without it, both of those would be lifeless. We must learn to treat elemental Water *and* the physical water of our planet with greater respect, or the consequences will be dire.

Air

The leaves of Air element plants tend to be feathery and hairy, and their stems are often hollow, as with much of the family *Apiaceae*. They often appear delicate, almost filigreed, and their stalks are topped with umbels of flowers that come in a variety of shades of white, yellow, and green or flowers that bear fruit that hurls seeds a very great distance. The notable structures of Air plants are greatly spaced apart, often shooting up and spreading out, as with mullein or lavender.

Blue spike vervain (*Verbena macdougalii*), one of the Air plants, is one of my absolute favorite herbs for nervous tension and insomnia caused by anxiety, but it is extremely bitter. The flavors associated with Air are bitter and astringent, sometimes pungent, though the latter is best reserved for Fire. Most Air plants are nervine and expectorant, having an affinity for both the nervous system and the respiratory system. They can also be carminative, as with chamomile and peppermint, meaning they help a person to pass wind, which does seem to bear out in a correspondence table. Air plants can also be trophorestorative, which means they have a tonic, nourishing, and restorative effect, such as with milky oat (*Avena sativa*), which helps to rebuild and remyelinate[46] the axons of nerves.

Air plants are most often related to the planet Mercury and often help to develop communication, establish healthy patterns of thinking and imagining, and aid one in clarity, focus, and acuity. They have other planetary resonances, of course, but they are most often Mercurial and are considered "study herbs," such as *Ginkgo biloba,* the leaves of which even look like little fans.

When constructing spells to open communication or to close it off, Air herbs come in handy. They can also ease the effort it takes to perform long-distance workings. Air plants also make for good purifying herbs, particularly as curse breakers, being gentle but thorough as they carry unnecessary energies away. They are also useful weather-working herbs. Air plants can be used in hexes to cause sleeplessness, shiftlessness, and a feeling of needing to leave a job or a house.

Air is the element of the mind, of logic and rationality, representing the *logos* of Nature. Being one of the volatile elements, Air is associated with motion and rapid movement, particularly upward and inward, which allows us to explore the impossible heights of our imagination and innermost thoughts. Air is highly flexible, able to surround and understand things from all aspects and angles, and lead us into free thought. But it can also whip us up into flights of fancy and delusion, miring us in patterns of thinking that can be detrimental. It is not only the breeze from the wings of butterflies but also the tornado and the hurricane wind that ravages cities, leaving swathes of unbelievable destruction in its wake. Air, along with Water, is related to the breath of life, what in Qabalistic terms is called the *ru'ach* or "breath, spirit." This is also related to the alchemist's Mercury as the "breath" or "spirit" of the substance that rises up to be purified.

---

46 *Remylienation* refers to the creation of new, thinner myelin sheaths (the fatty, enveloping cells that protect axons, which are sort of like the "mouth" of a neuron) on demyelinated, damaged axons, allowing them to propagate action potentials (the conduction of bioelectric impulses through a neuron) once again.

Fire

The plants that harbor the most elemental Fire inside them are the ones that bite back. They have spice and heat, bringing redness and pain. They are often red or turn red over time, but may also be orange or yellow. They are things considered *hot*. Fire plants enjoy hot, dry places and can withstand very difficult conditions. They are pernicious and persistent. Fire element plants tend to be thorny, prickly, or have leathery leaves with sharp edges. They are also often fragrant with a pungent taste, like rosemary.

Fire element plants have a proclivity for driving motion in the body, increasing circulation and gut motility, opening tissues, and stimulating immune function. They are warming and dispel stagnation and coldness, making them vital for things like edema, liver stagnation, and low blood pressure.

Magically, the fire element speeds up the effect of spells, bringing results faster. They also act as powerful protectors and banishers of negative entities and powers. They move energy, sometimes explosively, and push things up and out. In the vein of maleficium, fire element plants can cause irritation, anxiety, and paranoia and rile up the ire of angry spirits before you set them on your enemies.

This is the element of heat and action, of forward motion and taking charge. Fire is the quickest of the elements and helps to bring about fast results and transformation. The plants that harbor Fire tend to be very effective for works of *maleficia,* but also for protection and purification, increasing willpower, and opening channels for energy to flow through. The herbs of Fire are good catalysts, too, acting as ingredients that bring your spells to life.

Fire is the most active of the two volatile elements, with an energy that moves upward and outward, capable of vast expansion. It relates to the vital lifeforce of things, the energy of life itself. It is the fire that warms us and our homes when it is glowing warmly in the hearth or the campfire and also the bonfire that transforms the energy of our gloom and sadness during autumn festivals. Here in New Mexico, we have a festival every September called Zozobra, where artists build an enormous papier-mâché and fabric effigy called "Old Man Gloom," which is filled with petition papers to take away problems, illnesses, and all the things that bring sadness. It is then set alight in a grand ritual replete with fireworks and recorded groans that shake the ground, and the fire takes those sources of gloom and transmutes them into something better and more sustaining. To the alchemist, Fire is Sulphur, the essential soul of a thing that makes it wholly unique.

Fire can also be greatly destructive, especially when it is out of alignment with the other elements. It is the forest fire that wreaks havoc across the mountainside and the heat of the Sun bringing life to fields, but also death when there is no food or water to be had. It is the building pressure that leads to an erupting volcano, the heat of a lightning strike, a red-hot branding iron against the skin, the blistering tongues of flame licking at the legs of a person consigned to the fire. It must be approached with cunning and caution, but Fire can be revolutionarily transformative and is essential to the work we do.

AETHER

Aether is the "light that is not yet light," the element that, of course, precipitates the other four. It is also the element that is made by combining the four others in balance. If Earth, Water, Air, and Fire are the yarn a tapestry is made of, Aether is the *wool.* Aether is also called "spirit" and "quintessence," the latter coming from the Latin *quinta essentia,* the "fifth essence." This is the purest element that the alchemists and natural philosophers believed the soul, as well as planets and stars, to be made of. It is also the "fluid" by which the luminaries and even God influenced everything here in the sphere of Earth. Aether can be considered the consciousness of the universe, the permeating emanation from the very mind of God, descending through a series of rippling permutations to become...well, everything! In some veins of Greek mythology, it is the god Aether who rules the bright "upper sky," and it is said that "everything came from him." In the system I use, this includes Gaia (Earth), Thalassa/Pontus (Water), Ouranos (Air), and Hemera (Fire/Light).

When it comes to how they operate in herbalism and wortcunning,[47] it is important to keep in mind that aether is the mixture of all the other

47 *Wortcunning* is the knowledge of not only the remedial, medicinal qualities of herbs, but also their magical, spiritual qualities. The word *wort* means "useful herb," and *cunning* refers to the skilled application of the knowledgeable practitioner to create biological and magical effects.

elements, so it is part of them, not separate. It doesn't act on its own but suffuses everything. If there is a class of herbs that *can* be ascribed to it, it is the *Phantasticants:* entheogens, hallucinogens, and the others which help us to see the "world behind the world."

Tria Prima

These four elements and the quintessence were the building blocks of all things and the fundamental cornerstones of healing until an Arabic alchemist named Jabir ibn Hayyan, also called Geber, added two other elements: Sulphur and Mercury. Later, the alchemist Paracelsus added a third new element, which was Salt. These three new elements are called the *tria prima,* the "Three Primes," and are precipitated by the interactions of the four elements.

Earth and Water precipitate Salt, which represents the fixed, heavy, physical body and other gross matter. Water and Air precipitate Mercury, which is the spirit that unites all things, our connection to the *anima mundi*. Air and Fire precipitate Sulphur, the essential soul of all things that makes each one unique to itself. These are the constituents that make up the threefold nature of creation. Therefore, all things can be broken down into these three prime materials, which are physically present in calcined salts, alcoholic extractions, and essential oils. These are separated from each other through alchemical work, thus comminuting an original substance into three, which are then reconstituted as a new, more perfect thing capable of creating powerful effects in the body and the world at large. It is important to note that this process from *prima materia* to the *tria prima* to the products of alchemy is a series of expansions and contractions...a series of breaths. From one to two, from two to one, from one to four, from four to three, from three to one, and back to three, and finally to a thing so fully whole unto itself as to be indivisible. Alchemy is a beautiful, transformative, *living* art leading ever back toward its beginning: it is the great dragon, the cosmic serpent...it is the ouroboros.

Through these purifying processes, the hope of many alchemists was to turn base metals into gold or to produce the Philosopher's Stone, the *Lapis Philosophorum,* through a process called the Great Work. Today, thanks in large part to Carl Jung, many people believe that the aim of

alchemy was wholly spiritual, that any experiments to turn other metals into gold or to find the Philosopher's Stone were performed by fools; real alchemists knew the "Great Work" was a metaphor for enlightenment.

This is patently false, as there is an enormity of proof to the contrary. The spiritual aspect of alchemy existed, of course, but as a counterpart to the physical procedures alchemists undertook, for they were reflections of each other focused through the person's life. One of the most famous alchemical axioms from the *Emerald Tablet of Hermes Trismegistos* states this clearly, and I will include it in its entirety here:

> *Verum, sine mendacio, certum et verissimum: quod est inferius est sicut quod est superius; et quod est superius est sicut quod est inferius, ad perpetranda miracula rei unius. Et sicut omnes res fuerunt ab uno, mediatione unius, sic omnes res natae fuerunt ab hac una re, adaptatione.*[48]

All the parts of alchemy, of the alchemist's life, make up one whole; the parts cannot be separated without becoming whole again.

The above quote relates to our next section, which is on planetary magic. Our lives here on Earth are influenced by the stars, our bodies, spirits, and souls being forged in a celestial furnace made of starfire. As I'm certain you know, the zodiac is divided amongst the four elements: Earth governs Taurus, Virgo, and Capricorn; Air governs Gemini, Aquarius, and Libra; Water governs Cancer, Scorpio, and Pisces; and Fire governs Leo, Sagittarius, and Aries. The children of the elements, the *tria prima*, are also present in astrology as the fixed, mutable, and cardinal signs of the zodiac.

The fixed signs of Taurus, Leo, Scorpio, and Aquarius are Salt, for they are the most stable of the signs that embody their particular elements. The mutable signs of Gemini, Virgo, Sagittarius, and Pisces are Mercury because they are adaptable, flexible, and always changing and flowing. The Cardinal signs of Aries, Cancer, Libra, and Capricorn are Sulphur because they are the spark of their element, the beginning, and the essential nature of it, which is why they stand at the beginning of the seasons.

---

48 "True, without falsehood, certain, and most true: What is below is like what is above, and what is above is like what is below, to accomplish the miracles of one thing. And as all things were derived from one by the meditation of one, so all things are born from this one thing by adaptation."

These are the lenses through which the seven inner planets and three outer planets, as well as the other stars, asteroids, comets, and clusters we account for in astrology, shine to color our world in a panoply of hues. It is the signs of the zodiac and the seven classical planets, though, that were the particular interest of early alchemists, as they could relate everything they did in their work to those great lights as part of the Chain of Being. Every metal, every stone, every body, and every plant has a correspondence to a planet and the signs of the zodiac, which is where the work of the alchemists really ties into our discussion in *this* book and where we will turn our attention next.

CHAPTER 3

All Things In Their Time

PLANETARY MAGIC AND CELESTIAL INFLUENCE

Everything on our planet resonates with the music of the stars. It is the tune to which our lives dance, down to our very cells and the organelles inside them, to the fine, scintillating filaments of our souls and the water of the spirit we move through. Even time dances to their jig. The five elements, the signs of the zodiac, the energy of the planets, and how they relate to each other and our daily lives all concern the work of a wortcunner *and* the work of a witch.

These are some of the most integral and important threads we pull on to create our magic and shape the outcomes of events. The stars are inevitable. It is, therefore, a good idea to know how and when to work with them and around them. All these influences go into the "energetic architecture" of things, making the blueprint for who we are and how we walk in the world, a concept we will discuss later in this section.

Here, I want to relate to you not which plants resonate with which planet and which sign but rather *how* we discover their resonances so that you can figure them out for yourself. I also do not want to write an entire treatise on the nuances of planetary magic and astrology, as that is not the purview of this book. Rather, I include in the following discussion the general personality and feel of a planet, what sorts of things it has rulership over, and how it influences the morphology and herbal actions of plants. That way, if there is a plant you want to work with that no one has bothered to write about, you will still be able to figure out its nuances and integrate it wisely and well into your practice. This is the way with many of the invasive herbs, as most people think they aren't much worth talking about.

The Outer Luminaries

Pluto, Uranus, and Neptune are the three outer luminaries, a word meaning "lights" but referring to the planets. They do not have direct resonance with any of the plants, at least in the system I use. They are, rather, "higher octaves" of three of the inner planets: Pluto is the higher octave of Mars, Neptune is the higher octave of Venus, and Uranus is the higher octave of Mercury, so the outer planets harmonize with the inner planets and the things under their rulership. The outer planets also each correspond to one of the *tria prima:* Neptune to Salt, Uranus to Mercury, and Pluto to Sulphur.

Instead of ruling signs and plants and stones and all the rest of the things we ascribe to the *inner* planets, the outer luminaries oversee the organization of spirit and matter, as well as greater cosmic shifts; they make sure the Wheel of Fate continues to spin. They have very little to do with the individual on any mundane level, so they are not as wrapped up in the wortcunning practices of the alchemists and witches of the material world as the inner planets are. Therefore, we will not discuss them here.

The Inner Luminaries

In traditional astrology, alchemy, and much of the history of occultism and magic, the seven inner planets, which are visible to the naked eye, were the planets people dealt with and brought into their mythologies. These are the great gods that govern our lives here on Earth, the angelic beings that drive our lives and plan out our development. They are a symphony, each playing its own song, its own music. Each weaves harmoniously into each other. That symphony is the lock that opens the secrets of the cosmos.

Everything that exists for us resonates in various ways with the vibrations of these songs, so we must learn to listen deeply and well.

They have been incredibly important to the development of magic and to the evolution of herbalism and alchemy throughout the centuries. Understanding their energies and the way they have been described in occult philosophy is essential to having an effective wortcunning practice, so they are detailed in the following.

The Moon

Zodiac: Cancer
Metal: Silver
Color: Purple

The Astral World is the special purview of the Moon, particularly the traffic of energy and entities into and out of that place and how they affect us. It is the sphere of dreaming and of visions, though not necessarily prophecy, which instead falls into the wheelhouse of the Sun. It is also the planet associated with illusion, transformation (particularly shapeshifting), the tidal flow of magical energy, psychism and the ability to see the unseen, and invisibility. Lunar plants increase receptivity, making us more sensitive to the forces around us, including helping us to be more empathetic because the Moon rules over the emotions. The herbs of the Moon can also be useful for cleansing the subtle bodies, particularly the etheric and Astral, which can help put an end to nightmares and repetitive dreams.

While we are talking about the Moon, I feel it prudent to have a brief discussion on the Witch Queen. The Moon is her particular luminary, representing the magnetic part of magic, which changes, shifts, and flows through its polarities. The Moon deals with things as they go through phases, as things both wax and wane. The Moon is a shapeshifter, and so is the Witch Queen, who is represented by many faces. In my practice, the Moon and the Witch Queen are Selene, Diana, and Hekate, all of whom are important parts of how magic flows through our world, which is detailed in the later section on lunar phases.

The Moon rules all wilderness places and most watery things, such as streams, rivers, lakes, oceans, and seas. The animals of the Moon have inward-curling horns, fluffy white pelts, and skin that shifts between colors, or they begin or live their lives in the water, such as frogs and toads. Dogs (the particular animal of Hekate), pigs, and goats fall under the protection of this luminary. Owls and other night birds are the Moon's, as are the insects that prefer the dark, such as grubs, pill bugs, and spiders. The stones of the Moon are all white or clear stones, stones with holographic sheens, such as moonstone and other chalcedony, selenite, gypsum, and others.

The herbs of the Moon are often spherical, white, or have a silvery sheen to their leaves or fruits, much like many *Artemesia* species and willows. They may also exude a white, milky exudate. The flowers of Lunar plants are usually light in color, trumpet or cup-shaped, or appear to be falling to Earth like stars. They will also blossom at night, like Datura and jasmine. Lunar plants also like to grow in watery, shady places, as most plants that resonate with the Moon also harbor the Water element.

The nighttime music of the Moon weaves subtle enchantments, and it can be a lullaby, an excitation, or a requiem. The herbs of the Moon reflect this. They are often soporific, hypnogogic, and nervine, with actions that lead the body into sleep and dreaming. They may also be deliriant (a trait shared with Venusian plants) or hallucinogenic. Many of the nightshades are Lunar, particularly Datura, which can ease pain or send a person into raving lunacy.

The taste of Moon herbs is blandly sweet, like Siberian elm, and sometimes bitter, again like many members of the *Artemesia* family. These plants often have mucilaginous properties, like the mallows, or are filled with cooling gel, like Aloe vera. The main herbal actions of Lunar plants are demulcent, which is moisturizing for the *inside* of the body, and emollient, which is moisturizing for the *outside* of the body. They may also act on the uterus and have emmenagogic properties, sometimes acting as abortifacients, such as mugwort. They may also act on estrogens and progesterone. Though plants with an affinity to the ovarian system also have connections to Venus, it is the Moon that rules the hollow organs of holding, meaning the uterus, along with the stomach and bladder.

In an herbal energetic fashion, the Moon is harmonized with the Sun and harmonizes Mars. What the Moon puts to rest and brings into quietude, the Sun can excite and enliven. The pathological Lunar states of lethargy, moroseness, and delusion can be revealed and enlightened by the power of Solar herbs. The Sun is also the opposing planet to the Moon, meaning they naturally help to balance each other and are essential to each other in how they work in the cosmos. They are a natural duet in the symphony of the universe. The aggression and over-stimulation that Mars can evoke are put to rest by the Lunar herbs, which can relax and sedate the anger of the Red Planet. Its moist, cooling nature can bring the fires of the Martial imbalances to heel, particularly when those imbalances concern digestion, circulation, and mentation.

MERCURY

ZODIAC: Gemini and Virgo
METAL: Quicksilver and Aluminum
COLOR: Orange

The song Mercury sings makes it the planet of intellect, communication, and genius. Where the Moon rules over the emotional life, Mercury rules over the mental. When performing magic that is meant to increase your acuity, help with learning and memory, and open or smooth pathways of communication, Mercury is the planet to consider. It is also a planet associated with travel, both physical and Astral, and governs the pathways that lead between places. Mercury, as the messenger that darts from place to place and the psychopomp wandering between the worlds of the living and the dead, can help to create connection, particularly through the use of words, both spoken and written.

Mercury rules scholarship and the houses of the mind. Where study is serious and consequential, Mercury is there. It is also the ruler of casinos and other gambling halls, as Mercury loves a great risk and great reward. It also thrives on trickery, cunning, and subterfuge to gain that reward. It doesn't really care which side wins, so long as the game is entertaining, but a gambling charm in your pocket is always appreciated by this luminary.

It shares rulership with the Moon over many animals, including the hare, foxes, and dogs, but Mercury has particular resonance with birds, especially those that mimic human voices, such as parrots, mockingbirds, and nightingales. The very intelligent birds, like ravens, are also under the auspices of Mercury, along with the birds that symbolize intelligence and cunning, such as the ibis, crane, and heron. The ibis is also the bird associated with Thoth, the Egyptian god of wisdom, and also with Hermes Trismegistos, the legendary first alchemist, who is the amalgam of Thoth and Hermes. Species of quickly darting fish are also Mercury's, and so are bees, flies, and all manner of flying insects and pollinators. It rules over all stones that are multicolored or shift through various colors, though its special stone is emerald.

Mercury is the perfect, nonbinary[49] union of the Witch Queen and the Witch King as the balancing agent of the cosmos, the Trickster willing to aid and hinder as necessary or as they find amusing. It is a celestial representative of the divinity of the "serpent blood" and its course through the veins of the witch, of the liminality of what it means to be a practitioner of this kind of magic. This planet is the witch or magician enthroned in the cosmos and standing at the center of the magic circles. I suppose you could say that Mercury as a divinity is the Great Old Ones embodied as living vessels of magic and the vessel for the collective knowledge of the long line of our illustrious forebears of the Craft.

One of the primary physical characteristics of the herbs of Mercury is a hollow stem, which we have already stated is an Air element quality in plants. This is, in part, the reason that rulership of the brain and central nervous system is given to this planet. Mercury plants tend to be well-balanced between their upper and lower parts or may be well-wrinkled, as with lungwort or walnuts. They also tend to be slender, delicate looking, or feathery, which again calls back to plants of the Air. Mercury's plants are often very fragrant and oily, giving off a scent even from a distance.

Along with the nervous system, Mercury is the planet with rulership of the respiratory system. Many of its herbs aid with opening the lungs, easing respiratory inflammation, and act as expectorants. Because of their volatility, they also affect the digestive system in a carminative fashion, leading to the release of gastrointestinal gas. Plants of Mercury are also those that increase blood flow to the brain and help with overall mental function, plants like Ginkgo and Bacopa.

---

49 This does not mean "two-gendered" or "nonpolar" or "non-gendered." Nonbinary is all-encompassing, the "neither-and" of gender expression, which cannot be represented through a traditionally gendered lens. Mercury, like the metal named for it, is solid and liquid, fully formed and formless, allowing it to shift from state to state and fill the shape it needs to in order to accomplish its goal, whatever that may be.

The pathologies of Mercury are harmonized by the herbs of Mars and harmonize the energies of Jupiter. The dry, cold, airy nature of Mercurial imbalances can lead to immobilization, movement in the wrong direction, or a lack of moisture due to a loss of circulatory motion. Stuffiness, headaches, brain fog, and all of that can be mitigated by the use of Martial herbs, which get things moving in an orderly fashion, blast through blockages, and stop the sluggish motion of tissues affected by disharmonious Mercury. Jupiter's imbalances can lead to bombastic, overly expansive energies, which, when translated into the body, can lead to bloating and gas, possibly stagnant liver and overall digestion. The volatile oils inherent in Mercurial plants can be beneficial to those conditions, returning Jupiter to a balanced state.

Mercury has no oppositional planet, as it is the go-between for the other energies. It is the balancer for *all* the other planets and can help them reach a state of better communication between themselves. The addition of Mercurial herbs to any formula can help to bring the whole thing into better harmony, though it is not essential to do so. Sticking with the motif of music, if the other planets are the right and left hands playing over the keys of a piano, Mercury is the pedals that elongate and resonate the notes, enriching the emotional balance of the song.

Venus

Zodiac: Taurus and Libra
Metal: Copper and Brass
Color: Green

The sensual realm belongs to Venus, all things relating to beauty, eroticism, and pleasure. It has a strong relationship with desire and has much to do with the development of what Jung termed "the shadow."[50] Relationships of all sorts fall under her sway, for better or worse, and can lead to either peace or war, kindness or cruelty. Venus retrograde periods can be exceptionally brutal on an emotional level. Venus is the sphere of raw potential, pure and undiluted talent. Where Mercury rules over genius, especially the type

50 See Appendix A.

that comes from long learning, Venus is the planet that guides the savant and the naturally gifted, particularly visual artists and poets.

Venus is called "the lesser benefic," as it is considered a generally kindly planet that brings joy in its wake. Every planet has the potential to be malefic or benefic, however, depending on where it is in the nativity and which aspects affect it, so the idea that one planet is kinder or crueler than another is misleading and, frankly, silly. Venus has the power to help us process emotional information in a way that leads to greater strength and tenacity over time, helping our hearts to relax their hold on old hurts and soothe the ache of grief. We must beware, however, for the arms of Venus can help to lift us back onto our feet and find our way forward (like mimosa) or, like the beautiful rusalka, cradle us as we sink down into the depths of our inner darkness (as is the case with opium poppy).

Venus is one of the planets that has garnered the most attention and mythology over time. It is both the morning star *and* the evening star: Phosphorus and Hesperus, Lucifer and Vesper, Ninsi'anna, Ishtar, Innana, Astarte, Aphrodite, Frigga, Shahar, the assorted sacred twins, and many others. As the star of dawn and dusk, it is also related to the Witch Queen wreathed in flesh, the *Regina Incarnatus,* the ever-dying one, Persephone embodied.

She is the one who "lives deliciously" and covets all things pleasurable, who revels in the sensations of flesh, and who seeks the limits of experience. She is the light of the morning, ever young and ever beautiful, the maid who sings the seductive song that draws you onward along the *via tortuosa*. As the evening star, she is the night-haunting hag, the danger in the shadows that shrieks with madness, gnashing iron teeth that long to rip into youthful flesh. She is the shadow on the Moon, the heaviness on the sleeper's chest, the souring of milk, and the rot infesting the crops. Together, they are the seductive Dame Venus, who sprinkles the witching path with a trail of sweet promises and dire threats.

Venus brings into its domain animals such as cats, both large and domestic, swans, bovines, porcines, goats, mice, rabbits, doves, butterflies, peacocks, partridges, dolphins, and many more. Its special stones are green in color or white and luminous, such as pearls, as well as carnelian and corals. All the sparkling gems belong to Venus, including diamonds. Her sacred places are well-tended gardens or especially verdant wild areas, such as meadows filled with wildflowers or areas with wild fruit trees. Also, any place that evokes feelings of luxury, beauty, sexuality, and intimacy of all shades.

The elements of Water and Air resonate strongly with Venus, so the plants of this planet will often have their morphological markers. They are often fleshy and beautiful, having showy flowers that can smell rich, sometimes with a scent so overpowering as to be revolting, such as ylang-ylang and rose. They often have tendrils that reach out and grab things, though they may also have feathery, delicate physical traits. They will also often have sweet, delicious fruits that are juicy and tantalizing or that have sweet, sticky flesh. Venusian plants may also have hearts on them or have heart-shaped traits. Elegant death camas has green hearts on its petals; pothos plants have heart-shaped leaves; and bleeding-heart flowers look like…well, bleeding hearts.

The flavors of Venus may be sugary-sweet and flavorful, speaking to their affinity for moistening dry conditions and cooling hot ones, relaxing over tense tissues, or they may be astringent, helping to tighten loose tissues and heal wounds. Diuretic herbs may also resonate with this planet, as Venus rules Libra, which in turn rules the kidneys and the urinary system. The skin and hair, particularly of the face, belong to Venus, which also has a strong relationship with the ovarian system. Many of the herbs that affect estrogen and progesterone resonate with Venus, as do the uterine tonics.

The song of Venus harmonizes that of Saturn and is harmonized with Jupiter's. The Saturnine disharmonies are often those of over-tightness, especially of connective tissues, skin, and joints. The moistening qualities of Venusian plants can bring openness and softness to the tissues that have become too hard. Venusian imbalances may come as a result of excess, particularly sexual excess, or due to an over-abundance of moisture, such as discharge and weeping sores. Jupiter can harmonize these conditions by virtue of the dry, gentle coolness his herbs provide.

The oppositional planet of Venus is, of course, Mars. These two planets work together to achieve real, purposeful action. The dreams of Venus need the mobility of Mars to be achieved, and Mars needs those dreams to know where to direct its abundance of energy. Herbally, they harmonize with each other because Venus is cool, whereas Mars is warm, and a little bit of either can tip the balances toward better equilibrium.

The Sun

Zodiac: Leo
Metal: Gold
Color: Yellow

Divination, music, oratory, drama, performance, and prophecy are all under the guidance and rulership of the Sun. Perhaps it is better to say that the Sun is the ruler of what these activities root into—self-confidence. The Sun is the planet that shines a light on things and brings clarity, foresight, and personal power, even when things seem to be at their darkest. It is the planet of sovereignty and indomitability, offering magical dominion over spirits and creatures alike. It also reveals invisible things by virtue of its light and breaks through all sorts of binding and bondage. The Sun is also a planet associated with bravery and courage through illumination.

One can feel a closeness to the center of everything when working with the Sun, but one must be cautious of flying too close. Everything that the Sun's light touches casts a shadow, and the closer one is, the longer that shadow becomes and the more one must be aware of the darkness they trail behind them. It is also easy to lose oneself in the coldness of absolute light, to lose track of everything else that exists and all the nuance and uniqueness of things. This can lead to detached aloofness and arrogance, a feeling of being above and beyond, of inherent rightness. That is a dangerous place to be.

In this section, we will speak on the Witch King, the electric part of magic. He is best represented by the Sun, which goes through periods of greater and lesser intensity of heat. It can be warming and relaxing, distant and cold, or so ragingly hot and unrelenting that it becomes lethal. These all describe the Witch King, who, in my practice, is Lucifer in three aspects: Apollo, Dionysos, and Hermes. These are the deities of illumination through inspiration, intoxication, and instruction, respectively. We honor them at the solstices and equinoxes, as they represent the path of the Sun through the day and through the year, its ebb and flow. Solar herbs are used to prepare libations and smoke offerings, which can also be done for any face of the Witch King you work with.

The places of the Sun are places of governance, such as town halls and governmental buildings, particularly the centers of rulership. Also, places where there are great works of art made or viewed, such as museums, art schools, opera houses, and other performance spaces. The animals of the Sun include lions, bulls, rams, and baboons, as well as wolves and other apex predators. Among the birds of the Sun are falcons, hawks, vultures, roosters, and eagles. The scarab and other beetles, bees of all kinds, and the cicada are its insects, where the animals of the sea that are under its power are the manatee, the sunfish, the starfish, the bass, and the salmon. The stones of the Sun include the ruby and the bloodstone, but also all gems that are golden in color, such as citrine and amber, or those that carry asterisms.

Solar herbs are often narrow at the base, then wide and spreading at the crown with red, orange, yellow, or white flowers. These will most often look like discs with radiating petals, resembling the Sun, or will look like sprays of yellow sparks, like the flowers of St. John's wort. The flowers also tend to follow the course of the Sun throughout the day, as is the case with calendula and wild lettuce. Though they have a proclivity to grow in sunny, wide-open spaces, Solar plants can also grow in shady, moist areas and prefer coolness. These plants will have a heating, circulating, energizing effect when taken internally or cause redness and warmth on the skin.

The plants of the Sun are like sunlight brought into the body, dispelling gloom and stagnation and replacing it with something more uplifting and empowering. They strengthen us from the center out, particularly because the Sun rules the heart organ. The plants of the Sun will often have a tonic effect on the heart and cardiovascular system, being beneficial in cases of things like hypertension and arteriosclerosis.

Really, Solar herbs are circulatory regulators and stimulators and, therefore, help to maintain the systems of the body. It shares this trait with Mars, but where that planet's herbs are aggressive and hot, the plants of the Sun tend to be milder, coaxing the blood and other fluids through the body instead of forcing them. Because the Sun is the source of light amongst the planets, herbs that are beneficial for the eyes are also given to it, mostly through their action as circulatory stimulants that take healing fluids to the eye.

The Sun harmonizes the Moon and is brought into harmony by Saturn. The gentle warmth and energy provided by its plants coax the stagnant disharmonies of Lunar energy to move. They may express as a lack of potency, a general malaise, and a lack of self-worth, which the Sun can brighten. They can also bring the dreamy, delusional powers of the Moon into greater focus, turning dreams into visions and visions into prophecy. The Sun's disharmonies are related to massive self-aggrandizement and megalomania, especially when the imbalances are concurrent with Martial ones. Saturn can step up in these moments and constrain the expanding ego, instilling a sense of humility. Solar disharmony may also be due to an over-abundance of upward circulation, leading to over-burdened and leaky tissues, which the astringency of Saturnian herbs is greatly beneficial for.

Mars

Zodiac: Aries and Scorpio
Metal: Iron
Color: Red

Known as the "Red Planet" and the "Lesser Malefic," Mars is a luminary whose song speaks of war, unrest, aggression, action, and steady, fast movement. It speaks to us of persistence and short-term success but also sudden, violent failure and collapse. Mars is one of the organizing principles in the cosmos, bringing things into order, though it may do so rigidly. The song of Mars is about independence as part of a community, of maintaining individuality as part of a greater whole, of chiseling out a form from the greater block of stone. It is a song that feeds the Will, but it must be worked with in doses, as it can also lead to willfulness, obstinacy, selfishness, and manipulativeness. When the energy of Mars is woven well, it can be highly protective and is useful in all sorts of apotropaic charms.

Mars has rulership of battlefields, including things like boxing rings and other areas of sporting competition. It also rules over certain aspects of gambling and has some sway in places like casinos, though they are generally ruled by Mercury. The animals of Mars are, of course, the ram and the scorpion, but also all other stinging, biting, irritating insects, beasts who are easily enraged, as well as the pack animals, such as wolves. The stones of Mars are the ruddy stones, such as jasper, raw ruby, and bloodstone; the stones of martial defense, such as obsidian; and also stones heavy in iron, like lodestone, meteorite, and hematite.

Mars is another planet associated with the Witch King, especially in his aspect of the Devil or the gods and spirits of the wilderness places, which may be more in accord with his original godly portfolio. Mars may be the planet that has the most to do with our discussions on invasive plants and agriculture because Mars was a god of the wild, who became a god of agriculture, who became a god of war. Mars, in his role as Witch King, is *Rex Ferox Eremorum,* the Ferocious King of the Wilds, lord of those places it is too frightening by far to travel through incautiously. Then he became a god of agriculture, of domesticated Lands, a god inside a fence.

There was a tradition in Greece and Rome to ritualistically force Ares/Mars into bondage within a city, to keep the wild god as a protector but also to keep him from helping outside forces destroy the city. What is agriculture but the bondage of the wild in service to the polis? Mars is the Horned God of the wilds but also the god of tamed fields and regimented rows of crop foods. Perhaps this is why the Devil's Plantation[51] belongs to him. It is a taste of the freedom he once was master of.

As a wild god forced into domesticity, it makes sense that he became a god of war, as well. Most wars are started over resources, over access to water and Land for farming and building larger cities and larger fields. The captive god of the wilderness, his energy forcefully turned toward ever greater agricultural pursuits, became hungry for Land to cultivate, and so found ways of taking it by force. Working with invasives and wild plants, especially through witchcraft, is a way to set him free.

Martial herbs are often covered in thorns or spines, such as honey locust or devil's club. The prototypical plant of Mars is the stinging nettle, *Urtica dioica,* which is a Mars resonating herb of Scorpio. Outwardly, it is irritating and causes swelling and itching like a good Mars herb, but internally, it is cooling, bringing the Water element into the body via its Scorpionic nature. The leaves of Mars herbs are deeply serrated or sharp,

---

51 "...a plot of land that is set aside by farmers or a community, on which no crops are grown or livestock grazed. It is often triangular in shape, at the corner of a field, or where two or more fields meet.... It is a place where the Spirits, the Land Wights, or other beings live and where the normal rules of humanity do not apply." Nigel G. Pearson in *The Devil's Plantation: East Anglian Lore, Witchcraft, & Folk-Magic,* pg. 11.

as with *Mahonia* species. Martial plants will often have red or purple coloration, as with cinnamon bark, red chilé, echinacea, and pokeweed. These will also be very well ordered, meaning their leaves will be perfectly aligned along stems, or the venation of the leaves will be regimented and segmented in long lines, like with plantain. There will be a symmetry, an almost purposeful placement of elements, to Martial plants that is very obvious.

These herbs will often be superficially irritating and have a rubefacient action, bringing redness and heat to the skin. This means they are excellent for healing muscle sprains and soreness or loosening tight connective tissue, as they increase specific circulation via topical application. The plants that stimulate circulation or digestion primarily through intense heating are usually Martial, as are many of the stimulating herbs. This can include caffeine-containing plants that stimulate the nervous system, like coffee and tea, or things like mustard that stimulate digestion, cleavers that stimulate the lymphatic system, or cascara sagrada, a strong laxative that strongly stimulates the colon and peristalsis.

They will also act as pyretics, meaning they increase the heat of the body when they are ingested, as with garlic and other *Allium* species. This family also causes the eyes to water, which is another indicator of Mars plants. The flavor of Mars herbs is bitter but also often hot and burning, as with chilé peppers and mustard. Perhaps it is better to say their flavor is "pungent," which is just another way to say *intense,* which is a keyword for Mars generally.

When it comes to energetics, Mars harmonizes Mercury and is harmonized by the Moon. The hot, intense, and greatly over-stimulated nervous systems of the general populace today benefit from Lunar herbs, such as blue vervain and marshmallow. Its oppositional planet, which is Venus, can also help, as many of its herbs are moistening, cooling, and remind us to slow down and enjoy the pleasures life offers. The disharmonies of Mercury can lead to dry, cold states related to frigidity and nervous system impairment, but also things like asthma, bronchitis, and general illness. Martial herbs like echinacea and cleavers can help increase immunity and get the body into a state that is reparative rather than stuck in a damaging loop.

Jupiter

Zodiac: Pisces and Sagittarius
Metal: Tin
Color: Blue

The song of Jupiter is the loudest, most joyous of the planets. It is called the "Greater Benefic" and is said to bring all good things in abundance. As the largest planet in our solar system, it is the harbinger of expanse, growth, and freedom. This planet deals with business, especially growth and profit, and is the planet that can help the most in places of commerce. Jupiter is, of course, the king of the gods in Roman mythology and correlates to the Greek Zeus, who overthrew his father, Saturn/Kronos, and established the Olympian dynasty. What fetters Saturn lays upon us, Jupiter breaks, so the herbs of Jupiter can be put to good use as curse breakers and can help to remove bindings. Because of his role as a ruler, Jupiter is related to all things concerning law. Jupiter is also the planet most associated with religious and spiritual matters and with weather in general, but especially storms. As such, it can also lead to blind rage and extreme changeability, zealotry, spiritual bypassing, and what has been termed "toxic positivity," an inability or total unwillingness to acknowledge any sort of negativity, leaving us stuck and stupefied.

The sacred places of Jupiter are places of commerce, courtrooms, and places where lawmakers frequent. Dirt from these places makes a good addition to any poke for luck in a court case. Jupiter's especially sacred animals are the bull and the eagle, though it rules all large animals, such as elephants and whales, and any of the more regal, stately animals, like elk and horses. It also rules all of the animals associated with storms and tempests, like rams and sheep, as well as mythological beasts like dragons. The stones of Jupiter include amber (because it creates an electric charge when rubbed with wool), jacinth, beryl, and all blue stones, particularly lapis lazuli and sapphire.

The herbs of Jupiter are often large, with broad, rough leaves that droop toward the ground. They often have large, deep roots, which are sometimes yellow or orange in color. These plants also tend to grow in areas where they can have enough room to really spread out or take over, such as with Juniper barrens. Juniper plants can also be quite resinous, oily, and pungent smelling, though the oils tend to be less aromatic and volatile than in Mercury plants. The flowers of Jupiter plants also tend to grow or go to seed in spherical shapes, like dandelion and valerian.

Jupiter, as the ruler of Sagittarius, has rulership of the liver. Many Jupiterian herbs are hepatoprotective, cholagogue, and digestive, particularly in helping the body break down fats and filter wastes. Their flavor is often very bitter, which stimulates most of the digestive system to secrete its various enzymes and juices. Jupiter plants tend to be warm and moist, meaning they help to treat dry and cool conditions, such as slow gut motility or low secretion. Pathological Jupiter patterns include hot, swollen, sometimes weeping or seeping conditions, particularly in the joints and skin.

The song of Jupiter is harmonized by Mercury and harmonizes Venus. Jupiter can get a little overzealous when it comes to production and secretion and sometimes needs to be reined in by the dry, Airy plants of Mercury. It also has an energetic and psychological tendency to become self-centered and isolated in a way that leads to self-aggrandizement and megalomania, which the direct communication and cutting nature of Mercury can help to curb. When Venus is under-productive, leading to depressive states, skin disorders, and loss of vision, the plants of Jupiter may help bring that planet into greater harmony. Borage, a plant very much in Jupiter's resonance, is a must for languishing Venusian qualities.

Saturn

Zodiac: Aquarius and Capricorn
Metal: Lead
Color: Black

Saturn is the most misunderstood and maligned of the planets. Historically, it has been called the "Greater Malefic," as it is said to bring ill fortune to a greater degree than Mars and has been treated as a sort of astrological bogeyman. As I hope I've made clear, this is just not the case. Saturn is the planet of constriction, binding, or endings, but none of those things are inherently negative or harmful. I think it is better to think of Saturn as the Shaper of Ages, the great sculptor who skillfully whittles down possibilities until a fully realized form is created. Without that, nothing could exist. This is, in part, why Saturn is the

planet associated with Binah and the mythology of the Great Mother in traditional Qabalistic practices; it is the Womb of all Form.

As a god, Saturn/Kronos is the father of Jupiter/Zeus and the patriarch of the Golden Age, when everything was perfect. His own madness brought that age to an end. Due to his fear of a prophecy foretelling his demise, he ate all his children as soon as they were born. All except Jupiter, who was spirited away to safety by his mother, Ops/Rhea. When he was grown and ready, Jupiter tricked his father into vomiting up all of his siblings, who were now fully grown. They began the war called the Titanomachy, during which Saturn was deposed by his children, his genitals were severed with a flint sickle and tossed into the sea (from which Aphrodite/Venus was born), and he was sent to the Underworld to rule over the Elysian Fields, where the righteous and heroic go after death.

Saturn is the god of time and the boundaries of things, limitations, contracts, cycles of renewal, prosperity, wealth, generations, and even liberation. Because of that, he is also an agricultural deity, particularly of harvests and the end of the growing season. As with Mars, Saturn is a planet particularly involved with the topic of this book because of its links to agriculture. It is a constraining force in the wilderness, the *murus urbis,* which keeps the wild god from entering the city uninvited. Inherent in its power, though, is Saturn's inevitable ability to comminute and break apart the boundaries that it sets, so the end of the wall is there at its beginning. The song of Saturn is a requiem and a promise, a celestial *memento mori*, such as the Seikilos epitaph:

> "Ὅσον ζῇς φαίνου μηδὲν ὅλως σὺ λυποῦ πρὸς ὀλίγον ἔστι τὸ ζῆν τὸ τέλος ὁ χρόνος ἀπαιτεῖ."[52]

Saturn rules the cemeteries and graveyards, morgues, hedgerows, travel terminals, all other boundary areas, caves, deserts, swamps, bogs, and other places difficult for survival. Also, ruins and desolate places, fields ready for harvest, hollow trees, and orchards where the fruit lies rotting

52 "While you live, shine / have no grief at all / life exists only for a short while / and Time demands his due." (Translated by John Landels, 1999).

on the ground. The stones of Saturn are all black gems, such as onyx, jet, and obsidian, but also coal, anthracite, and all very dense and heavy stones. The particular metal of Saturn is lead due to its heaviness and dark color. It rules all creeping and solitary animals, as well as vultures and other animals that are predominantly carrion feeders. "Birds with long necks and harsh voices," according to Agrippa, like peacocks and ostriches. Its sea animals are things like eels, lampreys, cookie-cutter sharks, and other slithering, undulating creatures of the deep who have strong teeth and eat meat.

Saturnine plants are often strongly jointed or grow directly from the ground as if they are bursting up from the Underworld. They may also have a dry, roughness about them and will break apart easily or will have circles, whorls, and rings prominently. They may also be extremely angular in their growth patterns, looking almost tortured. The plants of Saturn can have an aroma like rotten meat, like the rafflesia flower and other carnivorous plants, or so astringent as to be somewhat sickening. The color of the plants may carry signatures of white, blood red, black, or deep shades of purple, and their flowers will often grow directly from the jointed stalk, as with gentian and Solomon's seal.

The flavors of Saturnian plants are drying, cooling, astringent, and sometimes burning and bitter, in the way many toxic plants are. All poisonous plants fall under his rulership, though they may be co-ruled by other planets. The Saturnian garden is one of growing and healing the skeletal system, reducing inflammation in the joints, and tightening tissues. Many of its herbs are also antilithics, breaking down calcifications in the body, whittling them down bit by bit like a stone in a river. The effects of Saturn are felt deep in the body and affect it greatly and obviously. Its disharmonies are often associated with senescence, things like arthritis, myopia, and brittleness.

Saturn is harmonized by Venus and harmonizes the Sun. The cool, dry disharmonies of Saturn, the stiff aches of age, and the paper-thinness of elderly skin can be harmonized by the effects of Venus's garden of moistening emollients and demulcents. The astringent nature of Saturn's garden helps in cases where the Sun has gotten too robust and moves fluids through tissues in such a way that they leak or become loose. Saturn can help by drying, tightening, and closing the tissues up.

Planetary Hours

Each of the seven inner luminaries rules a day of the week and a set of hours throughout the day. Knowing how the days and hours work together is important for knowing when to gather certain herbs, when to perform rites, and when the strength of some charms will be greatest. The order in which the planets are ascribed to the days and hours is according to the "Chaldean order," a geocentric model that stacks the planets from fastest to slowest in a great chain. These were understood to be spheres of influence that nestled one inside the other with Earth at the center, something like a series of matryoshka dolls, all leading up to the sphere of Heaven.

The order ascending from Earth is thus: The Moon, Mercury, Venus, The Sun, Mars, Jupiter, and Saturn. This is drawn out with the Moon closest to the Earth and Saturn furthest from it, abutting the sphere that holds the zodiac and the other stars. At first, the order of planetary rulership for the days of the week seems to deviate from this order and is assigned thusly:

Sunday: The Sun
Monday: The Moon
Tuesday: Mars
Wednesday: Mercury
Thursday: Jupiter
Friday: Venus
Saturday: Saturn

Though it may seem like the order of days does not follow the Chaldean order, trust that they *do* follow the order, just in an encoded fashion. If the planets are laid out in the Chaldean pattern but in a ring with the Sun at the top, and if one draws lines between the planets in the order of the days of the week, one will have drawn a heptagram, or the seven-pointed star of alchemy representing the seven planets and their corresponding metals. It seems that the occult has been with us even as we are writing out events or grocery lists on a calendar.

The first planetary hour of each day is ruled by the planet that rules the day, so the first hour of Sunday always belongs to the Sun. The hours then follow the Chaldean order but are attributed in *descending* order, with the hour of Mars coming *before* the hour of the Sun and the hour of Venus coming *after* it.

Another important thing to keep in mind when working with the planetary hours is that they are *not* increments of sixty minutes and are not measured at equal length unless they are calculated on either Equinox when day and night are equal. This is because they are split into daylight and nighttime sets, measured from sunrise to sunset and sunset to sunrise, respectively. This means that daylight hours in summer will be longer than nighttime hours, and vice versa in winter.

To calculate the length of daylight and nighttime hours, determine how much time there is from sunrise to sunset on a given day. Multiply the number of hours by sixty, then add however many minutes are remaining to get the total number of minutes for the daylight period. For example, today, a Tuesday in Albuquerque, the Sun rose at 7:09 a.m. and set at 6:37 p.m., which is 11 hours and 28 minutes. Multiply 11 by 60 to get 660, then add 28 to get 688 minutes of daylight. Divide that by 12, which would reveal that each daylight "hour" was about 55 minutes long, so the period between 7:09 and 8:46 a.m. was ruled by Mars. For nighttime hours, subtract 688 from 1,440 (the number of minutes in a 24-hour day), which equals 752. That divided by 12 gives nighttime hours of 62 minutes and 36 seconds in length, the rulership of which can be divvied up appropriately. As I am writing, the current hour, around 9:30 p.m., is ruled by Mars.

However, if you are unaware of the time for sunrise and sunset and do not have access to an internet calculator, of which there are several, then you may attribute the rulership from midnight to midnight, starting with the ruler of the day. That means 12 to 1 a.m. on a Sunday would be ruled by the Sun, 1 to 2 a.m. would be ruled by Venus, and so forth.

This is important because it is best to gather herbs ruled by a certain planet on the day that planet rules and in an hour ruled by that planet or one corresponding to your purpose. If I were to gather lavender flowers for a spell concerning better communication, I would gather them on a Wednesday in the hour of Mercury, or I would do likewise if I was just gathering lavender and storing it. If, however, I were gathering them to increase the ability of my words to charm and cajole people, as with some kinds of glamoury, I would gather them on a Wednesday in the hour of *Venus,* who rules over appearances, charm, and attractiveness. If it were for a court case of some sort, though, I would gather in the hour of Jupiter, who rules over law and judgments. Think of the day as a song being played and the hour as the key it is being played in. The song and its subject matter stay the same no matter what, but the key gives the feel of the song a total mood shift.

Lunar Phases

One more point to discuss on magical timing that I would be remiss to leave out: the cycle of the Moon. If you think of the days as songs and the hours as key signatures, think of lunar phases as the overture setting the stage for the performance of your work; it sets an expectation. Lunar phases are integral to the way magic moves in the world, and taking the Moon into account is an important part of figuring out when to perform various types of magic. Each tradition and practice will have different ideas of how to work with these energies, so what follows can be taken as merely an example from my own work. My own way of working with the lunar phases has changed much over the years, and it is still shifting and changing as I learn more about mythology, myself, and my practice. Just as the Moon is ever-changing, do not feel as though you must eternally act or think a certain way you've been told to or as you read to do in a book.

New Moon: *Hekate Moira, Dame Fate, ascends to the highest peak of the castle that ever turns without moving and readies herself through purification to sit before the wheel and loom underneath the illuminating flash of Lucifer Moiragetes.*

The new moon is the night after the dark moon, the time at which there is only a small sliver visible in the sky. Some would call this a *fingernail moon,* which is apt, as this is when to clean underneath your own. This is the best time to begin projects and to tidy your ritual area, clean and re-sanctify your altar, and make yourself ship-shape for the lunation to come. Long-form alchemical procedures are best started on or near a new moon. This is a good night for ritual baths, too, as well as clearings and cleansings of oneself and the home, but not for exorcisms, which should rather be done on the dark moon. When you think of the new moon, think of freshness and cleanliness.

WAXING MOON: *Hekate Klotho is at the spinning wheel, taking the Astral Aether and turning it to the red threads of Fate.*

For approximately two weeks, the Moon waxes to its fullness, building itself up bit by bit. This is a time to gather spell components together, gather some herbs,[53] and get your ducks in a row for later rituals. This is also the time to begin spells to grow prosperity and wealth, to make love charms for greater attractiveness or to spark relationships, to make healing charms that are meant to *increase* health, and for acts of glamoury. This period is also to foster the projects that were started on the new moon into the next phase of the operation.

FULL MOON: *Hekate Lachesis is fully at her loom, busily weaving forth the tapestry of Fate that shows the lives of all throughout the world.*

When the Moon is at its brightest, Selene, the goddess of the Moon, is in the heavens, fully present in the world and "bent on love," meaning she is with her husband, the shepherd Endymion, and in the moment of rapture. She is watching over all things in the night, as her brother, Helios, does in the day, meaning this is a time for divination, dream magic, and seeking answers. Selene, who is considered prudent, peaceful, and moderate, is watching, so do all that would please her on this night, which includes the rituals of love and lovemaking. This is a time for petitions and asking for blessings, for spells of protection, warding, and empowerment, and for large celebrations and rituals.

It is also a useful time for drawing into the material world that which you created in the Astral world during the previous phase of the moon. I have called this the "Gestation Moon" in the past, but I'm no longer sure I think of it in those terms. This is more of an "Embodying Moon," when there is enough Astral Light or Lunar Aether overflowing the gates of magic to create bodies and anchors for things that normally only exist in the Astral world. It is a time for visions and for bringing the gods into the world where we can commune with them, for giving body and form to spirits we have met or created, to enshroud them in "flesh." This

---

53 Think of herbs that build and bring things together, such as calendula, comfrey, and beet.

makes the full moon an appropriate night to accomplish your alchemical works, bringing the purified parts together into full union as you enliven and ensoul them.

I think this is also why it is considered a time for manifestation because it is a time that our dreams can be given real, permanent form in this physical world. As such, it is good to think that the full moon is also a time for hunting and is the night when Diana walks through the wild places. She can help you attain whatever prize you seek, help you to stalk it, find it, and bring it down.

WANING MOON: *Hekate lets fall the shuttlecock and examines the work, assuring Herself that all is done without error, then pulls tight the threads for cutting.*

The period when the Moon is waning is a time for bringing projects and procedures to a close and putting the final touches on things. Spells for decrease are also suggested at this time, such as charms to diminish disease (like the famous "abracadabra" charm), to remove obstacles, and to begin banishing rituals that take time to work. During this time, the things you manifested during the full moon are settling into their new forms or, if your operation was not a success, a time for you to reflect on what you can do differently going forward. Think of the waning moon as a time for rest and recalibration. This is also a good time for *maleficium*, as the waning moon can also be a *wasting* moon that slowly drains the vitality, luck, creativity, or other energy from an enemy.

DARK MOON: *Hekate Atropos takes up her fateful scissors and snips free the threads of Fate before she retires to the earthly surface, there to wander the rocky wilds and the desert places, to feast, and to revel with the ghostly horde.*

This is the night when the Moon is completely dark, a time for wild magic and communion with the Witch Queen. The Eye of Selene is closed, resting after her long sojourn with her husband, and Hekate has freed herself from the loom for a night. The dark moon is the night of *deipnon* (dinner), a ritual feast that Hekate shares with those who pay her homage and love her most.

The night of Hekate is a night of great power for witches, for She is the source of all magic walking in the world. As the Queen of the Dead and the shepherdess of ghosts, this is the best time to ask for her aid in exorcism and banishment of nonhuman spirits and disincarnate ones.

Another way to think about the phases of the moon is a mythopoetic approach I developed after reading *Practical Planetary Magick* by David Rankine and Sorita d'Este alongside *The Roebuck in the Thicket* by Evan John Jones. The mythology of sacred hunts, stories of ritually pursuing a divine beast for magical purpose, is ubiquitous the world over. The lunar cycle can be understood as a sacred hunt, and I have built a mythology around it that helps me understand the phases better. The "Hunter" is the witch or sorcerer, where the questing beast (what Jones called a "Shaper") is the source of power and magic, Hekate. If you don't like blood and hunting, you may skip this bit.

It begins with the new moon. The Hunter cleanses and purifies themself, readying for a long hunt. They set out and, over the course of the waxing moon, they hunt high and low, far and wide, until they find their quarry on the full moon, perhaps with the aid of Diana, lady huntress of the wood. Through ritual and invitation, the beast draws near, and the Hunter strikes with the holy dagger, slitting its throat in a sacrificial manner. They drink of the Shaper's blood and take its power into themself before leaving an offering for the beast. Its head is severed and mounted on a pole facing the east as an offering to the gods of the hunt and to protect the Hunter and their community for a time. It is at this point, however, that the hunter becomes the hunted.

The spirit of magic, Hekate Herself, hunts them over the course of the waning moon, setting traps, bringing them challenge after challenge, watching how the Hunter uses the power they have taken. On the dark moon, Hekate catches up, and a battle ensues. If the Hunter loses, the connections between them are slowly lost, and the hunt must begin again, but it will be a much more difficult one, for She now knows the Hunter's tricks. If the Hunter wins, Hekate opens Her *own* throat and feeds the Hunter from the font of Her power, gifting an eternal connection between that person and the source of magic; She becomes *Mater Sanguis,* the Blood Mother. On the new moon, once the hunt is concluded, She returns to Her place at the highest tower of the castle that spins without motion, ritually cleanses Herself, and prepares to spin the Threads of Fate, which now are very different for the Hunter.

SIGNS OF THE ZODIAC

As with the elements, it is important to remember that each plant is a complex mixture of the zodiacal lenses, just as we are, though they will reflect certain of their energies more than others…just as we do. The overall energy of each zodiac sign and the systems or body parts they rule over must be taken into account, as well as their elemental associations. These can be tricky to pin down, and everyone seems to have a different idea of which plant belongs to which sign, so work within your practice to figure out what works for you and your magic.

Still, understanding the elemental character of the zodiac signs is essential to being able to figure out which herbs reflect them. First, each sign is part of one of the four elements, or perhaps it is better to think of them as reflections of certain aspects of the elements in the world. Second, they are classified by three modes, either *cardinal, fixed,* or *mutable,* which describes not only their position in a season but also their energetic character, which is explained below. Also, remember that if the herbs act like mirrors for the zodiac, reflecting their qualities through their shape and action, they may reflect more than one. As we are all of the signs woven together in a complex web, so are the herbs.

The Modes

Cardinal: The cardinal signs begin a season and have the energy of initiating things, getting things going, and gaining access to things. The cardinal signs are *Aries* (Fire), *Cancer* (Water), *Libra* (Air), and *Capricorn* (Earth). When it comes to herbs, think of the plants that initiate the energy of an element in the body or in your spell.

Fixed: Fixed signs rest in the middle of a season and are wholly immersed in their element and the general energy of the season they are a part of. These are also the signs that represent the four living creatures on the World trump of the tarot and are the representative faces of their seasons. The fixed signs are *Taurus* (Earth), *Leo* (Fire), *Scorpio* (Water), and *Aquarius* (Air). The herbs that belong to these signs will be tonic, helping the body maintain balance and homeostasis, and herbs that help sustain a spell or charm.

Mutable: The mutable signs come at the end of a season and are *Gemini* (Air), *Virgo* (Earth), *Sagittarius* (Fire), and *Pisces* (Water). They bring the energy of the sign preceding them through themselves into the new season, so become admixtures of two elemental energies feeding another. Herbs associated with these promote change, flow, and removal of obstacles in the body and to your spellcraft. If the herb promotes movement, particularly toward another elemental state (such as moving stuck emotions toward action or moving edema from one part of the body to the kidneys so it can be removed from the body), then it may be one of the mutable signs.

The Signs

Aries: Mythologically, Aries is the winged ram from which the golden fleece was stripped, a beast named Chrysomallos. It became the object of desire for many adventurers, eventually falling into the hands of Jason after a very heavy amount of help from Medea. Aries is known as a head-strong sign and rules the head, the eyes, the face, the circulatory system, the arteries of the neck, and memory. It also rules over the adrenal cascade and the hormones related to stress. Aries is associated with inflammation, redness, minor burns, and swelling, so herbs that deal with circulation, the head, and memory will likely reflect Aries. The herbs of Aries also share in the energy of its cardinal nature, having the ability to spark and stoke heat and begin stimulating the systems related to the Fire element. They make excellent hasteners in magic or can act to aggravate enemies, as with hot-foot powders. Plants like edible peppers and ginger reflect Aries.

Taurus: This is the ruler of the neck and throat, including the thyroid (and the metabolic hormones), trachea, larynx, the veins of the neck, as well as the muscles of the upper back. Herbs of Taurus tend to alleviate pain in these areas and have a relaxing, tonic quality. Taurus tends to deal with stagnant conditions that dig their heels in and become chronic. Issues reflected in Taurus are things like thyroid disorders and swelling, laryngitis and loss of voice, as well as meekness and feelings of being too small or weak. Magically, these are herbs of prosperity and growth. Herbs assigned to this sign include many cooking spices, particularly things like fennel, clove, fenugreek, and cardamom.

Gemini: Gemini rules the arms from the shoulders to the fingertips as well as the Thoracic cavity and muscles, the diaphragm, and lungs. Sometimes, the lower parts of the brain, especially the cerebrospinal nerves, are given to Gemini. It has a strong relationship with the respiratory system and the way the body exchanges gasses. The herbs of Gemini will help to amplify oxygenation in the body, open the bronchi, or act as expectorants. They may also have an effect on the acuity of the mind, helping the hands remember what they need to do or to do those things more efficiently. Gemini herbs help clear the air and help you speak your truth more effectively, to have a direct link between what you really think and what you do with it, and how you change the world by the power of your mind. Herbs like lavender, mallow, and Ginkgo belong to this sign.

Cancer: Cancer rules the breast, the upper alimentary canal, the stomach, and the pancreas. As the Cardinal sign of Water, Cancer deals largely with the emotional life of a person and how emotions affect the body. Cancer herbs have an affinity for uplifting the mood and aiding in cases of indigestion. They also have effects on general fluid motility in the body, getting them flowing. They help in initiating change and motion so a person feels less stuck, particularly emotionally. They are gentle-yet-powerful supporters of emotional breakthroughs and help to unknot the stomach, remove tummy butterflies, and ease digestive upset caused by anxiety, depression, and obsessive thinking. The herbs of Cancer count amongst themselves plants like lemon balm, passionflower, and jujube.

Leo: Leo rules the heart, cardiovascular system, and the spleen. As the fixed sign of Fire, this sign is linked to tonic herbs of the heart that help to sustain the thrum of life and move blood through the body. The herbs of Leo may also be herbs that bring confidence and ease panic. The emotions that make the heart batter at the breast are part of the reflection of Leo, and the herbs that make the heart lay easy are the ones to give to this sign. Also, the herbs that build the blood, help with circulation, and tonify the cardiovascular system, such as hawthorn, linden, sunflower, and beet.

Virgo: Virgo rules the intestines and colon. The herbs of Virgo are Earthy and, as a mutable sign, have quite a lot of downward motion, helping with elimination and release. The plants that ease tension, particularly in the gut, are attributed to Virgo, especially those that deal with constipation, diarrhea, IBS, and ulcerations of the lower GI. Energetically, they can also help to ease the mind out of repetitive thinking, helping us to ground ourselves, particularly through food. The herbs of Virgo may also help to increase one's ability to trust in one's intuition. Herbs such as horseweed, turkey rhubarb, and bindweed strongly reflect Virgo.

LIBRA: Libra rules the kidneys and the urinary system. The herbs associated with Libra are balancing to the body and widely useful, not just to the systems ruled by Libra, but generally. In this category, I include most of the adaptogens, which are tonic for the nervous system and help the body to meet stress more effectively. Also, herbs that help to stimulate the urinary organs and are beneficial to the functionality of the urinary system belong to this sign. Herbs of Libra are often astringent, drying, and diuretic and are best balanced against a more demulcent one, like marshmallow.

SCORPIO: Scorpio rules the genitals and reproductive organs. As such, many aphrodisiacs are reflected in this sign, as are those that are meant to increase vital force. Herbs that help us plumb the depths of our emotional selves and help to move emotional stagnation may be Scorpionic, such as skullcap. They also help to move fluids through the lower body, such as with ocotillo. Other Scorpio herbs include nettle, catnip, and coriander.

SAGITTARIUS: Sagittarius rules the hips, thighs, and muscles of the lower back (the flanks). It also rules the liver. It has a powerful forward motion as the mutable sign of Fire and helps drive the energy of the Earth through the roots of plants, where it can be safely fostered through the cold of January. Herbs that help with the motility of muscle in the body, heal skeletal muscles, and give the body boosts of energy reflect this sign, as do herbs that energetically speak to honesty, truth, and running toward goals like there may be no tomorrow. These include things like ginseng, sage, arnica, and devil's claw.

CAPRICORN: Capricorn rules the skeletal system and the joints, particularly the knees. Herbs of Capricorn include Solomon's seal and comfrey, things that have powerful action on the densest parts of the body. When in doubt, give herbs that lend aid to the eliminatory systems to this sign. Capricorn, being the cardinal sign of Earth, initiates slow, gentle healing and helps us to reach deep down into relaxation and quiet to begin the process of grounding. These herbs are often helpful for joint health and deep aches and pains, which can keep us up at night and make sleep difficult. These include cat's claw, turmeric, and horsetail (which is one of the oldest plants on Earth).

Aquarius: Aquarius rules the lower leg and ankles. As the fixed sign of Air, the herbs that reflect this sign will help ease the mind and steady our thoughts, helping us to focus and think deeply. They are also tonic for the brain and nervous system. Aquarian energy is also interested and curious, always seeking to know more about things, so these make good herbs to keep your mind (or the mind of an enemy) on the subject at hand. These herbs include blue vervain and Bacopa. Herbs of Aquarius will also help with circulation in the lower limbs, which can be problematic in some people and lead to things like varicosities. Herbs such as witch hazel and horse chestnut show reflections of Aquarius.

Pisces: Pisces rules the feet and, therefore, the paths we walk. Piscean energy is constantly shifting, as it is the mutable sign of Water. Though it is a Water sign, it is also moved by currents of Air, making it particularly flexible and prone to radical uniqueness. The mythology of Pisces relates this sign to Aphrodite and Eros, for it is on the back of these two fish that they escaped the monstrous Typhon and traveled to safety down the Euphrates. Herbs that reduce anger, ease the heart, and bring it back to feeling secure reflect Pisces, which includes things such as mimosa and violet.

THE DOCTRINE OF SIGNATURES

This is an idea that pervades cultures the world over, but, in the West, is most often talked about in relation to Paracelsus, the alchemist and physician said to have kept a true Philosopher's Stone in the head of his walking stick. The Doctrine of Signatures states that we can identify what a plant is used for and whether it is edible by observing its "signatum," the physical attributes of the thing. Thus, a walnut is good for the brain, and saxifrage can break up kidney stones in the same manner it grows through rocks, and purslane can be used for worms in the intestines since it looks like a wiggling worm as it grows. This is, of course, a dangerous and not very accurate way of determining which plants to use, especially internally. It's lucky that, due to their fatty oil content, walnuts *are* good for your brain, but saxifrage doesn't really help with kidney stones, and purslane isn't good for worms (though it *is* good for your brain, contrary to its signatum).

NEVER put something into your mouth that you have not been able to identify completely, without doubt of what it is, after watching its entire life cycle and seeing its flowers. It isn't worth it to severely injure yourself. Here in the mountains where I work, there are several species of geranium that grow right alongside aconite, one of the most deadly plants in the world. Their young leaves look almost exactly alike, especially to the untrained eye, though their differences become apparent when the flower stalks begin to grow. Without that surety, you might be gathering a root with the intention to stop bleeding or treat ulcers, but instead, gather one that will stop your heart altogether in almost no time at all.

Where the Doctrine of Signatures shines is in the attribution of planets to planetary energies and zodiacal signs and to sympathetic magical uses. Thorny plants are often Martial and are good for protective magic or aggressive acts of maleficium; the brittle joints of Saturnian herbs are good for breaking enemies or curses. The heart-shaped petals of roses are used in love magic, and calendula flowers, so much like great, big golden coins, are used in Solar magic of wealth and power. My advice is to never use the Doctrine of Signatures to decide what is good or bad for the body, but rather how it can be used symbolically to achieve the greatest degree of sympathy in your magic.

USING THE PLANETARY PENTACLES

One of the best ways I've discovered to draw on the energy of the planets is to use the planetary pentacles as found in the *Lesser Key of Solomon,* which was my first grimoire. My mother got it for my twelfth birthday, along with Francis Barrett's *The Magus,* which also goes over some aspects of Solomonic magic. I don't bother with many of the trappings of the system, especially because I'm not a Christian or anything close to adjacent to it, so the prayers and such hold little meaning for me. I use my normal spellwork tools, such as my wand and dagger, brass bowl and tripod, bells, candles, and the rest, and I call on my usual spirits, which is mainly Hekate. I consider her a suitable intermediary and translator between myself and the Solomonic tradition, and what I do seems to work, so I won't be making any direct invocations to Yahweh any time soon.

Instead, I use the names of the angels, spirits, and intelligences (daimons) of the planets as given in most of the grimoires and call on a chain of command that ends with Hekate as Dame Fate, the arbiter and mother of all things that exist and occur in the manifest universe, for which there is plenty of precedent.

So, how do we use the pentacles? Choose the one you think suits your operation best. Draw out the pentacle in exacting detail, but also feel free to change the names of Yahweh to those that make more sense to you. There isn't really a need to, but if it makes the operation more efficacious for your work, there is no real reason not to change them. The pentacles should be drawn out on vellum or very thin leather, like the head of a drum, or just a new sheet of printer paper (which is a bit janky, really, but sometimes all you've got). They may also be engraved on the correct metal for the planet, which gets pricey for something like the Sun, whose metal is gold. In this case, a gold-colored metal is fine, but so is a piece of parchment. What is important is the pentacle itself and the color you choose for drawing it.

Like we consider the day as the song that is being played and the hour as the key it is being played in, the pentacles and the color they are drawn in will have a similar feel. If I draw the Fourth Pentacle of Mars to gain victory over an enemy, but I draw it in purple, the color of the Moon, then I effectively create the overall effect of the pentacle (its song) in the key to the subconscious (the realm of the Moon). This brings a lot of nuance to the functionality of the pentacles. They can also be combined by drawing them out and connecting them in the line of a circle in which your work will take place. That way, you can use the Fourth Pentacle of Mars in conjunction with the Fourth Pentacle of Saturn, connected as the north and south curvature of a circle, in which you perform a poppetry curse. This is a particularly nasty and effective way of damaging an enemy.

To empower the pentacles takes a little bit of incantation, though. Because we have been using Mars, we will continue to do so and go about it in a simple way. We will say you are using the Fourth Pentacle of Mars on the day of Mars in the hour of Mars, and you have drawn it out in red ink on a piece of vellum and are burning five red candles and a suitable incense of Martial plants. So far, so good, but it is just a drawing on a bit of paper. So, we enliven it. You don't have to do this part in a circle, as you're not really invoking a being but rather connecting the device (the Pentacle) to a power source (Mars). Also, prepare the sigils of Samael, Kamael, Graphiel, and Barzabel, then set them aside. Draw a circle before you, about a foot in diameter. This can be drawn on poster board or on the floor or a working table, wherever you are doing this rite.

Begin by naming the pentacle:

"I have prepared upon my altar the Fourth Pentacle of Mars, so that, without doubt, I shall attain victory over my enemy, NN."

This you will set aside for a bit, then call out to the spirits who are in charge of the Martial powers, starting at the top and working your way down:

"I call to Hekate Moira, Queen of Fate, who stands upon the highest tower of the Castle that, without motion, turns. Open the gate for Pyripnos and spin the threads in my favor that I may attain victory over NN. Hekate Pyripnos, She Breathing Fire, I call to you. Open the gate for Mars himself and let loose your heat upon this pentacle, that I may burn away my enemy, NN. Mars, god of war and victory in battle, I call to you with the Fire of my throat and ask you: open the gate for your servants, Kamael and Samael, commanders over your armies, who shall stand against NN."

At this point, you will place the drawn-out sigil of Kamael on the right-hand curvature of your circle and Samael's on the left-hand curvature.

"Kamael, archangel of divine and proper justice, and Samael, dark archangel, venomous adversary, servants of Mars, I call to you and all the spirits under your command. Open the gates for Graphiel, Intelligence of Mars, and for Barzabel, Spirit of Mars, the daimons great of power, that they may wreak their wrath upon my enemy, NN."

Lay the sigil of Graphiel at the uppermost curvature of your circle and the sigil of Barzabel at the lowest curvature. Now you have a crossroads of Martial powers, at the center of which you will now place your pentacle.

"Kamael and Samael, Graphiel and Barzabel, angels and daimons of the Martial powers, and all the spirits under your leadership, by virtue of the authority from the gods who have opened the gates for you, let loose your power into this, the Fourth Pentacle of Mars, that it may come alive with all your Fire and rage to burn away all that is my enemy, NN.[54] *May NN have no restful night, no fruitful day. Let NN be broken down and ground beneath my foot, for I stand above NN in the glory of the power of the Martial Chain. So it is."*

The above is only an example, but something like that will call down the power of the hierarchy of the Martial powers into your pentacle, making it alive and ready to work magic. They work well enough without incantation, but they work *so much better* with the actual powers of Mars backing your work. Every orchestra needs a conductor and a series of lead chairs for the sections of the composition to follow, and the power of a pentacle is clearer when the powers that govern it are orchestrating the work it is meant to do.

54 Where you see NN throughout any ritual in this book, replace it with the person's name for whom you are performing the rite.

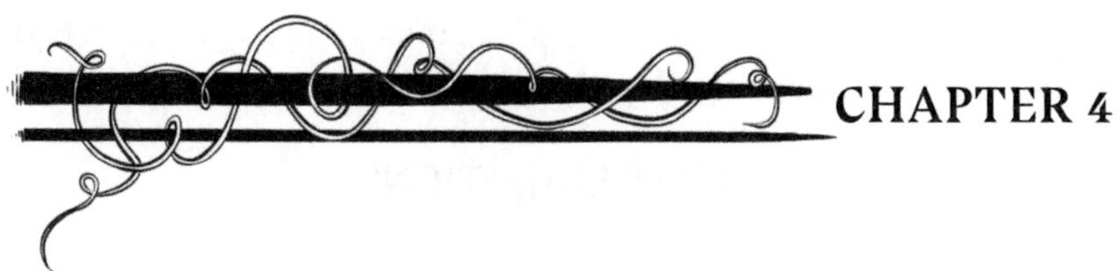

CHAPTER 4

A Wortcunner's Handbook of Methods

THIS SECTION OF THIS BOOK is to help you figure out which preparations to make and how to do so. Very basic methods for the creation of remedies and charms are presented here, so feel free to tweak them in ways that make sense to you.

There are also a few words to be familiar with before we go any further. First, a *marc* is the herbal, chunky, nonliquid part of your formula. This is something that will be tossed, composted, calcined, or in some other way transformed or gotten rid of. The *menstruum* is the liquid part of your formula, the solvent matrix to which your herbs, resins, and spell components will infuse to create the basis for your preparation. This can be water, oil, wine, vinegar, or any other liquid or solvent thing.

The marc and menstruum will be used mostly for making infusions or extractions. An *infusion,* usually made with water, is a short process, usually no more than fifteen minutes. There are also infused oils used for salves, which can take a few minutes to weeks to complete. *Extractions,* on the other hand, are part of longer processes meant to preserve the constituents of an herb for a very long time, sometimes indefinitely, in something like alcohol or vinegar. These are then made into other things, such as liniments and compresses and almost every other kind of preparation you can think of.

In this book, the word *preparation* is used to denote anything you might make, be it magical or not, whereas the words *remedy* and *remedial* are used to indicate something meant to have a positive effect on one's health. We do not use the words *medicine* or *medicinal,* as *nothing in this book is intended to be a substitute for medical treatment.* Please consult your medical care provider before using any of the remedies presented here, particularly if you have a known medical condition or if you are pregnant or nursing. If you intend to utilize herbal protocols in any way, it is best to also be in the care of an allopathic physician.

DRY PREPARATIONS

Tisane: Any blend of herbs meant to be infused in water and imbibed is a tisane. They are commonly called "herbal teas," but a tea must include the leaves of *Camellia sinensis,* the true tea plant. It seems a bit arbitrary to split hairs over this, but using separate terms *does* help to alleviate some confusion when discussing remedial preparations.

Smoking Blend: Any mix of dried herbs meant to be smoked can be termed a "smoking blend." These are also often burned on charcoal tabs as incense rather than being literally smoked. This is a dry incense that does not incorporate honey, molasses, or any of the other binders most incense utilizes. I have several blends I make to smoke in a pipe with tobacco and other sacred herbs during ritual and spell work, though I will often take from these and use them as incense instead.

Strewing Herbs: These blends are made to simply toss on the floor, on fires, across thresholds, and various other places. The word "strew" just means "spread by untidily tossing," so don't feel too precious about using them. They're meant to be a bit messy. One way to use them is to make a "vacuum powder," which is merely a cleansing blend of herbs meant to remove malicious or negative influences strewn over your carpets, then vacuumed up. They can also be useful for blessing houses and people (think rice at a wedding), offering to the Land or Water, and so much more.

Incense: I include incenses in the "dry" section because they can be prepared that way to great effect. Just mix herbs together that have magically or spiritually cohesive properties and drop them onto a fully reddened coal placed in an appropriate thurible with a thermos-diffuser like salt or sand. The way I usually create incense is as follows:

1. Choose your herbs and think your formula through carefully. Once you've decided on the herbs you'd like to include, use a

grinder to powder them as completely as possible (the finer, the better).

2. Mix the herbs with honey or molasses until they are about the consistency of kinetic sand. They should hold a shape but flake easily apart. Let them sit in a container or plastic bag for about 2 weeks. This should be kept in a cool, dark place like a cabinet.
3. After this period, I take small amounts of the herbal mixture and either roll them into spheres or use a mold to shape them.
4. They then dry in the molds for about 2 more weeks until they are hard and ready to use. This kind of incense makes a particularly potent offering smoke for deities and spirits. Incense like this will still need a coal to burn.
5. Alternatively, you can mix the herbs with water, shape them, and let them stand for 24–48 hours, at which point they are ready to burn. This is an especially useful method for formulas meant for clearings or spell work.

In my experience, it has also been important to add a resin to whichever incense you are concocting. This produces more fragrant and thick smoke, as well as helping the overall incense to stay together. The three main resins I see being used are frankincense, myrrh, and storax. There are also plenty of others, like dragon's blood, gum arabic, copal, guggul, and opopanax. Really, if it's a tree sap, it can be used in incense. Some of the other resins I've used and enjoyed that I find in my area are juniper, pinon, and ponderosa. Also, other resinous plants can count toward your resin content, such as rosemary, chaparral, and bindweed root. There are also liquid incense blends, which are usually made with reductions of wine or cider and honey.

1. Figure out what your intention is and pick fragrant herbs, spices, and resins that can work together in harmony with each other toward that purpose.
2. Choose a menstruum, which is the liquid part of your formula. It ought to be something that is mostly water but also a preservative, such as wine, cider, rum, vinegar, or the like.
3. Bring this to a near boil, put it in an appropriately sized mason jar, then put your herbs, spices, and resins in as well. Allow

it to cool before you put the lid on (preferably with plastic between the lid and the lip of the jar), and let it sit for a few weeks. Shake it at least once per day.

4. Once the menstruum is infused, strain it from the marc into a bowl and measure the volume you've got. Add the same volume of honey to the menstruum and mix it together well.
5. In a saucepan over low heat, reduce the honey and menstruum mixture. This will take some time, probably a few hours, but you will be left with a very thick, viscous substance that can be dolloped onto coals or embers and burned in much the same way as resins. The liquid will bubble and sputter and send up big plumes of smoke, which is very cool-looking and smells divine.

WET PREPARATIONS

Aqueous Infusion: This is simply herbs steeped, simmered, or boiled in water. It includes teas and tisanes, as well as any other preparation made primarily with water.

Cold: Cold infusions take time, which is their drawback, but they are the best option for certain herbs. Mucilaginous herbs, such as marshmallow and elm, and herbs with delicate flavors, like lavender, are best prepared as cold infusions. To make a cold infusion, simply pour room-temperature water over your herbs and let them steep for a few hours or overnight. Strain the marc from the menstruum, and *voila!* You've got a cold, aqueous infusion of your herbs.

Hot: When it comes to hot aqueous infusions, most people tend to oveboil their water, which scalds the herbs they are using, rendering them much less effective. The rule of thumb is to form the "string of pearls," which is when small bubbles form steady streams from the bottom of your vessel to the surface of the water. This means your water is at about 195–205°F, which is just about perfect. If you decide to use water where bubbles are just barely forming on the bottom of the pot, that is also effective, especially for delicate things like petals and actual tea leaves.

Decoction: A decoction is a prolonged simmering of herbs in water to create a concentrated infusion, usually of denser components like roots, barks, berries, and some mushrooms. To decoct herbs, fill a pot with the volume of cold water you want, then put your herbs into it. Let them sit in the cold water for about five minutes, then put them over medium heat. Remember to put a lid on the pot so you don't lose all of the volatile constituents! Bring the water to a simmer and let it go for about 20–30 minutes. Remove the pot from the heat and allow it to cool.

Compress: Also called a *fomentation,* a compress is made by dipping a clean cloth in an aqueous infusion and applying it topically. Strain your infusion first to avoid getting herbs all over the person you're working with, as a compress does not have the marc in it at all. These are often used in cases of fever or headache or to ease the pain of burns, rashes, itchy skin, and other maladies that benefit from coolness and evaporation. They can also be done hot, but these are rarer because they tend to cool quickly.

Poultice: A poultice is very much like a compress, except the marc is wrapped in a cloth and then laid on the body. This creates a sort of seeping pack that can be applied to a wound for long periods of time. A poultice of comfrey root is useful for sprains and breaks, and a poultice of Oregon grape can be beneficial when applied to the site of an infection. Think of a poultice when you want to apply something topically for an extended time. If you want to apply a hot poultice to an area of the body for an extended time, as when you are trying to draw out infection, or you want to bring circulation to the surface, you may apply the herb to the skin, wrap it in plastic wrap, and put a hot water bottle or heating pad over it, thus prolonging its efficacy.

Plasters: These are a type of poultice used most often with red or green chilé (or other peppers) and mustard, things that heat up the skin and underlying tissue quickly and effectively. They are usually placed between layers of cloth, not directly on the skin, and then wrapped with a heat source laid on the top. They must be checked every few minutes, though, to avoid blistering the skin.

Tincture *(Alcoholic Extraction):* These are some of the better-known herbal remedies among the laypeople of the world. The menstruum for a tincture is usually vodka or grain alcohol, but you can use things like tequila, rum, or any other alcohol that is 40% abv (alcohol by volume) or above. The process can be either easy or difficult, depending on the method you choose, which will probably be determined by how quickly you need the preparation.

The usual weight-to-volume ratio for a tincture between marc and menstruum is either 1:4 or 1:5 for dry herbs (usually with vodka or another 80-proof alcohol) and 1:2 for fresh herbs (usually with grain alcohol or anything with 95% abv), though for more potent or toxic plants this becomes 1:10 or higher. What does that mean? If you have 8 ounces of dried lemon balm, you'll need 32 fluid ounces of vodka for a 1:4 ratio or 40 fluid ounces for a 1:5 ratio. If you have 8 ounces of fresh lemon balm, you'll need 16 fluid ounces of a menstruum made with grain alcohol.

Once you have your math figured out, you can make your tincture in an appropriately sized jar by simply adding your herbs to your menstruum and letting them sit for about 4–6 weeks in a warm, dimly lit place (the top of the fridge is ideal). I like to powder my dried herbs as much as possible before I add them to my menstruum, and I like to run my fresh herb tinctures through a blender for about 3–5 minutes before I put it all in a jar. This exposes more of the possible surface area of your herbs to the menstruum, meaning a stronger tincture in the end. Also, make sure to shake your tincture as often as you think to do so, as the motion of your herbs through the liquid will make your tincture more potent than one that was never moved around.

Another point to make on tinctures is when to use grain alcohol and when to use something like vodka. Fresh herbs should be tinctured in grain alcohol, which doesn't have to be diluted in any way, as the inherent water content of the herbs will do that naturally. This precludes them from a menstruum like vodka, however, as they will water it down too much, and the preparation *will* grow mold, thus ruining your tincture. To figure out the necessary volume of alcohol for your fresh herb to make a 1:2 tincture, weigh the herb you're going to use and multiply the weight by 2, which will tell you how many fluid ounces of alcohol you'll need. For example, if you're tincturing 4 ounces of fresh lemon balm at a 1:2 ratio, you'll need 8 fluid ounces of 95% alcohol. Grain alcohol is also useful for resins, like frankincense and myrrh, for resinous or hard roots, dense wood, and bark, though these should be reduced to 65–70% abv by adding water to your grain alcohol.

To figure out the reduction, divide the overall alcohol content (which will usually be 95%) by the percentage you desire, then take the dividend and divide the volume of tincture you're making from the overall percentage, which will yield the volume of water you need to add. Here is an example using 95% abv. To make 40 fluid ounces of a 75% abv tincture: 95 / 75 = 1.26, 40 / 1.26 = 31.7, so your tincture will have 31.7 fluid ounces of 95% abv alcohol in it. Then subtract 31.7 from 40, which yields a difference of 8.3, so your tincture will have 8.3 fluid ounces of water.

Vodka and other lower alcohol content liquors are best for dry herbs, as the water content will help to extract a fuller spectrum of constituents in most cases, though they will be at a more divergent ratio, such as 1:5. If you have 4 ounces of dried vervain and you want to tincture it at a 1:5 using 40% abv menstruum (which is the case for most varieties of vodka you'll buy at the store), then you multiply 4 by 5 to get 20, which is the volume of alcohol you'll need to make the appropriate strength tincture. For any of the above methods, you can substitute gram-to-milliliter ratios, which are more exact.

For dosing, the rules are pretty simple. In a 1:5 tincture, you have extracted 1 ounce of herb in 5 fluid ounces of menstruum, which means you've extracted about 1 gram to 5 milliliters of fluid. So, if you decide the dose of your herb should be 5 grams per day, the dose will be 25 milliliters per day, which is almost a full ounce of tincture. Each dose should be broken up throughout the day, usually into 3 times daily, but it can be spaced out more if necessary. This is information you should have under your belt so you are as informed as possible when you are working with a trained herbalist who can help guide you and your personal protocols.

Then, of course, there is the folk method, which is simply putting herbs in a jar and pouring alcohol over them. This is a fine method, but it becomes difficult to dose. There is no need to measure anything; you just have to make sure that your herbs are covered by about one inch of alcohol after you've filled your jar, then just let them sit for a few weeks. Do try to shake your jar every day, but I've had good results by just forgetting the jar is there until I need to decant it.

You will also want to label your tinctures very clearly. Remember to write down the name of the plant, including the Latin binomial (scientific name), the ratio, the percentage of ethanol, the menstruum used, and the date you started it. Once the tincture is ready and you've strained it, make sure to relabel the bottle and replace the date with the day you decanted it. If you plan on handing out tinctures to friends and family, give the stock bottle (the bottle you pour from) a lot number and put that number on every smaller bottle of the tincture you hand out. That way, you can keep track of your batches.

Maceration: This is the easiest thing in the world to make. A maceration is just extracting herbs in alcohol by soaking them for a period of time. If you are using the folk method, you just put your alcohol and herbs in a jar for a month, and that's it. If you are using any of the more exact extraction methods, the same process applies: soak your marc for a month in alcohol.

Percolation: This process is *much* more complicated than maceration and requires a series of tools, making it a pain in the keister, yet useful to know how to do. You can buy a percolation setup, but making one is relatively simple. You just need a glass cutter and a glass bottle with a twist-off lid. You need to carefully remove the bottom of the bottle. Afterward, it is also a good idea to grind down the edges to avoid cutting yourself as you work. You also need 2 coffee filters, a rock, a jar, something to hang your bottle from (a chemistry stand works well), and your herb must be as finely powdered as you can get it.

You will need to put one coffee filter in your bottle between the opening you made at the bottom and the neck. The edges of the filter should be pressed evenly against the sides all around. The herb is placed on top of this and must be *very* well packed down. Make sure that your bottom filter doesn't move as you do this. Next, the other filter goes over the top of the herbs, and there absolutely *must* be no gaps between the bottle and the filter. Then, place your stone on top of the filter, so you will have a tower of things that goes filter-herb-filter-rock. *Slowly* pour your alcohol over this, filling the bottle. You will see the liquid begin to percolate through the herb powder, and if your bottle is light enough in color, you will see colored liquid begin to pool in the neck. Place your jar under the neck of the bottle and untwist the cap until the liquid in your percolation bottle begins to drip out very slowly.

This will take many hours to complete, but the final product is a fully functional tincture that can be dosed in the same way as a maceration tincture but takes hours to make instead of weeks. I hardly ever use the percolation method, as it is more trouble than I usually tend to put myself through, but it is a handy method to make tinctures quickly. If, for some reason, your percolation gets messed up, like the alcohol flows too quickly or the filters shift and everything gets mixed together, just put the herbs and alcohol into a jar and turn your percolation into a maceration.

Cordial and Elixir: I include these together because they are so very similar. They are basically sweet or more palatable tinctures that are often sipped at or meant to be an uplifting treat. The real difference is that an *elixir* is usually sweetened with honey, and a *cordial* has honey along with fruit. They are also not necessarily made with vodka but something sweeter, like brandy or rum, though vodka, tequila, and gin also make appropriate menstruum, depending on the flavor profile of what you're making.

Glycerite: Sometimes, you don't want to make a tincture with alcohol, especially if it is meant for children or people who would prefer not to ingest alcohol. In that case, glycerites are a good alternative. To make one, you simply mix 70% vegetable glycerin with 30% water to make your menstruum, then measure as you would normally to get the right ratio.

Liniment: A liniment is just a tincture that is applied topically. I like to mix oil into the formula, only about 5–10% of the total product, so that it sticks to the skin better and has a nice, slick texture.

Vinegar: When making herbal vinegars, you are almost always going to make them with apple cider vinegar (ACV), though they can be made with any type of vinegar. These are prepared via the maceration method (see *tinctures* above). They are excellent choices for making liquid extracts of digestive herbs, such as anise, bay, caraway, chamomile, and ginger. One of the most famous vinegar preparations is called "fire cider," which is a vinegar extract of chilé, ginger, citrus, garlic, onion, and any other anti-bacterial or anti-viral herbs.

OXYMEL: An oxymel is a vinegar extract mixed with an equal (or nearly equal) amount of honey. The word comes from the Greek words οξυς, meaning "acid," and μελι, which means "honey." For those who have a hard time with the flavor of vinegar but want to utilize its properties, this is a sweeter, more palatable option.

OIL INFUSION: Oil is one of the oldest and most versatile tools in the herbalists' kit. The most ancient infused oils were made with animal fat, herbs, and other ingredients (such as soot, bone, ochre, and other such things). Though we more often turn to things like olive, safflower, sunflower, or other vegetable-derived oils, there is no reason that we cannot still use animal fats in our work. In fact, they tend to make more effective preparations overall, though vegetable oils make perfectly serviceable remedies.

The thing with animal fats is that they have to be properly clarified before using them, or they will rancidify and smell absolutely horrid, so they can be time-consuming to make. Animal fat can also sometimes be costly, depending on the fat you choose, whereas most vegetable oils are cost-effective, ready to use, and available at the local grocer. Whatever you decide to go with, the appropriate ratio for an effective oil is about 1:1 for heavier herbs, meaning 1 ounce of herb to 1 cup of oil, or 1:2 or 1:4 for lighter herbs.

STOVETOP: I tend to use the stovetop method over others, as I am impatient, and this is a quick and easy way to make an oil. All you need is a double boiler, your oil, and your herb. I usually combine my oil and herbs in a blender and let them mix for about 2 minutes before putting them into the pot. I leave this for about 2 hours, maintaining steady heat. As the herbs infuse into the oil, it begins to change color and becomes fragrant, which will indicate to you that it is done.

Another method for stovetop infusions is to put oil and herbs into a skillet directly on the burner. This is a bit more risky, as it is easier to burn your herbs, but you can get an oil done in under an hour. You need to bring the oil up to medium heat, stirring consistently, then turn it off for about 10 minutes. Then, turn the heat up again, stir, and take it from the heat. This should be enough to get a well-infused oil or fat.

Oven Method: I usually reserve the oven method for things like resins, as they need a higher heat and a longer period to fully infuse into an oil. It can be used for other herbs, too, though, particularly woody or dense marcs. For this process, you need a glass jar with your resin or herbs, ¾ filled with oil. You do *not* want to fill your jar to the top because oil expands as it heats up, and you will have a huge mess to clean up or a house fire on your hands.

Heat your oven to about 200°F and put your jar of oil directly on the rack. Leave the door of the oven cracked and allow the oil to infuse for a couple of hours or until you begin to smell your resin scenting your space. You will filter this through a fine cloth to remove any of the insoluble elements, like bugs, bark, and gum, and then you can use the oil to create whichever preparation you'd like.

Alcohol Intermediary: This is another quick way to make oil, and has become one of my favorite methods. The oil comes out beautifully every time. You will need a very small amount of grain alcohol, well-powdered herbs, and a blender. In a bowl, mix just enough alcohol into your powdered herb to make it the consistency of kinetic sand, and let it sit for about 2–4 hours. Take this and put it in a blender with your alcohol. On a medium speed, let it blend until the cradle becomes warm, then pour it into a jar and let it sit for a few hours, if not overnight. While it sits, leave the lid off the jar, but loosely drape a cloth over it so that any remaining alcohol can evaporate out. Strain the oil from the mark with a tightly woven cloth, then use the oil as you see fit. Alternatively, you can pour the alcohol into the herb, wait for it to evaporate, and, when you can't smell alcohol anymore, use the stovetop method to infuse the oil.

Maceration: As with tincturing, an oil maceration is simply putting herbs and oil into a jar and letting them sit for about 4 weeks. When I make these, I leave the jar in a warm place out of direct sunlight, usually on my countertop. If the oil is for magical purposes, you can leave the jar sitting on top of a sigil or sacred symbol, place it in a shrine or on an altar, or even write a sigil, symbol, or sacred phrase down on paper and put that inside the jar with your herbs. You can also soak metals, animal parts (ephemera), charms, crystals, and other objects in the oil, lending it their power.

Solar Method: This is the method I see most often online and in beginner herbalist groups. I personally do not use this method at all these days, but it is the one I started with. I found that the oils sometimes had a tendency to go rancid as they sat, which is why I now use the stovetop method more than any other. This is technically a maceration, but you use the light of the Sun to warm your oil. Put your herbs and oil into a jar, place that in a sunny place, and let it sit there for a few weeks. This is an excellent method when making oils dedicated to the Sun or to Solar deities.

Ointment: Also called an unguent, this is a category of herbal preparation. Ointments are defined by being remedial applications made from infused oils. They have a variety of consistencies due to varying water content and have an array of uses.

Salve: A salve (pronounced sav) is an oil or fat mixed with beeswax or another solidifier and has no water content. The perfect consistency can be garnered almost every time by adding 1 ounce of beeswax to 1 cup of oil and melting them slowly together in a double boiler. A properly made and kept salve can last for several years without going rancid. Salves are very useful for applying oil to a specific area and for keeping wounds moist while they heal.

It is important to note that these may keep in moisture, but they also keep in heat, so they should not be applied directly to a fresh burn. Instead, use aqueous infusions as washes until the heat of the burn subsides completely, then begin to keep the healing skin moist with salves.

Cream: These have a larger amount of oil than water but may also contain things like butters that make them thicker than a lotion. Creams can also be whipped to make them lighter. Because these are about 20–30% water, they have a shorter shelf life than salves but longer than lotions. They are also moisturizing but also more remedially effective than a regular lotion.

Lotion: Meant to moisturize and ease topical pains, a lotion is equal parts oil and water mixed together with a blender. For each cup of oil in your lotion, melt into it 1 ounce of emulsifying wax.

Measure the volume of oil you've got, then heat the same volume of water, which can be infused with herbs and turned into a tisane. This will increase the remedial quality of your lotion.

Put the hot water into the blender and turn it on at a medium speed, then very slowly add your hot oil to the water while the blender is going. The liquids will begin to emulsify, slowly uniting into a creamy lotion. You may need to chill it in the fridge and blend it again several times, but eventually, it will become a smooth, creamy texture that feels wonderful on the skin.

Enfleurage: This is a fat-based extraction to obtain the *scent* of a flower, though other things, such as leaves and even smoke, can be enfleuraged. Some of my best friends are enfleurage experts and run a small botanical perfumery here in Albuquerque. They taught me about this process.

1. Use a fat that is colorless and odorless. De-fragranced coconut oil is a useful one, though historically, well-clarified tallow was the base.
2. This is melted down with about 3–5% beeswax and poured into glass trays (such as cake pans) or chassis with wooden frames and glass bottoms. A layer of about ⅛ of an inch is the desire here. Allow this to cool completely.
3. Very carefully harvest your chosen flower, which you will need quite a bit of. Lay them in rows in the fat, though they can also be lightly sprinkled over the fat until it is well covered. You want one layer with room for the flowers to "breathe."
4. This is allowed to saturate the fat for perhaps 12 hours, and then the flowers are removed. The fat is "recharged" by adding more flowers, which are then allowed to infuse the fat for another period. Pay attention, as you do not want the smell of wilt and rot in your enfleurage (unless you do, and then it doesn't matter). Change the flowers as soon as they smell "off." This is done as many times as it takes to get the scent of the flower fully into the fat so that when you rub it on your body, you can still smell the flower.
5. This can be added to solid perfumes or further washed and extracted in alcohol to make an *extrait,* which can then be added to liquid perfumes.

6. Enfleurage can also be done hot. Using oil or fat heated to about 140°F, macerate the flowers for about 2 hours or until they have lost their scent. This is a useful way to get the scent of leaves and resinous items that don't infuse easily using the cold method. This is then re-charged multiple times until the desired scent is achieved.

Scrub: When you need to exfoliate your skin to remove dead cells or to soften the skin in a certain area, nothing works quite like a scrub. This can be made with sugar, salt, cornmeal, sand, or any other abrasive material mixed with oil or put into a lotion or cream. Scrubs can be made with remedial oils and dried herbs, too, giving them a bit of remedial action as well as their exfoliating use. I have also seen them sold as polishes and cleansing grains.

MAGICAL PREPARATIONS

Flower Essences: I learned about flower essences when I went to school for my natural therapeutics certification, and many people use them as a sort of homeopathic remedy, though I think they belong here in the section on magical preparations. They are basically the energetic imprint of a plant's consciousness recorded in water and preserved in brandy, which is then used to treat emotional issues and energetic blockages. To make one, you need a crystal or glass bowl completely free of markings, distilled water, and fresh flowers that have just opened. These are laid atop the water for about two hours in the Sun, then removed. That's all you need to do, really.

I preserve the stock essence by adding 30% ethanol, then create 1-ounce dosage bottles, which are 20 milliliters of water and 10 milliliters of brandy with 30 drops of the flower essence. This diluted ("potentialized") essence is stronger than what is in the stock bottle, according to the homeopathic philosophy they are based on. Just 1–3 drops from the dosage bottle are added to a glass of water, turning the entire glass into a further potentialized essence. Each sip you take thereafter is a dose, so be cautious. It sounds insane, but I have seen these do some remarkable things and have had some very trippy experiences with them, including my ability to see the unseen being greatly amplified. If you want to know more, do further research into Edward Bach and his works, as well as the work of the Flower Essence Society, which has tested (a process called "proving") a large number of essences.

Fluid Condenser: Aerik Arkadian defines them as: "Any substance or combination of substances, in any state of matter, that have a high capability to conduct energy between planes (i.e.,—the astral and the physical)."[55] Based on the philosophy and work of the magician Franz Bardon, these are items that act like a sort of magical battery or conductor of magical power. Really, anything can be a fluid condenser because what the term "fluid" refers to is not liquids but "electromagnetic fluid," which is the same as "astral ether," "spiritual energy," or the power that magic is made of.

Therefore, something like a wand or ritual dagger counts as a fluid condenser. Anything can be made into an effective conductor of magical energy through ritual, but they can be made more effective by virtue of combining various congruent items together, which is why I include them here. One of my favorite methods is to use resin made and poured at an appropriate astrological time and filled with gems, herbs, and charms that align to the purpose I need the condenser for. I've made these for planetary, apotropaic, and necromantic magic, and I have plans for a lot more. They are a blast to make.

Hash: This is just a combination of dried, loose herbs, gem powders, ephemera, and other ground-up bits and bobs meant to be used for a magical purpose. They are just a chunky magical powder.

Libation: A libation is the ritual pouring out of a liquid on the ground as an offering to an entity. This is most often a type of gift for the dead but is also poured out for deities, nonhuman spirits, and any other entity you can think of. Libations can be as simple as water, wine, beer, milk, or blood. They can also be complicated, ritualistically made liquids that draw on the power of planets, stars, and sacred places channeled into the preparation by using gems, metals, ephemera, and herbs at the appropriate time in the appropriate manner.

Poke: This is another term for a charm bag. Various gems, powders, ephemera, trinkets, herbs, and roots are placed into a pouch made of cloth or leather and tied or sewn shut. The pouch can be of an appropriate color for your operation, as can the thread you use to close it. A poke may also be strung with charms and amulets or painted over with sigils, incantations, and other symbols of importance.

---

55 Arkadian, "What is a Fluid Condenser?"

Phylactery: The Jewish *tefillin* are called phylacteries, though they are not the only kind. A phylactery is a particular sort of protective amulet that relies on the power of words. A spell of protection, a prayer, or some bit of sacred text is written on a scroll or a lamella (a thin sheet of metal), then rolled up and placed into a box or other vessel, along with various herbs and other tokens of power. These can be used to protect a household, oneself, important ritual items, and spirits. A very interesting version is meant to act as a repository for a part of oneself, especially when one makes a vow or offers one's heart to a god or other powerful entity. This is then locked and put in a sacred place, never to be opened again. These can sometimes be transferred between deities if everyone is amenable to that situation.

Spirit Trap: Sometimes, spirits can get out of hand or are just mischievous or malicious by nature. Spirit traps come in handy in these cases. They are built to tempt and ensnare a spirit, which keeps them out of your hair. Once a spirit is caught, the phenomena that keyed you into their presence should cease. A spirit should not be kept in the trap for a long period of time, so your trap should be regularly purified by smoke, fire, or sunlight.

Spirit Vessel: These are like a home for a spirit. They can be anything from a mason jar to an ornate, solid gold chest. Most of mine are porcelain dolls or boxes with idols of the spirit they are a home for. These are places where spirits can commune with you, where they can be fed, and act as a physical anchor that links them to this world. They should be well cared for and will sometimes need to be re-enchanted, depending on the parameters of your relationship with the spirit.

ALCHEMICAL PREPARATIONS

Calcination: The repeated burning of the herbal marc used in an alchemical preparation is called calcination, which returns the marc to its constituent salts. The result is a light gray, light yellow, or white ash, though very prolonged calcination may produce a red ash. This can then be washed to derive the pure, alchemical Salt by evaporation.

This means that the ashes must be strained through a fine cloth or coffee filter with a bit of distilled water or hydrosol from your distillation process. The finest ash will be solute in the water, while the dross, called the *caput mortuum,* is discarded. This is the only part of the original herbal material that is thrown away. The water and ash solution is placed in a ceramic vessel fit for use on the stovetop, and at a temperature between 150°F and 200°F, the water is evaporated until only the fine residue of the ash remains. You will end up with an extremely small amount, but this is all you need for your purposes.

Distillate: I include distillation here because it is an important part of most alchemical processes and is one of the primary ways to purify a liquid.

Rectification: Continual or repeated distillation of a single liquid is called rectification, one of the essential parts of alchemy. It is so integral to the very heart of the Great Art[56] that it is part of the great alchemical motto, V.I.T.R.I.O.L.: *Vista Interiora Terrae Rectificando Invenies Occultum Lapidem.*[57]

Aqua Vitae: This is a rectification that purifies the ethanol out of red wine (or other liquors, usually brandy), turning it to a clear liquid, though it retains the scent of the original substance. It was used in the golden age of alchemy as a sort of vital force enhancer, a pain reliever, a wound healer, and also as an enjoyable additive for drinks.

---

56 Though the term "the Great Art," or *Ars Magna,* is often used specifically to refer to the careful creation of the Philosopher's Stone, it really refers to alchemy in general. Only through long study, risky experimentation, and skilled application of their ideas and tools could an alchemist make any headway in their work, meaning they had to make an art of everything they did. The practices of alchemy are even told artistically in the language of image and symbol, as the wide array of woodcuts and engravings show (and sometimes even songs, such as those in *Atalanta Fugiens* by Michael Meyer). In 2016, the Getty Center put on an exhibition that also brought light to the ways in which alchemists and their art were not wholly occult and hidden, but rather driving forces for art and science in the wider culture. See the online article "The Transformative Influence of Alchemy on Art" for more about the exhibit.

57 "Visit the interior parts of the Earth; by rectification, thou shalt find the hidden stone."

Spagyric: These are a type of alchemical, herbal tinctures derived by the purification of an herb or other substance by comminuting it into alchemical Salt, Sulphur, and Mercury and then recombining them as an elixir. A true spagyric is made following an exact alchemical process that separates Salt, Mercury, and Sulphur from the plant material and then recombines them in perfect unity. The celestial timing for gathering the herbs, as well as for distillation, rectification, calcination, dissolution, and cohobation, should be considered. If you are potentializing a Jupiterian plant, it is best to gather it on the day and in the hour of Jupiter, then perform the spagyric process only on Jupiter's day in Jupiter's hours. As the spagyric process proceeds, you are essentially drawing down the energy and power of whichever planetary rulers you are performing your operation under, so the most potent Jupiter formula will be done solely in Jupiter's time, not any other planet's.

For the sake of ease, I suggest starting with a 1:4 ratio, such as 8 ounces of herb to 32 fluid ounces of water, though you may want to add more water to your flask if it seems low.

1. **Distillation:** The first step is to remove the Sulphur from your herbal marc, meaning that you must distill the essential oils from it. This will require a distillation train, which consists of a flask (cucurbit), a condenser, and a receptacle. The herbs can be placed directly into the flask, which will be filled a third to half-way with distilled water. You will need a source of cold, running water or a basin of ice water with a pump of some kind, as the condensing tube needs to be chilled.

   As the water vaporizes, it takes with it the volatile oils from the herb (which is fixed), separating the soul (Sulphur) from the body and spirit (Salt and Mercury). It will sit on top of the water in your receptacle and is easily siphoned off using a pipette. The water is used in the next step, though a portion should be set aside to perform the dissolution of Salt after calcination (steps 4 and 5).

2. **Fermentation:** This is the process of removing the spirit (Mercury) from the body (Salt), a process during which the marc putrefies, disintegrating the body from the spirit. The water from your distillation is poured back into the flask,

and then all of it, herbs and water, are poured into a jar. A bit of yeast is added, about 5 grams to 1 quart of liquid, and a bit of fermenting sugar, then the jar is closed up with a fermentation lid.

Everything can be kept in the flask instead by plugging it with a stopper fitted with a fermentation airlock. Barring either of these, the herb and water mixture can be placed in a wide mouth jar or earthen vessel, a pinch of yeast is added along with some fermentation sugar, then a piece of fabric is loosely draped over the mouth, and a plate or other smooth, flat surface is placed over it. This begins the process of fermentation, during which alcohol is produced directly from the plant you've been working with.

Place your fermentation in a warm, dark place, preferably where the temperature stays around 70°F. The darkness represents your formula entering the Underworld. It must traverse the realm of shades during its *negredo,* its "black phase" or "dark night," which will lead to the separation of body and spirit. The process ought to take about 40 days and nights, but you will know it is done when the fermentation stops bubbling. This will be purified in the next step.

3. **Rectification:** The alcohol produced during the fermentation period must be strained from the marc (which is set aside) and purified by rectification. By so doing, the alcohol is separated from the water in your ferment and made pure Mercury, ready for your spagyric. Sajah Popham, in his book *Evolutionary Herbalism,* suggests that the ferment be rectified at least seven times to symbolize the harmonization of the celestial spheres.

4. **Calcination:** The marc, which is now merely the body (Salt) of the herb, must be purified next. This is done by calcination. The marc must be set alight and burned to ash, then ground in a mortar. This is done repeatedly until it is lightly colored or reddish. This is the body on the pyre, where it passes through Fire to further separate the Air and Water from the purest part of the Earth.

There is another salt that can be found in the watery leftovers from the first rectification of Mercury, which is called Salt of Sulphur. This is obtained by gently heating the leftover water and evaporating it until you are left with a honey-like, reddish substance that can be scraped out of the flask and readied in a crucible separate from the one you will calcinate your herbal marc (salt of Salt) in. They must be calcined separately and undergo dissolution separately. They will be added together again during cohobation.

5. **Dissolution:** The calcined ashes must undergo dissolution or washing to remove the *caput mortuum* from the purified Salt. See "Calcination" in this section for clearer instructions.

6. **Cohobation:** Now you are ready to mix the Sulphur, Mercury, and Salt together again, which should be done in a spiritually descending order.

    - Ensouling the Spirit: The soul (Sulphur) must be poured into the spirit (Mercury), then mixed thoroughly.
    - Enlivening the Body: The mixture of the soul and spirit (Sulphur and Mercury) is poured into the salt of Salt and mixed.
    - Embodying the Soul: The enlivened mixture (Sulphur, Mercury, and Salt) is poured into the Salt of Sulphur and mixed.

You may also choose to combine the Salts and then mix them with the Ensouled mixture. At this point, the mixture is done, but it can be placed in an apparatus meant to circulate the mixture, evaporating and condensing the liquid, allowing your spagyric to rise and fall from Heaven to Earth again and again for as many as forty days and nights.

This can be left as a liquid, called a *spagyric essence,* or dried down to a crystalline substance called a *spagyric elixir* that can later be dissolved in a small amount of alcohol or water. There are also other spagyric preparations, but these are the two most common.

Lazy Man's Spagyric: This is done with the use of a Soxhlet extractor, which is a three-piece chemistry apparatus made of a cucurbit, an extraction chamber, and a condensation chamber. I believe the process removes all of the impurities that keep a substance from being fully unified within itself, which is a reflection of what the spiritual effects of alchemy do within the alchemist themself.

To explain the Soxhlet: The cucurbit, the lowest part of the Soxhlet, is filled with grain alcohol and placed over a heat source. Next, very well-powdered herbs are packed into a paper thimble or cone and placed into the extraction chamber, which is then fitted into the cucurbit. Next, the condensation chamber is attached to a set of tubes, one in and one out, that pumps ice-cold water through an outer casing of glass surrounding an inner tube that is usually either a spiral or a column of bubble-shaped chambers. This is fitted into the extraction chamber, forming a tower of three glass pieces.

A low-medium heat is applied to the cucurbit, which causes the alcohol to evaporate into the condensation chamber (in a process called *ascension*), where it condenses into droplets that fall into the thimble, thus creating an extraction of the herb you chose. The colored liquid leaks out of the thimble into the extraction chamber, which fills up to the level of an outer tube—called the return tube—and creates a vacuum that returns all of the liquid from the middle chamber back into the cucurbit and begins the process over again. Eventually, the liquid that fills the extraction chamber becomes clear, at which point you know your extraction is done. The resulting liquid is alchemical Mercury.

In order to complete a spagyric, you must calcinate the marc and wash the ashes to extract alchemical Salt. The essential oil of the plant has been separated from the marc with the alcohol extraction, so it does not have to be separated on its own. There is usually so little oil in any given plant that this is the most efficient method. If you want to separate it, though, you'll need a distillation train meant for essential oil extractions and enough herbs to make the oil, which can then be added to your marc to be calcined.

For more on alchemical philosophy and spagyric preparations, consult the following books:

- *Herbal Alchemy* by Phillip Hurley
- *Spagyrics* by Manfred M. Junius
- *The Herbal Alchemist's Handbook* by Karen Harrison
- *Evolutionary Herbalism* by Sajah Popham

Vegetable Stone: This is basically a solid spagyric. Instead of recombining the Salt and Sulphur into the Mercury, the latter two are added to the Salt during the calcination process. Through repeated calcining and addition of Mercury and Sulphur, a small stone is produced that is said to have wondrous abilities. Small chunks of the stone are eaten or dissolved in water or alcohol before being used in a way similar to a tincture. Not quite the philosopher's stone, but still pretty cool. If you would like more information on the process for making the *Lapis Philosophorum*, see Philip Hurley's *Herbal Alchemy.*

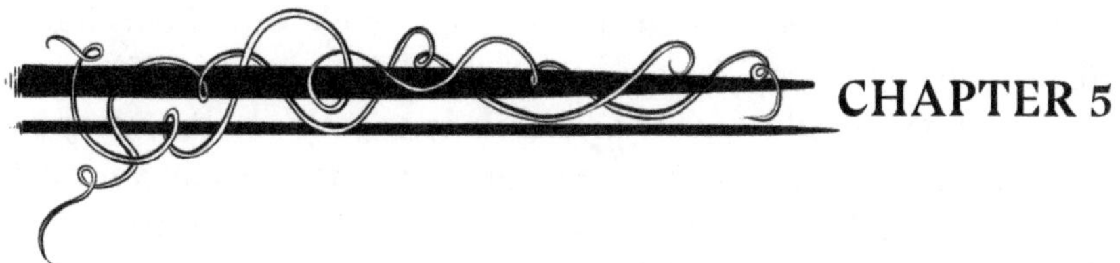

CHAPTER 5

Materia Medica-Magica

The following monographs are meant to help introduce you to some of the invasives you may encounter in your region and may choose to work with. This is not an exhaustive list, as there are thousands of plants that are considered invasive for one reason or another, and the list is different depending on where you live. These are simply some of my favorites, plants I've built a good relationship with over the years and use in my own practice. Some are plants that friends of mine use more often than I do, but they have introduced me to the plant and its powers.

Each monograph will have general information on the plant as well as its elemental and astrological attributions, at least the ones I think fit best. If you disagree with me, that is also okay. That's why I wrote out the "why" for assigning rulership to one planet or another, so you can do what makes the most sense to *you*. Each will also have foraging advice along with recipes, remedial uses and suggestions for preparations, and magical uses with some spell and charm ideas. Use these as a springboard for your own research, then let your imagination, your magic, and the plants themselves guide you onward. As for common names, they can be a bit confusing and are just folk names people come up with based on the lore of the plant, how it is used, or how to describe it. If the common name listed is one personal to me, I've marked it with an asterisk.

When it comes to whether to take any of these herbs internally, especially when pregnant or breastfeeding, it is important to do your own research and decide what you are comfortable with. Many herbs are "considered unsafe" because there hasn't been enough Western, clinical, allopathically-oriented research done on them. There may be centuries of traditional knowledge to guide you; however, the voices of our forebears and their relationship to the Land, which was experiential. Though there is much traditional knowledge gathered here, do not take what you learn in this book only and apply it directly. Utilize it as a part of a deeper study with as many authors as you can muster and with the teachers you can find in your area, all of which will help deepen your understanding of these practices and how they can fit into your own life.

Also remember that you should never harvest herbs for food or medicine from contaminated soils. Never harvest close to a road, especially those that are covered in asphalt or near factories. Do not take from parking lots or areas that may have been sprayed with herbicide and insecticide, and do not gather from areas where contaminated runoff may be present. This is partially to protect your health and the health of those you seek to aid with your harvest and partially to protect the Land by allowing these plants to do their job of remediating ecosystems. Wildcrafting, the harvesting of wild herbs, must be done with a holistic reciprocity in mind.

First, it is important to remember to ask for permission to harvest a plant and to really, truly listen…meaning there will sometimes be firm answers of "no." If you're always hearing "yes," you're not listening. Second, always gather in a way that leaves the area better off than you found it. Spread seeds of native plants and desirable medicinal plants, clear out overpopulated invasives so they don't outnumber the other plants, do not take the first or the last of a plant, take only what you need and will use, pick up trash, and tend to the area. Third, always leave an offering when you harvest, something that will help the plants. I take water into my mouth and spit it back onto the soil from where I've gathered, trading the water of my body for the water of the plant's body, but my teacher leaves cornmeal and tobacco, and others give back in other ways. These are the basic steps to having a reciprocal relationship with the Land. Give back and be respectful; do not simply take.

Robin Wall Kimmerer, who I learned about through Jade Alicandro of Milk & Honey Herbs, has a set of guidelines for what she calls "The Honorable Harvest," which I will list here. They really are fantastic and will help you think through what to do when you go harvesting.[58]

1. Know the ways of the ones who take care of you so that you may take care of them.
2. Introduce yourself. Be accountable as the one who comes asking for life.
3. Ask permission before taking. Abide by the answer.
4. Never take the first. Never take the last.
5. Take only what is given.
6. Never take more than half. Leave some for others.
7. Harvest in a way that minimizes harm.
8. Use it respectfully. Never waste what you have taken. Share.
9. Give thanks for what you have been given.
10. Give a gift in reciprocity for what you have taken.
11. Sustain the ones who sustain you, and the Earth will last forever.

Remember that we are not in this alone. The Earth and the Land are part of a vast, entangled, complex network of relationships, and we must learn to see our environment and the work we do in the context of the "big picture." We cannot allow ourselves to get bogged down in short-term and short-sighted visions that see one plant as bad and another as good. We cannot let ourselves become lazy and selfish and take too much with nothing in return, and we must be aware of the health of the Land. Being a conscious steward of the Earth is hard work, but there isn't much that is more important right now as we face down the barrel of the future.

58 Kimmerer, 2015.

ACACIA

(*Acacia spp.*) Sun—Air—Sagittarius

AKA: *Wattle, golden rods, Crown of Thorns,* burning bush, Lord's casket,* most common names are species-specific*

There are several species of Acacia in the US that are considered invasive, such as *A. melanoxylon, A. dealbata, A. mearnsii,* and *A. longifolia.* Each species is a beautiful tree, though, with spheres or racemes of fragrant yellow flowers that grow directly out of the branch. Most Acacia species are native to Australia but have naturalized to almost every other continent. There are some that are native to Africa, India, and the Middle East, however, such as the incredibly important *Vachellia nilotica,* better known as *Acacia nilotica* or gum arabic tree. The resin of this species was used in Ancient Egypt as the adhesive for bandages used during mummification and as a preservative for mummified flesh, not to mention in various sacred preparations of incense and oil. The resin has always been an important part of trade and has been a source of wealth for farmers who provided gum arabic to the world for use in perfume, ink, medicine, baking, candy making, incense making, carpentry, and an extremely wide variety of other things.

Acacia has also been a food product in the areas in which it grows. The seed pods are a preferred forage for some animals and have been a food eaten by humans, as well. The resin is also edible and has been used as a dietary fiber and thickener of foods for millennia. The hard inner wood of this tree has also been used for carpentry and tool making, and the bark is used as a black dye.

Among their ecological impacts, Acacia trees are nitrogen fixers. They draw nitrogen up to the surface of the soil and fix it in their roots, thus leading to greater soil fertility overall. This *does* alter the soil and reduces biodiversity among rhizobia communities, which enhances this tree's ability to grow in novel areas, though this has only been studied in areas that are already nutrient-poor. It provides food, shade, and nutrients for the soil, which can't be bad things.

As with many of the other plants that similarly alter soil, such as garlic mustard, it is not a guarantee that Acacia is creating a positive feedback loop so strong that it decimates the ecosystem it begins to grow in. Rather, it begins to change the soil, which, in turn, begins to work on the rhizomes and root bacteria of the plant, altering the soil further and allowing for new plants to grow. Eventually, everyone reaches a mutually beneficial compromise…or the plant dies. That's how evolution and adaptation work; it's a conversation.

An interesting bit of folklore surrounding the Acacia: it is part of Jewish tradition that the "burning bush" described in Exodus is, in fact, an Acacia tree. There is also some lore suggesting that the crown of thorns placed upon the head of Jesus was made from this tree, giving it a link to the idea of divinity, resurrection, and holy blood. Acacia is also one of the possible woods from which it is said the Ark of the Covenant, the Tabernacle, and Noah's Ark were built. In Egypt, Acacia is sometimes the tree in which Osiris was entombed, though it shares this role with tamarisk.

Foraging Uses

The flowers and beans (not the pods) of many Acacia species are edible, and the bark is to some extent, though the leaves of the tree must be collected cautiously, as they tend to harbor hydrogen cyanide. Always make sure of the species of Acacia tree you're harvesting from, and do your research to make sure it is an edible variety.

The flowers can be eaten directly off the tree and taste something like honey, if a bit greener. They make a lovely honey infusion and can also be made into a jam or jelly. The leaves, as it is with garlic mustard, must be harvested when they are young, fern-like shoots. They harbor very little hydrogen cyanide at this point, but they accumulate more as they mature. They are often used in Southeast Asian cooking.

The seeds should always be toasted before consuming them and have a nutty, chocolatey flavor that lends itself to coffee substitutes and chocolate baked goods. If you're searching for recipes, you may confuse this tree for black locust (*Robinia pseudoacacia*), which is also called *Acacia* and is an invasive tree included in its own section in this book, but do not conflate the two. They are very different trees. It is better to look up "wattle seed" if you're looking for recipes using Acacia species.

Acacia Bean Coffee

- 1 c. Acacia seeds, toasted
- ½ c. dandelion root, toasted
- ½ c. chicory root, toasted
- 2 Tbsp. beetroot powder
- 1 Tbsp. mushroom powder of your choice

1. You will want to dry toast all of your ingredients in a skillet. Chop the roots, beets, and mushrooms (if you bought them fresh or gathered them) into very small chunks first. Mix these with your Acacia seeds and put everything into a skillet on the stove over medium heat. Toast them until the seeds start popping about, somewhat like if you were popping corn.
2. When everything is a nice golden brown and smells sort of nutty, you can remove them from the skillet and allow everything to cool down.
3. Using a grinder or a blender, grind your Acacia seeds and roots until they become a dark brown, uniform powder.
4. If you bought pre-powdered ingredients, toast them as well to kill off any mold that might have been integrated with or growing in them. That is a risk you take when buying powders, so it is best to heat them to at least 160°F before using them.
5. Once everything is toasted, powdered, and mixed, you can use it to make a delicious coffee-like drink!

Beignet d'Acacia

This is a recipe I've modified from one written out by Laura Tobin on *Your Guardian Chef,* just to make it a bit more invasive and to use actual Acacia flowers rather than black locust.

- 2–3 c. Acacia flowers, loosely packed
- 1 c. flour of your choice
- ½ c. Acacia seed flour
- 1½ tsp. baking powder
- 1 c. milk
- 1 large egg
- 1 tsp. rose or orange blossom water
- 1 pinch of salt
- Vegetable oil for frying
- Powdered sugar for dusting

1. To make Acacia (wattle) seed flour, toast the beans until they are golden, nutty, and sort of popped open. Grind them into a dark brown powder, which is the wattle flour. There are lots of recipes for other things you can make with this, so have fun finding new ways to use it!
2. After picking your flowers, place them in a large strainer or a colander and rinse them thoroughly. Set them aside to dry a bit.
3. Mix the flour together with the baking powder and whisk them well.
4. Slowly mix in the milk.
5. Mix in your egg, salt, and flower water.
6. Heat your oil and get ready to fry. Put a plate with a paper towel on it nearby so you can use it to remove excess oil from your beignets.
7. Toss your flowers in the batter. Use an ice cream scoop or small ladle to pour even amounts of battered flowers into the oil. Once each dollop is golden brown, remove it from the oil and move it to the paper towel.
8. Let them cool for about 1–2 minutes, dust lightly with powdered sugar, and serve them warm.

Remedial Applications

The Acacia tree has been used remedially for all sorts of things, particularly the sap, which, when gathered from certain species, is called gum arabic. The gum is a potent source of dietary fiber and has been used traditionally in cases of high cholesterol and arterial diseases. It *has* been shown to reduce high levels of LDL-C (low-density lipoprotein cholesterol), which is an indicator of possible ischemic cardiovascular disease. It has also been shown to reduce systolic blood pressure, which is also a benefit to an overtaxed cardiovascular system. There is some evidence that it has some effect in preventing diabetes mellitus through its action on cholesterol. Gum arabic also has beneficial effects on the GI (gastrointestinal) tract and, thus, on IBS (irritable bowel syndrome), particularly in conjunction with pre and probiotics.

The leaf extract of *A. auriculiformis,* one of the invasive species found in the US, has shown efficacy in aiding memory and mentation. They act as an acetylcholinesterase inhibitor and prolong the activity of that neurotransmitter (ACh) at synaptic junctions, leading to better functionality of the brain and its memory centers.

The leaves of the Acacia have been used as an astringent wound healer but also to help with cases of diarrhea and dysentery, though the bark is more astringent and is more often used. The bark has also been used for internal bleeding and to treat blisters, sores, hemorrhoids, and ulcerations or bleeding in the mouth. The bark makes a useful antirheumatic agent, too, especially when made into a sitz bath or herbal soak. The bark is also incredibly high in tannins, meaning it is useful in tanning, as well.

Magical Applications

Perhaps because of its twisted branches and its thorniness contrasted with the joyful yellow and spherical shape of its flowers, Acacia has been a symbol of overcoming adversity and immortality and has been used as a funerary plant. The leaves of the plant are useful additions to incenses meant to aid in divination. An incense made from the flowers of Acacia can also be used to sanctify a space, particularly altar spaces and vessels dedicated to deities, and can act as a ward to protect you and your working area from malicious energies.

Anima Deorum Incense

This is an offering incense to the deities you work with and as a protective smoke to suffumigate your working space with. Powder and mix the ingredients together on a Sunday in the hour of the Sun, then let the mixture sit for about two weeks in a jar before molding them into the shape you intend.

- 1 oz. Acacia flowers
- ½ oz. chamomile flowers
- ½ oz. flax seed
- 1 Tbsp. gum arabic
- 1 Tbsp. honey

Lampad's Lantern Hash

Acacia has been associated with the dead, the lore going as far back as Ancient Egypt, and can be used to give form to the spirits we conjure and to draw them to our working area. This preparation is a "hash," or a mix of loose, crushed-up, dried herbs meant to be used for various purposes. Rolling a prepared candle in the hash before lighting it or lighting an oil lamp with the infused oil draws the dead toward it like a beacon.

- 1 oz. Acacia flowers, crushed
- 1 oz. dandelion root, pulverized
- ½ oz. dittany of Crete, crushed
- ¼ oz. tobacco leaf, crushed
- ¼ oz. bay leaves, crushed
- 3 anise stars, pulverized
- 3 datura flowers, dried and crushed

BINDWEED

(*Convulvulus arvensis*) Saturn—Earth—Virgo

AKA: *Small bindweed, lesser bindweed, common bindweed, wild-morning glory, withy wind, creeping Jenny, possession vine, Devil's guts, bellbind, creep-n-catch**

Found mostly along roadsides and in the cracks of sidewalks, field bindweed is a lovely relative of the morning glory. It grows in long tendrils that twist counter-clockwise and are lined with tiny leaves and dozens of small, pinkish cup-shaped flowers that are a joy for all sorts of pollinators. These flowers are also called "Our Lady's Little Glass" due to their association with Mary, Queen of Heaven, who drank one drop of wine from a bindweed flower. The drink was a thank you from a wagoner after Mary helped him when the axle of his cart broke on a rugged road. Of course, Mary has been syncretized with many other goddesses and spirits, one of which is Hekate, particularly in her role as a goddess with dominion over Heaven, and I have taken to calling bindweed "Hekate's chalice." Another spirit that I have heard associated with not only Mary, but takes her place in the story related above, is the Queen of Elphame, or Fairy Queen, which has also given bindweed the name "fairy cup."

Ecologically, bindweed can be a menace if left unmanaged. It can strangle out crops and garden plants, but really only in areas that are overly worked, often disturbed, nutrient-deprived, or where they are allowed to go rampant. If they are tamed, they will be good denizens in the garden, providing color for the gardener and food for the bees. As Barbara Pond says in her book *A Sampler of Wayside Herbs,* "It is scorned as a weed because its tight embrace strangles out other plants and its extensive root system depletes the soil; but it is forgiven when one sees it quickly covering some unsightly spot with its lovely bloom."[59] Not to mention, they are a useful herbal remedy and one of the most potent magical plants I have ever worked with.

Bindweed prefers dry, alkaline-rich soils in waste places, disturbed areas, and along roads. It will also grow in pastures and grasslands, along slopes, and near streams. Because of this preference, it also enjoys growing in tilled fields, meaning it can become a major problem for farmers and one of the reasons it is considered dangerous. Any plant that threatens human profits is a threat to humanity itself, it would seem. They grow mainly from seed, though they can very easily sprout from even tiny fragments of rhizomes that may be unknowingly deposited in garden beds. The seeds may stay virile for over fifty years and are really only spread through human activity, such as the movement of topsoil and the use of farming equipment. They require little water and, if soil conditions are right, can withstand extremely hot weather.

Though it is generally pollinated by many insects, it is specifically pollinated by sweat bees of the genus *Systropha,* which are small and thin with an entire abdomen designed to pick up pollen from the funnel-shaped flowers of bindweed. They even have modifications on their backs, so they can carry more pollen than most bee species. The males lay claim to a patch of bindweed flowers and protect it by ramming into conspecific males and dive-bombing other bee species to keep them away from their territory, then actually sleep inside the flower when it closes for the evening. Females live in underground tunnels near bindweed patches and emerge in the early morning to forage on nectar and pollen through the afternoon. It is during this time that most copulations occur. If you spend a little time near the bindweed, perhaps you'll get the cutest peep show of your life!

59 Pond 93.

Foraging Uses

Every part of bindweed acts as a laxative and can bring on diarrheal issues. It is, therefore, to be eaten with utmost caution, but that said, it is used culinarily. Various peoples, particularly in parts of Europe and Asia, will eat the leaves, either dried or fresh. They are added to gruels and porridges, soups and stews, or fried with butter. They are a somewhat bitter green but quite delightful. The flowers should not be eaten but can be removed from their calyx and sucked for their honey-like nectar.

Medicinal Applications

Field bindweed is a cholagogue, diuretic, laxative, and purgative as well as having antipyretic properties. The greatest evidence is for its laxative action; only about a tablespoon of the dried vine will lead to softer stool and motility in the gut. It contains multiple alkaloids, which include pseudotropine, tropine, tropinone, and mesco-cuscohygrine, the latter being a pyrrolidine alkaloid also present in the *Coca* plant and some nightshades. It also contains some ergot-alkaloids derived from ergot-like micro-organisms that live endophytically in the cells of bindweed, meaning this is a plant that must be used in limited amounts.

The most often used part of the plant for any remedial function is the whole vine, which is simply the easiest to get. The vine is used as a laxative, as a cold remedy, to treat fever, and to wash insect and spider bites to reduce redness and pain. Because of its diuretic properties, it makes a great addition to kidney and urinary tract treatments. It pairs well with the mallows, puncture vine, and things like uva ursi. The root is the most potent part of the plant, but it takes a bit of effort to dig up and process. By boiling and cooking down the root, a resinous substance can be obtained that is a strong laxative and cholagogue.

An aqueous infusion of bindweed should be taken twice daily for no more than 7 days. To make a cup, only about 1 teaspoon of the dried aerial parts should be steeped for 6–8 minutes in about 8 ounces of water. If you prefer to use a tincture, it should be used sparingly and considered a low-dose option. No more than 5 milliliters of a 1:5 tincture made with dried aerial parts and no more than 2 milliliters of a 1:8 tincture made with fresh root should be used in any formula.

Constipation Formula

- 1 tsp. field bindweed, dried aerial parts
- 1tsp. cheeseweed, dried aerial parts
- 1 tsp. Siberian elm, dried, powdered inner bark
- 8 oz. of water

1. Steep this formula in 8 ounces of nearly boiled water for approximately 10 minutes.
2. Drink this three times per day for no more than 4 days or until bowel movement occurs.

Bindweed Resin

- 16 oz. field bindweed, fresh root, chopped
- ½ gallon water

1. Place the chopped root in about 64 ounces of water over medium heat.
2. Simmer and reduce the water content of the pot until it becomes thick, then pour off.
3. Place liquid on waxed paper in the oven at about 175°F for about 3 hours or until it is a thick, sticky resin.
4. Use only a very small amount, no more than the head of a pin, to create a laxative effect. It can be melted into hot water to make it more palatable.

Magical Applications

The category of magic in which bindweed finds its greatest potency is in its name: binding. The word *convolvulus* comes from the Latin *convolvere,* meaning "to entwine, to roll together." Because of its Venusian resonance, it has an affinity for love magic, particularly those spells meant to bring another person under your sway or to bind their thoughts obsessively to a particular pattern. Bindweed is one of the ultimate enchanter's herbs, as it has the power to evoke dreams and desires that become obsessions. Bindweed is also tied in with the lore of destroying love, as it is said that to pick a bindweed may lead to the death of one's lover. That said, it can also be used in magic for bringing or keeping people together. Two poppets made of wax bound together with bindweed vines and red thread, then pierced together through their hearts by a red-headed pin, will make a strong love charm to join two people.

The flowers or the root make good additions to incense meant to conjure up the darker, more aggressive aspects of Venus-Aphrodite, particularly in her role as avenger, and can be added to formulations that aim towards working with Kedemel, the Planetary Spirit of Venus in charge of the planet's baleful influences. Even when using the plant to create love, it is a binding, twining, entangling sort of love that bindweed conjures, so it is best not to think of it as an addition to sweet little love spells.

This herb is also linked to the power of storms, particularly thunder. In Shropshire, it is said that picking one of the bindweed's flowers will surely bring thunder before the day is through. It is, therefore, suitable for use in offertory incense or libation waters for thunder or storm deities and spirits. The spirits of thunder and lightning are fearsome and often surprising, often linked to both destruction and fertility. They are often bringers of great change and upheaval. Bindweed can help us tap into that power and bring great shifts in events, binding up and toppling some things so others may rise. It can be used in an incense to conjure the Anemoi, the four winds, a recipe for which follows.

Bindweed can also be used in spells meant to halt things and bring them to a stop. This can be used in *maleficium* and *beneficium,* as one can just as easily use it in magic to halt the advancement of an enemy or to break up a relationship as to stop a court case, the growth of a tumor, or the occurrence of bad dreams. On this latter note, bindweed can be used in spirit traps meant to stop harmful entities from getting near you.

The link it has to the Queen of Elphame also makes it an appropriate herb to use when working with her or other fae. I'll admit I know very little about the Faery Faith, but from what I've read, the fae are the spirits of the ancestors of the people in Scotland, meaning the Queen is also a leader of the dead.

Incense of the Anemoi

- ½ oz. field bindweed
- ½ oz. Tree of Heaven seed
- ½ oz. St. John's Wort
- ¼ part powdered amber or copal
- ¼ part lapis lazuli powder
- 1 small bit of wool roving

1. Once the parts of the incense are gathered, powder them together thoroughly, then mix in just enough honey to make the powder the consistency of kinetic sand.
2. Roll this out flat between sheets of wax paper and allow it to sit for about two weeks.
3. Once it is tacky but stays together well, it can be pressed into molds or rolled into little marbles. These should be allowed to dry completely, which will take 2–3 weeks or the use of a dehydrator.
4. These can then be burned on a charcoal tablet lit in an appropriate thurible. The smoke from the incense can be used when laying the compass at each of the cardinal points to summon in the four winds: Eurus, Notus, Zephyrus, and Boreas.

Incense Offering for the Dead

- ½ oz. bindweed, aerial parts
- ½ oz. mullein leaf and flower
- ½ oz. Siberian elm leaf
- ½ oz. oregano leaf

1. Take these ingredients, break them up with your hands or in a mortar, and mix them together thoroughly.
2. Light a charcoal tab, such as a hookah coal, and blow on it until it turns red.
3. Sprinkle the incense over the coal and allow the fumes to billow. Allow the smoke to wash over or blow the smoke over the ritual space you've created or over your ancestral or necromantic altar.

Crown of Success Oil

One of the most famous and well-used oils for abundance, Crown of Success, can bring rapid victory and great rewards in all areas of life. This is a recipe I've written using some invasive herbs as replacements for the more traditional ones that will make a powerful version of this preparation to be applied to candles, charms, money bowls, and all sorts of things. Use sunflower oil in this recipe and perform the rite on a Sunday in the hour of the Sun.

- 1 bindweed root
- 3 allspice fruits, dried and whole
- 3 bay leaves
- 3 dandelion heads, gone to seed
- 3 gold or brass coins or 3 pieces of gold
- 3 keys
- 3 mimosa tree beans
- 3 Siberian elm twigs
- 3 sweet clover flower stalks
- 3 tsp. chamomile flowers
- 3 tsp. cinnamon bark chunks or 3 cinnamon sticks
- 3 tsp. mustard seeds
- 3 tsp. orange peel, dried
- 3 tsp. resin of choice

1. Gather the ingredients together, preferably on a Thursday in the hour of Mars, to increase indomitability and the likelihood of conquering whatever obstacles lie before you.
2. Allow the dandelion heads to begin to go to seed before you put them in the jar, which should happen almost immediately.
3. Prepare an icon of Hekate or prepare the First Pentacle of the Sun in yellow or gold ink on a Sunday in the first hour of the Sun. This is what you will place your jar upon as you work.
4. Prepare three candles. These ought to be yellow, gold, green, or white. Anoint these with olive oil and roll them in a hash of powdered allspice and cinnamon. Mark them with the following symbols and incant the associated words as you light them.

- Candle 1:

"Constrain all that would oppose me. Let them gnash their teeth to nothing and let all obstacles decay. Let them be vexed until they waste away."

- Candle 2:

"All that stands against me shall fall and shall be trampled underfoot. The arrows of my enemies and the tooth of every beast shall turn to cinder and to ash."

- Candle 3:

"I shall be crowned in glory all my days. All that I desire I give unto myself, for I, child of the Queen of Night, lay claim to them."

5. Bless and purify each item in the smoke of Russian olive leaves and incant the following for each one.

   "By virtue of this purifying smoke, be made clean, holy, and sacred before the eyes of the gods. May you be a jewel set in the crown that rests upon my head and proclaims me Sovereign of all that I desire."

6. Start with your herbs, putting them into the oil one by one. As you do so, incant the following:

   "For love, for gold, for honor and glory. I will choose the path of my story. Crowned by success, by victory armed, so is this oil true and well charmed."

7. Add your coins or pieces of gold one at a time.

   "A coin to pay the way I've come and one the way I'm walking. One to pay the path to come, now cleared of darkness stalking."

8. Next, add the keys one at a time.

   "These keys shall open the doors to success: For all victories missed in the past, for all victories available in the present, and for all the victories that lay before me. I shall not miss an opportunity, for all the doors are open, and I am the master of all desire, all want, and all need."

9. Now, to charm your root. Oil it with olive oil, incanting the following as you do so:

   "Let this root be my scepter, the sign of my rule. By it may I direct and command the armies of my fortune and the cavalries of my desire, that they may bring the bounty of conquest to my hands. By virtue of this scepter, do I command Agathos Daimon, the great good spirit, that it may never leave my side and shall ever bring me good fortune, victory, and success. So it is."

10. Put your root in the jar, seal it, and swirl it forty times in a clockwise fashion as you recite the following verse from Hesiod's Theogony.[60]

    "Hekate whom Zeus the son of Kronos honoured above all. He gave her splendid gifts, to have a share of the earth and the unfruitful sea. She received honour also in starry heaven, and is honoured exceedingly by the deathless gods...For as many as were born of Gaia and Ouranos [i.e., the Titans] amongst all these she has her due portion. The son of Kronos [i.e., Zeus] did her no wrong nor took anything away of all that was her portion among the

60 All quotes from the *Theogony* are from Hesiod, *Homeric Hymns, Epic Cycle, Homerica,* Translated by H.G. Evelyn-White, (Loeb Classical Library, 1914), www.theoi.com/Text/HomericHymns1.html. The Transcription can be found on theoi.com, and the full book can be found on gutenberg.org at www.gutenberg.org/files/348/348-h/348-h.htm. This comes from the "Hymn to Hecate," lines 404–454.

> *former Titan gods: but she holds, as the division was at the first from the beginning, privilege both in earth, and in heaven, and in sea. Also, because she is an only child, the goddess receives not less honour, but much more still, for Zeus honours her."*
>
> Add the following:
>
> *"I, a child of Hekate, avatar of great-bosomed Nyx and Queen of Witches, share in Her heritage of honour. I duly receive all that is my portion upon the earth, in the heavens, and in the deep places. I wear my crown and regalia, and, by virtue of this oil, am anointed in honor of my mother, Dame Fate. May the wheel spin out the golden thread and may the triple maidens weave me victorious, crowned in glory."*
>
> Repeat this every time you anoint yourself or anything else with this oil.

You may choose to bury the jar of oil on a "field of battle" for a time, perhaps on a new moon, then dig it up on the full moon. This can be a historical site where a victorious battle took place or at a sporting stadium where many victories have been won.

BLACK LOCUST

(*Robinia pseudoacacia*) Mercury—Air—Gemini

AKA: *False acacia, acacia, green locust, yellow locust, pea flower locust, white locust, devil's thorn,* blasting thorn**

This tree is an interesting one because it is native to eastern North America, yet considered invasive in many places in the US because of its tendency to sucker and, therefore, create forests of itself. It has also been introduced to other parts of the world as an ornamental, though there is fossil evidence of the plant existing in Europe as early as the Eocene epoch. How and why it disappeared from there is a mystery, but it has found its way back via human intervention.

The tree can grow up to seventy feet tall in the appropriate conditions and has a wide canopy that narrows toward the top. The leaves are alternating and oddly pinnate, meaning there is one leaflet sticking off from the tip of the leaf grouping. The flowers resemble those of other pea family plants and are arranged in drooping clusters of white blossoms with yellowish centers that give off the most heavenly perfume. The smell is…indescribable, really. Maybe honey mixed with the sweetest dream you've ever had and topped with the most perfect version of your favorite fruit. The fruits are small, two-fluted, flat beans that seem to twist in on themselves. The bark is dark and twisting, forming geometrical patterns superficially. The youthful growths have spines in pairs that grow at the base of leaves; each set looking like the Devil's horns, which gives it credence as our North American choice for blasting rods. It is dark, beautiful, and has a powerful history here.

Black locust is one of the hardest woods, if not *the* hardest, on the North American continent, having a Janka hardness rating of 7,560 N. This served the naval forces of the burgeoning United States during the War of Independence, as their ships were jointed with trunnels of black locust while the British ships were fitted with trunnels of English oak, which has a Janka rating of only 6,000 N. The superior hardness and durability of the trunnels in the North American ships allowed them to outlast the British and take more artillery damage.

It was this tree that early colonizers used to build their settlements, too. The ruins of the original site of Jamestown were reduced to almost nothing after merely a century, but the corner posts, which were made of black locust, still stood firm. The wood has also been used as fence posting, to build decking, and to create very durable windbreaks. Native American peoples have used it for bows, arrows, and spears and as a construction wood, meaning it has millennia's worth of historical value. There is evidence that, as part of their aggressive modification of the Land, Native Americans moved the black locust from inland forests to coastal areas because of its usefulness, particularly as a bow wood. It is one of the strongest woods available and the third most traded hardwood in the world, though it is susceptible to wood borer damage, which can cause weakness and cause it to spit when used in fires, firing embers several feet.

Like the Acacia trees it shares a name with and other plants of the *Leguminosae* and *Fabaceae,* black locust is a nitrogen fixer that remediates soils. It can overshade other plants, including natives, but will be overshaded by other plants in time, meaning it is not a huge threat to the ecosystems it grows in. Rather, it aids the growth of plants by not only harboring nitrogen but also returning its own biomass to the Earth, which breaks down into nitrogen, carbons, and all the other essential nutrients plants need to grow. It's almost as if plants like this one evolved over millions of years to know how to co-exist and coregulate within ecosystems...

Foraging Uses

The flowers of black locust are the most often eaten part of the tree and can be taken raw off of the tree and added to salads or just munched on. They have a delicious, almost honey-like flavor. When looking for Acacia recipes, you are likely to find these flowers listed as *beignet d'acacia,* a recipe for which is found in the section on actual Acacia on page 89. They can also be added as a floral note to pancakes. The beans can be eaten raw, though it is better to cook them because the toxic constituent, robin, which resides in all parts of the tree *except* its flowers, is broken down by heating. Better to be safe and either toast or boil and leech the beans. The leaves and bark ought never to be eaten.

Hekate Cakes

This is a recipe for a sort of honey pancake from the second century CE that I've adapted to include black locust flowers. Because of the tree's ties to liminal magic, I associate it very closely with Hekate and find it to be a suitable offering. On *deipnon,* the night of the dark moon, I sometimes offer these at the crossroads and eat a few myself.

- 1 c. flour of your choice
- 1 c. water
- ½ c. honey
- 1 c. locust flowers, loosely packed

1. Mix everything in a bowl.
2. Heat a skillet on medium heat and melt a good amount of butter into it.
3. Pour out cakes about 3 inches across. When you see bubbles forming through the batter, flip them. Continue to flip the cakes until both sides are golden brown. They'll be a bit flat and dense but very tasty.
4. Serve them with a drizzle of honey or berry coulis.

Remedial Applications

The applications of this tree are not numerous, as it harbors a toxin (robin) that can be quite deleterious to the human condition. Vomiting, dizziness, dry mouth, and a weakening of the muscle of the heart leading to dysrhythmia are among its symptoms. However, it is broken down through the application of heat and rendered inert, or the poison can be taken advantage of. One of the ways the tree has been used is by chewing the root bark as an emetic. As with many toxic substances, the bark has a numbing quality. The roots of the tree were beaten against stones to make them pulpy and then placed against aching teeth by the Cherokee.

The flowers are antispasmodic, diuretic, and laxative and can be prepared as an emollient for the skin. A tea of the flowers, which smells quite nice, can be turned into a cream fairly easily. The leaves can be used as a cholagogue and the bark as an immune tonic, but both act as better emetics, and you're more likely to vomit than gain any health benefit.

Magical Applications

Black locust lends itself to workings of all sorts of magic, particularly the making of tools like wands, staves, and the hilts of knives. It can also make a very fine set of divination tools, such as runes or simple throwing sticks. It has a powerful and shifting connection to life and death, to light and dark, having an inherent liminality that can be put to good use by a savvy witch. In the lore of the Cherokee people, it is said that a splinter of black locust placed in the skin of a person by a malicious magic user can bring rapid death. This may be a sort of "curse of things inside you," where sharp thorns and poisonous items are sewn into the stomach of a poppet so that the target will wither with pain. It is also a tree of durability and strength, though, so it can be used to bring those qualities to the forefront by magic.

Blasting Rod

To make one with black locust, simply find a stick of adequate size. If you're making a cane, make sure it comes to just above your hip, and if you're going for a staff, up to the shoulder is a good height. Wands are often the length of the forearm and hand from the tip of the middle finger to the crook of the elbow. Gather this on a Sunday in the first hour of Saturn or on a Saturday in the first hour of Mars. On a Thursday in the hours of Mars and in the hours of Saturn, carve a spiral into the stick, creating a twist in the wood. Smooth it out as you wish, sculpt it into a serpent, or some other such thing. This allows you to direct power into and out of the rod in a spiraling, twisting manner that can be used offensively or defensively.

A blasting or turning rod or wand is one of the traditional instruments of the witch. Often, a sort of shillelagh made of blackthorn wood (*Prunus spinosa*), also called the sloe tree, is the instrument *nonpareil* for maleficium and abjuration. In North America, however, we do not have many blackthorns, so a suitable replacement can be found in black locust. A blasting or turning rod is used to set spirits upon an enemy or to direct one's power in such a way as to hex a person through the eyes or a simple gesture, but also to turn that sort of spell craft aside and return it to its sender (thus "turning"). It can also be used to strip luck and good fortune from a person and turn it toward oneself or to warp the threads of fate using probability-directed magic.

As a finishing touch, paint the wand in specially prepared lacquer. Make a tincture of aconite flowers (be *incredibly* cautious with this plant, as it is one of the deadliest toxins on the planet), nettles, datura blossoms, and black locust flowers. Add one cup of gum arabic and enough India ink to turn the tincture thickly black. If you are inclined and have the means, crush human bone (preferably the bones of the left middle finger), burn it to ash, and calcine it until it is a fine powder. Add this to the lacquer and enchant the resulting product with whichever incantation you find suitable. Once the mixture is prepared, apply it to the rod, staining it a traditional, glossy, jet black.

DALMATIAN TOADFLAX

(*Linaria dalmatica*) Mars—Earth—Aquarius

AKA: *Butter-and-eggs, flaxweed, wild snapdragon, python,* golden turn skin,* toad skin,* fith-fath weed**

How I love to see this plant! It is like joy growing from a stalk, dozens of laughing, full-bellied yellow dragons laughing with deep mirth. The flowers are bright yellow snapdragons, each having a spike trailing down the backside of the flower like a larkspur. The lower lip of the dragon's mouth is marked by a slightly orange bit of fur that acts as a landing pad for pollinators, specifically long-tongued bees that can reach down into the nectar spike. The leaves of this species are shorter and narrower than the common toadflax (*Linaria vulgaris*). They are short and heart-shaped, with their tip pointing upward, a lot like spurge.

It is native to the Mediterranean, but it has been introduced to most other continents. It is considered noxious in both the US and Canada for its pervasive growing habits in grassland habitats. As with other pioneer, first-stage succession plants, dalmatian toadflax has a deep tap root and branching lateral roots that bring out nutrients and make the soil ready for the next stage of colonization.

They can form thick stands that overshade and outcompete natives and grasses, but only for a while and only in places where there is already low competition, meaning there are few, if any, healthy plants in the area.

They tend to grow in overgrazed areas, scraped-down lots, gravel pits, roads, and the other neglected, forgotten, destroyed edges of ecosystems. Here, they grow along the ditches next to paved, trafficked roadways that are periodically mowed, which reduces the viability of native plants and degrades the soil, meaning they have to keep repeating their job again and again. Eventually, they die, other plants move in, and they reach balance in the habitat. In the meantime, they are an important source of food for bees and other insects; their seeds feed birds and small animals, and they do the best they can in areas that have been greatly disturbed.

Foraging Uses

I have never found evidence of people eating this plant as a part of their diet, and I don't think there is a reason to. A few of the flowers on a salad probably wouldn't hurt you, but they also wouldn't taste very good. Its flavor does not live up to the folk name "butter-and-eggs," that's for sure. Some people eat the young shoots, but because of its potentially toxic nature, only small amounts at a time can be eaten, anyway. It's better to harvest other greens and leave this one to the remedial uses.

Remedial Applications

Toadflax is a plant that needs to be used with other plants. Michael Moore describes it as a "raw, disorganized remedy best used in formulas," which is true. It is a strong hepatoprotective but lacks a directive force by which to get things truly moving. Therefore, it is better with other herbs such as Oregon grape root, burdock, loosestrife, bindweed, and tamarisk. This is in cases of liver stagnancy. If the liver is inflamed for some reason, toadflax can be of use in relieving that inflammation on its own or with anti-inflammatories like willow and sweet clover.

Toadflax also has an effect on the kidneys, as it has a diuretic effect and the crushed seeds of the plant have been historically used to treat kidney stones and gravel. It has also been used as a remedy for "dropsy" or edema by way of removing excess water from the body via urination, so it makes a good companion herb for dandelion. Because of its astringent properties, it has been used to treat hemorrhoids, the fresh plant being made into a salve by heating the leaves and flowers in a fat until they become crisp. The resulting oil is a lovely green color and is relieving when applied to hemorrhoids externally but also to other sores and swellings. Combined with lemon balm and yellow dock, it makes a nice topical application for herpes and shingles outbreaks.

It should be noted that toadflax influences the metabolization of some pharmaceutical drugs, such as ACE inhibitors and barbiturates, causing them to last longer and be more intense than anticipated. There are also constituents in the plant that can make one feel queasy and have a profound laxative effect, especially if you don't need to be taking the herb for hepatoprotective problems.

TOADFLAX LIVER TONIC

- 1 tsp. toadflax, flowering parts
- ½ tsp. bindweed root, dried and crushed
- ½ tsp. burdock root, dried and crushed

Make a hot aqueous infusion about 4 times per day for no more than 7 days. If you begin to feel queasy or begin to feel the laxative effect of these plants, stop using this immediately and switch to something else, like burdock alone.

MAGICAL APPLICATIONS

Toadflax is put to good use as a protection against malicious magic and the effects of jinxes, hexes, and curses. It is also a handy herb for invisibility as well as skin-turning, shapeshifting, and therianthropy.

SKIN-TURNING UNGUENT

First, a brief discussion on skin-turning and shapeshifting. The body is made of various layers, from the physical body to the very most subtle layers of the spirit, all of them being connected. The layers that are more subtle than the physical one are often collectively termed the Astral body, Sidereal body, or body of light, and what I term the "free body" or the Lunar Body.[61] I see it as having three basic layers: the Animal Body, the Emotional Body, and the Mental Body. The more connected and

61 See my first book, *Ars Granorum: The Six Seed Arts of Witchcraft* for a discussion on my thoughts on this subject, though they have evolved since that book was published.

awake each of these subtle bodies is, the better able you are to control and remember what you've done across the hedge, for it is these that are able to flit off and go about dreaming and traveling the Astral world and of shifting shape. As you gain proficiency in the art of skin-turning, you may be able to call the animal spirit into your daily consciousness at will, though it can be a dangerous thing to shift shape for too long or too often. It is easy to forget oneself when one becomes better accustomed to another shape and loses attachment to the original one. Proceed with cunning and caution.

Even so, this recipe is a sort of flying ointment meant to help you change your shape during transvection. It is meant to be applied to the neck, armpits, and feet, though it can be spread in a thin layer over the whole body. Avoid *all* mucosal membranes (meaning *any* orifice of any kind). You may also wish to set up an altar to the spirit of the animal whose shape you are learning to take, including an incarnadined (reddened) skull to which you apply this unguent, further linking you to the spirit and its shape. On a Monday in the hour of Mercury, preferably on or near a dark moon, create an oil infusion of the following ingredients. Add half an ounce of beeswax per cup of oil to make an easily spreadable, oily unguent, or use the fat of the animal you wish to turn into (or a suitable relative).

Just in case you have trouble returning to the body as it usually is, trouble coming out of animal form, have colloidal silver on hand or an oil made by heat infusing sterling silver into it, and apply this to the body. It will help realign your Lunar Body to its particular form.

- 200 datura seeds, dried and ground
- 1 oz. toadflax, dried
- 1 oz. yarrow, dried
- ¼ oz. blue vervain, dried
- 1 handful of harebell, fresh or dried
- 1 handful dandelion heads, going to seed
- 1 small length snake shed (optional, but strongly recommended)

GARLIC MUSTARD

(*ALLIARIA PETIOLATA*) JUPITER—FIRE—LEO

AKA: *Hedge mustard, poor man's mustard, garlic root, jack-by-the-hedge, penny hedge, garlicwort, sauce-alone, spice Jupiter,* greenglow**

This is probably one of the tastiest of the invasive plant species in this book and is considered one of the most dangerous of them all. Because of its ability to seed and spread rapidly and because it is an early sprouting plant, many people think it outcompetes native plants in their habitats and reduces overall biodiversity in forests and fields. It is believed that this plant allelopathically changes the mycorrhizal network and bacterial microbiome of the soil in such a way that native plants cannot survive. It is also considered useless, as many people think that it is not foraged by animals such as deer.

According to Vikki L. Rodgers et al., "Compared to uninvaded plots, plots invaded by *A. petiolata* were consistently and significantly higher in N, P, Ca and Mg availability, and soil pH," and "Similarly...the colonization of native soils by *A. petiolata* roots did not alter soil nutrient cycling, implying that the exudation of secondary compounds has little effect on soil processes."[62] They also discovered that the presence of *A. petiolata* in an area increased the rate at which native leaf litter was decomposed, meaning that nutrient availability increased, as mentioned above. The study found that garlic

62 See Rodgers et al.

mustard *does* indeed alter mycorrhizal activity in the soil, however, which is a detriment to native species. That does not mean that this is a bad plant in need of eradication at all costs or that the data indicates that garlic mustard is as strong a competitor as the authors may have feared.

In his article "Is Garlic Mustard an Invader of an Opportunist," Michael Anderson, resident naturalist of Macalester College, says, "[An] inconsistency in the garlic-mustard-as-superior-competitor scenario is the fact that continuing field surveys have failed to observe the clear negative impacts on native communities that were initially expected."[63] He goes on to point out that in his own studies, "Some native species do seem to get beaten out in such trials (head-to-head competition experiments), based on how strongly they are inhibited by garlic mustard and how strongly they inhibit the invader in return. However, many native species seem to be a relatively even match, and a few even outcompete garlic mustard."[64]

Over time, it is becoming more and more clear that garlic mustard becomes less and less competitive the longer it stays in an ecosystem, reaching a balance with the native environment, biological pathogens and predators, and stressors other plants are also susceptible to. It is important to make clear that garlic mustard is not the monster it was made out to be; it is merely taking advantage of environmental conditions brought about by human conduct, and its ability to invade is slowing, showing that it, along with most other invasives, will come into symbiotic balance with their environments, unlike humans beings. Anderson points out:

> *The North American environment to which garlic mustard was introduced in 1868 is not the same environment across which its population has been recently expanding. In the past century and a half, human populations in garlic mustard's invaded range have exploded in number, carved our way deeply into the pre-European landscape, and changed our technology and lifestyles in ways that have increased the environmental footprint left by each one of us. These human-made changes have ripple effects in the ecosystems associated with us—affecting even native species—favoring some organisms and disfavoring others.*[65]

---

63 See Anderson.

64 Ibid.

65 Ibid.

When it comes to foraging by animals, it is true that they do not preferentially eat garlic mustard and have been seen to avoid it. That does not mean it is never eaten, as there are photographs of white-tail deer eating garlic mustard, and it has been observed to happen, if rarely. Still, that is not an indicator that the plant is useless, as white-tail deer populations are at an all-time high because we have cultivated for ourselves the same environments that deer seem to flourish in: areas without predators and with ample food and water availability. Their populations have expanded with our own, and because they forage preferentially on native plants, they create ideal opportunities (more sun where plants have been eaten, disturbed soil from their hoof tracks, fertilizer from their manure, among other things) for invasives like garlic mustard to grow. Again, it is because of human-driven ecological change that garlic mustard has proliferated, not because it is an aggressive killer of native species.[66]

All of that said, *A. petiolata* needs to be managed, which is a daunting task, to be sure. However, if the common person knew that garlic mustard is edible when cooked or eaten young, that it has medicinal qualities that outperform other plants, and that it is a potent magical tool...well, maybe everyone would be gathering it for one reason or another, so it would have less opportunity to spread unchecked. Coming into right relationship with a plant like this means learning how to develop a reciprocity between it, us, and the Land.

Garlic mustard was brought to the US in the mid-1800s by immigrants from Eurasia and is now considered invasive in the Northeastern US and Canada, with some invasive pockets in the Pacific Northwest and Alaska. It was brought as food and as a medicinal plant, something considered too valuable to the people who carried it across land and sea to be left behind forever, something that was deeply meaningful to them. Learning why that was the case will help us to figure out how to utilize this plant in the best way possible.

The leaves of garlic mustard are heart-shaped and deeply toothed, resembling serrated violet leaves, though the basal leaves are more often kidney-shaped. They have a characteristic smell of garlic, which is where the common name for *Alliaria* (meaning "garlic-like") comes from. The flowers are four-petaled like those of other Brassicaceae plants. In this

66 See Anderson.

plant, they are of a median size, white, and clustered at the top of the stem. They give way to long, upright seed pods called silique, which produce many hundreds of seeds that are hurled up to six feet from the plant when they burst open. The root is usually S- or L-shaped.

These plants have a two-year life cycle, with one year as a rosette and one year growing a stalk and seeding with no winter dormancy period, meaning they remain green the entire time they are alive. Their first year, after they sprout in May, is spent gathering nutrients that are then stored in their root. They wait for the *following* spring, usually early May, earlier than most native plants, when they send up a stalk. They will flower and seed quickly and widely, then die back before most natives are even fully developed or ready to seed. Seeds can stay viable in the soil for about ten years.

The entire plant harbors cyanide (as hydrogen cyanide), though it accumulates in the plant over time, meaning younger plants are safer and can be eaten raw. Older plants can also be eaten, though, if they are chopped and cooked thoroughly. This is an ingenious adaptation to avoid predation by herbivores and works well for the plant, as it has very few natural predators, especially in areas it has naturalized to. However, it remains an important plant to pollinators, who are finding it harder and harder to find food in their native habitats. Being human, though, we can figure out ways around this defense and enjoy their particular flavor.

Foraging Uses

Contrary to what many people still think, garlic mustard *is* edible. The younger the plants, the better, and the tastiest ones are those that can be snapped easily with your fingers, about six to ten inches from the top of the plant. Gather these when the flowering tops are either unopened or very few have opened. This inhibits their ability to seed, so if you are trying to rid an area of a stand of the plant, return to the same stand of garlic mustard again and again, taking their tops to eat.

The whole plant is edible, though it is the young stalks that most foragers find to be the most enjoyable. These can be stripped of their leaves and flowering tops and then steamed like asparagus. They taste a bit sweet and a bit garlicky and are absolutely delicious. The stalks can also be pickled, which is a real treat on a hot summer day. The leaves and flowers can be added to various dishes and dips and can even be used to stuff mushrooms and squash blossoms. They make a very nice salad green and can be used fresh or dried to flavor soups, to season meat, and to add a kick to sauces, dressings, and other culinary infusions. The root and the flowers both taste a lot like horseradish with a slightly bitter aftertaste that lends itself very well to a slew of flavor profiles, including as a red wine marinade for things like steak.

On top of that, it is high in vitamins A, C, E, and some Bs and provides a number of minerals and vitamins that are getting harder to get through conventional food sources. Eating wild weeds is one of the most nutritious things you can do in your diet, really, and garlic mustard is such a delightful way to do so. There is no way to lose from eating garlic mustard.

Garlic Mustard Stuffed Buffalo Gourd Flowers

- 3 Tbsp. of oil *or* other fat of choice
- 3 c. water
- ½ oz. garlic mustard stalks, steamed
- ½ oz. garlic mustard flowering tops, finely chopped
- 1 bunch of lamb's quarters, finely chopped
- 3 oz. of goat cheese
- 8 buffalo gourd flowers *or* other squash blossom, stamen removed

1. Preheat your oven to 375°F or a little hotter.
2. Put 3 cups of water in the bottom of a pot and place a metal colander in the bottom, or use whatever setup you usually use to steam things. Bring to a boil and steam your garlic mustard stems until they are tender (about 10 minutes). Move to step 3 while you wait.
3. Mix the minced garlic with 1 tablespoon of your chosen fat and sauté on low heat for about 1 minute. Stir in your chopped garlic mustard flowering tops and your lamb's quarters, cooking for about 9 minutes.
4. Remove the stems from the steamer and the flowering top or lamb's quarters mix from the heat and allow to cool for about 15 minutes.
5. Chop the steamed stems into small chunks and mix in with the flowering top or lamb's quarters mix. Remove excess moisture with a towel.

6. In a bowl, stir all your cooked parts in with goat cheese and mix them thoroughly.
7. Make sure your buffalo gourd blossoms are clean and that the stamen (the pollinating structure in the center) has been removed. Stuff these about ¾ full with your herb and cheese mixture, then gently twist the ends closed.
8. Place the filled blossoms in a glass or ceramic pan (preferably, but steel or iron will work). Drizzle 2 tablespoons of your chosen fat over the blossoms, then sprinkle with salt and pepper to taste. Roast these for about 10 minutes or until they are hot. Any extra mixture can be stored in the fridge for about a week. Use it to top your next batch of pasta!

Garlic Mustard Ravioli

- 1 c. of flour, heaping
- 4–5 egg yolks
- 4 oz. garlic mustard flowering tops
- 3 oz. goat cheese
- 3 oz. ricotta
- 3 oz. shredded gouda
- 2 cans chopped tomato in tomato juice
- 3 cloves garlic, minced
- 2 oz. of fresh horseweed, finely chopped
- ½ c. fresh blackberries, mashed (optional)
- Ravioli stamp, maker, or cutting wheel

1. First, you will make your ravioli stuffing so it is ready. All that is required for this is to finely chop your garlic mustard flowering tops, then mix your ricotta, goat cheese, and gouda together. Make sure it is not runny at all, as runny stuffing leads to sticky pasta.
2. Next, make your pasta! Take the cup of flour and make a heap in the middle of a sizable cutting board. Make a well in the middle and put your egg yolks into this.
3. Using your hands, break the yolks and swirl them about in the well, then begin to gently mix them with the flour. Knead this

together until it is completely mixed and becomes a slightly sticky, firm dough, then roll it into a ball. Halve the ball, then wrap the balls of dough separately in plastic wrap and let them sit for about 30 minutes out of the fridge.

4. Flour your cutting board or working space, then roll the dough balls out until they are thin-but-not-too-thin, about ⅛ of an inch. Using something like a melon baller or a small spoon, place small dollops of the cheese mix on one sheet of the dough, about an inch from the top and an inch and a half apart from each other. Make as many rows as you can in this way.
5. Place the second sheet of dough on top of the first as evenly as possible. Allow it to settle, and you will see little lumps where your filling is. Gently press down *around* the lump.
6. Center your ravioli stamp on the lump of stuffing, and begin to cut out your pasta. Lift the edge of the dough, and all your ravioli should simply come loose! If there is a problem with the edges not sticking together, use your dampened finger to seal them.
7. Any remaining dough can be used to roll out again to get as many ravioli as possible out of this recipe.
8. Now, you'll need to start your sauce. In a saucepan, mix 1 tablespoon of your chosen fat and your minced garlic together and sauté them together for about 1 minute; do not let it brown.
9. Set a pot of water to boil for your pasta, but wait to add it for a few minutes.
10. Add your tomatoes, using a bit of water to rinse the cans to get as much out as possible. If the tomatoes are very chunky, use a potato masher to even them out. Add a heavy pinch of salt to the pan and simmer on medium heat for about 10 minutes. Feel free to add any herbs you want to at this point.
11. After about 6 minutes of simmering the sauce, add your pasta to the boiling water. It should take about 4 minutes to complete.
12. Add the pasta and the sauce together, stirring them gently together until everything is evenly coated. Serve hot, with cheese and chopped garlic mustard on top. Enjoy!

Medicinal Applications

A. petiolata is actually a very powerful medicinal, which is one of the reasons that it was brought over from Eurasia in the first place. It has been used as an anti-asthmatic, an antimicrobial, an anti-inflammatory, a vasodilator, a vermifuge, a vulnerary, and as a sternutatory (meaning it promotes sneezing). The latter method is simply snorting a powder made from garlic mustard leaves, and it is quite effective. Mustards are also highly useful for digestion, so eating them and making medicinal vinegars with them can help balance out digestive issues from upset stomach to IBS. The medicinal aspects of this plant are similar to other mustards and can be used in conjunction with them or in place of them.

Garlic Mustard Chest Plaster

A garlic mustard plaster can be used to ease the pain from bronchitis or other respiratory illnesses or to ease pain in muscles. They can also be used on the forehead for headaches. Be aware, as plasters can cause burns.

- 1 oz. powdered garlic mustard root
- 1 oz. powdered yellow mustard seed
- 1 oz. flour of your choice
- Olive oil
- Warm water
- Cotton towel
- Larger cotton cloth
- Heating pad

1. Mix the garlic mustard and mustard seed powders and the flour together in a bowl, then add enough warm water to create a batter-like consistency. If it ends up runny, add flour. If it ends up thick, add water.
2. Lay your smaller cotton cloth flat on a counter space. Spread the garlic paste onto one half of the cloth, then fold the other half over the paste so it is "tacoed" inside. Then, gently fold that in half as many times as it takes to get the size of plaster you want.
3. Wrap that inside of another, larger cloth to give a layer of protection that will lay against the skin.

4. Rub a good amount of olive oil (or butter, tallow, lard, or other fat) over the area where the plaster will be placed, usually on the chest. This will reduce the risk of burn.
5. Place the plaster against the area you are treating, then lay the heating pad on top to heat the plaster up and activate it. Check under the plaster every 2–3 minutes to make sure the skin is not becoming overly red or blistering.
6. Let this sit for no more than 20 minutes at a time, taking at least an hour break between plasters.

Garlic Mustard Fire Cider

Fire cider is an old remedy for all sorts of colds, flus, and stomach issues, but they are also very useful for stomach and digestive complaints, as well. Anything can be added to a fire cider recipe, so the following one will be fairly simple to allow you to add things as you wish.

- 1 qt. of apple cider vinegar, just about
- 8 oz. of garlic mustard root, chopped
- 4 oz. of garlic mustard flowering tops, chopped
- 1 oz. hot cayenne powder
- 1 garlic bulb
- 13 hot peppers of your choice
- 2 lemons
- Juicer

1. Clean and sanitize a quart jar.
2. Separate the garlic cloves and remove them from their husks.
3. Finely chop the garlic mustard root and flowering tops along with the peppers and garlic. Put this into your quart jar.
4. Cut your lemon in half and juice it. Add the juice to the jar and let it sit for about 30 minutes to an hour.
5. Cut your lemon rinds into quarters and add them to the jar along with your cayenne powder.
6. Pour enough ACV into the jar so that all of the ingredients are fully submerged. You may wish to place a small piece of cotton cloth between the ingredients and the neck of your jar to ensure they stay submerged.

7. Allow this to rest for 3–4 weeks, gently shaking the jar at least once daily. Also check to make sure everything stays under the vinegar.
8. Once it is ready, strain it and keep it in the fridge for up to a year. Take about 1 tablespoon 3 times daily when you feel tickles in your throat, sinus pressure, get a cough, or any other symptom of cold and flu. Taking 1 teaspoon in the morning and one at night can also be used as a preventative measure if you are around people who may be sick.

Garlic Mustard Circulation Tincture

This tincture can be used to treat sore, achy muscles, arthritis, and overall pain in the body.

- 1 oz. of garlic mustard root, wilted and finely chopped
- 1 oz. Russian olive fruits, fresh and pulverized
- ½ oz. hawthorn berries, pulverized
- ½ oz. of horseweed, wilted and finely chopped
- 1 oz. wild lettuce leaves, fresh, finely chopped
- 32 oz. of 150-proof grain alcohol
- 32 oz. mason jar
- Blender (optional)

1. To chop your Russian olive fruits and hawthorn berries, you may need to use a food processor or blender, so you may as well add everything together at once and blend it together for about 2 minutes, then decant everything into a jar. Allow that to sit in a warm, dark place for about 3–4 weeks, shaking at least once per day.
2. If you don't have a blender or food processor, finely chop all your leafy ingredients together. Place your Russian olive fruits and hawthorn berries into a plastic bag and stomp on them, smash them with a meat tenderizer or hammer, or in some way mash them to pulp. Mix your leafy bits in with the pulp and mix thoroughly.
3. Put the resulting paste into your 32-ounce jar and cover the contents completely with your alcohol. Allow to sit in a cool,

dark place for about 3–4 weeks, and shake it vigorously at least once per day.

4. Strain and decant into an amber jar, then fill an amber dosage bottle (1–2 ounce dropper or serum sprayer) and take about 60 drops (2 sprays or droppers full) about four times daily.
5. This can also be made as a glycerite for those who do not want to use alcohol.

Magical Applications

Garlic mustard is a wonder when it comes to hastening spells, amplifying power, and bringing prosperity. Most mustards can be used the same way, as they all fall within the resonance of Jupiter and make useful additions to all spells that fall under the category of "business" or "acquisition."

Poke for Prosperity

Carry this charm on your person or keep it in your place of business.

- A pinch of garlic mustard seeds
- A pinch each of cinnamon, chamomile, and basil
- A poke of royal blue[67] cloth
- Golden thread or embroidery floss
- 3 bees, ethically harvested or charms
- 1 of each type of coin in your region
- 1 magnet
- The Fourth Pentacle of Jupiter

1. On a Thursday in the hour of Jupiter inscribe the Fourth Pentacle of Jupiter on a circular piece of tin, a piece of vellum, or a very thin piece of skin, such as a natural drumhead. Write it out with regular ink of a black or blue color. You may also create a different pentacle or sigil that has more meaning to you or write down a spell. When it is done, slip it into the blue poke.

67 Blue is chosen for this charm because it is the sacred color of Jupiter and resonates with wealth and prosperity.

2. Then, drop in your garlic mustard seeds along with your herbs and the coins you've chosen. If you have some, add in some five finger grass (*Potentilla gracilis*).
3. The bees should be gathered after they have already died of natural causes. Check windowsills or look around flower beds, but *do not* kill bees for this charm. You need their sympathy, not their lives. If you can't find three bee carcasses, you may use charms or beads or whatever else you can find. Put them one at a time in the bag, saying:

   "One to go and find the gold, and one to fetch it home. The last to keep the gold all safe inside its honeycomb."

4. Tie the bag shut with the gold thread while reciting whichever knot charm you find appropriate. The easiest one I can think of is:

   "By knot of one, the spells begun. By knot of two, the spell comes true. By knot of three, so shall it be."

5. Hang this bag in your business in the highest traffic room, in your home in the "nicest" room, whatever that means to you, or wherever you plan to draw this wealth. Where are the bees going to and from? Make that the place you keep the bag.

Gambling Oil

Rub this on your hands, feet, and lucky items when you go to the casino or other places of gambling.

- 16 oz. of sunflower oil
- 16 oz. wide mouth jar
- ½ oz. chamomile
- ½ oz. cinnamon
- ½ oz. garlic mustard flowers
- ½ oz. cayenne powder

- 1 tsp. garlic mustard seeds
- 1 lodestone
- *Optional*: 7 crickets, ethically sourced *or* 1 dried pig ear, ethically sourced

1. You simply need to macerate all of the ingredients together in a jar for a lunar cycle, starting on a Wednesday in the hour of Jupiter and ending on a Thursday in the hour of Mars, which aligns your working to gambling, increase, and conquest.
2. The ephemera are optional. Crickets are considered lucky, as is the number seven. Here, you can instruct them to each sing a song to pacify the planets so that none of them bother you and your profits. Pigs are also lucky creatures, and their ears will listen for the best opportunities and help increase your winnings.

Invasive Protection Dust

Sprinkle this in front of your door or around your home to protect it from malicious spirits and aggressive magics.

- 1 Tbsp. of Tribulus fruits, powdered
- 1 Tbsp. of arrowroot, powdered
- 1 Tbsp. of saltcedar leaves and flowers, powdered
- 1 Tbsp. of graveyard dirt
- 1 Tbsp. of salt
- 4 Tbsp. garlic mustard seeds

1. On a Tuesday in the hour of Mars, preferably when the Moon is waxing or full, gather the above ingredients, cleanse and bless them, then mix them together in a bowl.

   EXAMPLE:
   "Be cleared and cleansed, purified completely. May Fire remove all dross from you. May Water wash away all impurities. May Air raise you up to unity with your essential nature. May Earth give you new form, complete and pure. May your Spirit be amplified to the end of ages, throughout the multiverse."

2. Using a thorny wand (pyracantha or Russian olive branches work well, as do rose stems), stir them in a clockwise manner, telling the powder what it is for and conjuring the powers of whatever spirits and entities you work with.

   EXAMPLE:
   "Apotropaia, She Who Averts Harm, I do summon, stir, and conjure you unto this altar. I ask that you touch this powder of protection that it may keep me, my home, and my loved ones from all harm, all malice, all directed hate, and baneful magic and spirits. May it take on all your power, Great Lady, and may it keep me safe."

3. Once the enchanting is done, use the powder to sprinkle in front of your doorstep and around your home to create a barrier across which malicious spirits or magics cannot go.

HORSEWEED

(*Conyza canadensis*) Mars—Fire—Virgo

AKA: *Canadian fleabane, Devil's duster,* coltstail, marestail, butter-weed, pick-n-fly,* upsie-daisies**

This plant can grow very tall, upwards of six feet, with very evenly spaced whorls of toothed leaves all along the stem. The plant is covered in a coarse fur, and when it flowers, it blossoms in a spray of yellow flowers at the tip, giving the overall appearance of an ox tail or a very interesting riding crop. When it seeds, all the flowers go to fluff at the same time and make it look very much like a duster.

Horseweed can seed itself aggressively, and the seeds require no period of dormancy to germinate. It can adapt itself to most types of soil, even growing in loose gravel if the sun and water conditions are even minimally met. If its stalk is damaged, it will grow more stalks, branching like a hydra. It is considered a great nuisance to farmers as it has developed a tolerance to most herbicides. The suggested chemicals are 2,4-D or dicamba, but even with those, it requires some manual management as well. Farmers have indicated nearly total crop loss if horseweed is allowed to run rampant.

As with most invasives, horseweed is an important food for pollinators of many kinds and for various beetles. Its taproot is very shallow, so it doesn't really bring nutrients up to the topsoil, but it *does* accumulate toxic metals. Zinc and copper are accumulated in the highest amounts, then lead and barium, and sometimes chromium. When the elements are present in toxic levels in the plant, the above-ground biomass of the plant is reduced and stunted.

Even so, it still serves its purpose as an edible, remedial, and powerfully magical plant. The essential oils have been used for centuries as an additive and binder for perfumery, making them useful for glamoury and virility magic. The dried stem has also been used as a drill-style fire starter. Simply place one end in a depression filled with kindling or in a soft spot on a log and roll it rapidly back and forth between the palms, sliding the hands from the end nearest your face downward toward the log or depression as you go. Continue to do so until you see smoke and blow on the embers to ignite a fire. It takes practice, but this is a method used for time immemorial and *does* work when done properly.

Foraging Uses

When spring and summer come around, I gather this weed like there's no tomorrow. I love it as a remedy and as a spice. It tastes a lot like horseradish and has such a pleasant *bite* to it. When it is dried, it has a spicy tarragon flavor that is quite nice infused in vinegars, raw in salads, and in a very wide variety of dishes. Because of its spiciness, it is very useful as a carminative and benefits the GI tract in general. The whole plant is heavy in phosphorus and calcium, so it makes a useful nutritive addition to soups, stews, and steamed veggie combos. The essential oils derived from horseweed are used in flavoring candies.

Asparagus and Horseweed Caesar Vinegarette

- 1 bunch of asparagus, woody ends removed
- 1 shallot, chopped
- ½ c. champagne or white wine vinegar
- ⅓ c. olive oil
- 4 Tbsp. parmesan cheese
- 2 Tbsp. horseweed leaf, fresh
- 2 Tbsp. lemon juice
- 1 Tbsp. oregano, dried

- 1 Tbsp. honey
- ½ Tbsp. Dijon mustard
- 3–5 anchovies, packed in oil
- 2 garlic cloves
- 1 large egg yolk
- Salt and pepper to taste

1. Bring water to a boil and cook your asparagus until it is tender but bright green and crisp, which takes about 4 minutes, maybe 5. Transfer your asparagus to an ice bath to cool.
2. In a blender, combine your chopped shallot and vinegar, then blend until they are integrated. Set this aside.
3. Bring two forks and a large bowl to your workspace. Use these to rip and mash the garlic, anchovies, and asparagus into a very fine paste.
4. Chop your horseweed very finely and crumble the oregano into a chunky powder. Mix this well into the paste.
5. In the same bowl, whisk the egg yolk, lemon juice, mustard, and your vinegar and shallot mixture together until they become frothy.
6. Whisk in the oil slowly, in tiny portions, until the mix becomes lighter in color. Add water to thin and oil to thicken. Once it is the texture you want, mix in salt and pepper to taste and serve with Caesar salads, steamed veggies, or anything you'd like.

Horseweed Tzatziki Sauce

- 2 c. Greek yogurt
- 1 c. lebni
- 1 c. feta
- 1 cucumber, peeled
- 1 oz. horseweed
- ½ oz. oregano
- 1 Tbsp. lemon juice
- 1 tsp. black pepper
- 2 tsp. salt

1. Peel the cucumber and chop your horseweed finely.
2. Place these and your other spices into a small bowl with the lemon juice. Let this sit for about 10 minutes.
3. Combine the yogurt, lebni, feta, and cucumber mixture in a blender and blend until well integrated.

Remedial Applications

Horseweed is one of my favorites for the GI tract, particularly the colon. It makes a delicious tisane or vinegar and tinctures up very well. When it comes to herbs for IBS and other such things, this herb is a welcome friend, as it eases intestinal distress, diarrhea, gas, and upset stomach. It also helps with digestion and even stops the bleeding of hemorrhoids. Horseweed is also somewhat diuretic and can be used in conjunction with things like dandelion leaf and yerba negrita to help upkeep and soothe the kidneys and to benefit conditions that appear with edema. Another use I've tried is to roll the leaves between the fingers to release the volatile oils, then huff them into the nostrils to promote sneezing. It certainly works and is useful for stuffiness and runny noses.

Rapé For Rhinitis

A rapé is a finely powdered formulation that is snuffed or blown into the nasal cavity to stimulate activity there. My mentor uses them for sacred purposes and opening the subtle senses, but they are just as useful for clearing stuffy noses.

- ¼ oz. horseweed leaves, dried and powdered
- ¼ oz. black pepper, powdered
- ¼ oz. yarrow flower, dried and powdered

Once the items are powdered, shake them through a fine mesh sifter or sieve, thus making sure your final product is only the finest particles. You only need to use *very* little at a time, just the smallest pinch. Place that on your hand at the junction between your index finger and thumb, then breathe it into your nostril. You will feel a burn and then sneeze, hopefully relieving some of your stuffiness.

Magical Applications

Horseweed is an herb that I haven't read much of in magical herbals and the like, I imagine mostly because it is a silly little weed. We know better, though, and can make good use of it in our magic. I also use these as additions to flying ointments, sort of with the idea that my spirit rises on the back of a brilliant mare and right out of the keyhole! It also helps to increase virility and attract spirits.

Hag Tapers

Hag tapers are usually made with dried stalks of mullein, which is a lovely plant that offers us much. They do not *have* to be made with mullein, though, and horseweed's association with Mars and Fire makes it a perfect plant for this purpose, especially to call in the wild, dancing spirits of this volatile element.

1. Collect horseweed and dry it flat, trying to keep the stalks as flat as possible. As you do so, while they are still wet, chop the stalks into roughly equal lengths. This will increase the number of stalks you've got and keep your tapers manageable. If you are using the fresh leaves of horseweed for something, feel free to strip them as you go.
2. Once they are dry, which should take only a couple of days, strip the plants of their leaves if you have not already done so, leaving only the long, dry stems. Gather these together and tie them into bundles with fine thread, each of roughly the same diameter and length.
3. Gently melt down a non-paraffin wax, such as beeswax or soy. Scent it if you'd like to, but that is unnecessary. Essential oils can be added later with an appropriate anointing oil.
4. Dip the bundles in the wax repeatedly until they resemble something like a candle. They will not look like a store-bought taper but rather like sticks covered in a few layers of wax. This is what you want.
5. Feel free to sprinkle them over with some other herbs that are in sympathy with your purpose and roll the tapers through an anointing oil that makes sense. Burn them with great caution, as these burn less like a candle and more like a torch.

COLOGNE OF THE STALLION

This is a sort of glamoury preparation for attractiveness and virility. The preparation should begin on a Friday in the hour of Mars, preferably during a waxing or full moon.

1. Take the leaves and flowers of horseweed, about a cup loosely packed, and macerate them in a hot enfleurage using a low-scent oil.
2. Do this repeatedly until you can smell the spicy tarragon of the horseweed.
3. This oil is then dissolved in 190-proof alcohol in a mason jar for a period of about 3 weeks or until the next waxing or full moon. Shake it daily, as many times as you can. It can also be dissolved in a glass crank churn, which will help to diffuse the highest number of molecules from the oil into the alcohol.
4. Strain the oil from the alcohol using a dairy filter. The result is your *extrait*, which can be used as a cologne. On a Friday in the hour of Venus, bless the cologne to your purpose, placing the liquid in a copper or brass vessel set atop the Fifth Pentacle of Venus. Store the liquid in a green glass bottle. You may add 6 freshwater pearls and 3 emeralds to the bottle.
5. Other herbs that can be added, such as rose, coriander, and dill, among the traditional herbs, and Russian olive, mimosa, and Acacia flowers, among the invasives.
6. Alternatively, you may create a strictly alcoholic preparation from start to finish. This is called "folding" a tincture, which means you recharge the tincture every day with new plant material to avoid the smell of rot from settling into the alcohol. Simply strain the alcohol into another jar and add more plant material until the alcohol smells like horseweed or a combination of it with the other herbs mentioned above.
7. You may also choose to do *both* an enfleurage and a folded tincture and combine them. Whatever works for you and makes your preparation feel and smell "right," whatever that means to you.

JUNIPER

(*Juniperus spp.*) Jupiter—Sun—Fire—Gemini

AKA: *Enebro, ghost berry, ghost bead, ginepro, ginevra, ginny, gin berry, bladder berry,* yeast berry,* ghost-be-gone bush**

Juniper is known as "the tree that ate the West," which isn't inaccurate. Due to overgrazing, infrequent natural burns, climate shift, and the incredible adaptability of this tree, it has managed to quickly spread into sagebrush steppes and other open areas. Because of how the tree grows, it inhibits the growth of other plants, particularly deep-rooted prairie grasses and native trees. It is also a prolific pollinator, producing enough that the roads will seem to be paved in yellow and creating a very real problem for allergy sufferers.

Even so, the juniper is a wonderful and interesting tree. Its wood grows in strange, twisting patterns, creating an almost Daliesque quality in some of the oldest members, which are quite old. The oldest living juniper in the US, called the Bennett Juniper in Stanislaus National Forest, has been estimated to be at least 1,600 years old, though estimates as high as 6,000 years have been put forward and are possible. Wood rot in the center of the tree makes accurate aging impossible, but we know that the tree has stood longer than multiple civilizations.

Though it has been believed that juniper expansion decreases ambient water flow in streams and creeks, recent studies have shown that this is likely not the case. It is actually the *removal* of junipers that may create decreased water availability due to exposed soil and wind exposure, both of which lead to greater evapotranspiration. Studies also show that increased numbers of junipers do not lead to further soil erosion as previously thought, as the studies are incongruent, and further observation has made it clear that soil erosion is site-specific and cannot be blamed on one tree or another. Erosion certainly isn't worse in encroaching juniper woodland than in the over-grazed areas where soil is trampled, exposed, and degraded that juniper is expanding into. Over time, in fact, studies show that simply having trees of *any* kind in areas where soil exposure is heightened can only be beneficial to water and soil health and to the overall ecosystem in the long term.

Another accusation against juniper is that it decreases biodiversity in the areas it encroaches on. It is true that it displaces some species, but it is also a harbor for many others. Up to 150 animal species may live in juniper-pinon forests, though herbage is decreased. However, even in cases where juniper was removed, the herbage that grew in its stead was dependent on what had already seeded there, and those plants were most often invasives, such as cheatgrass and medusa head grass. Removal areas saw a decrease in wildlife overall. This proves that juniper is an important member of the ecologies of the landscapes it inhabits, even if the way it does so goes against the way we think the ecosystems should work.

Juniper is most often used in making gin. The berries, actually fusiform cones, are used to flavor grain alcohol, giving gin its distinctive flavor. The fragrant wood is used in building and furniture-making projects, especially cabinets, chests, and wardrobes. The oils from the reddish-purple heartwood of certain juniper species (particularly *J. virginiana,* called "Eastern Red Cedar") are used to prevent infestation by moths and other insects, meaning things like "cedar" closets and chests are usually made with Juniperus plants. In fact, the smell we usually associate with cedar, especially in the context of insect repellents, is more often juniper than true cedar. It has also been used to make pencils and paint brushes, as well as more common household tools such as pails, tubs, and utensils that are often subjected to water, as the oils in the wood also make it fairly water resistant.

Also, as a part of the commerce associated with juniper, the essential oil is a highly sought-after product in perfumery and medicine. It is usually derived from steam distillation of the berries, though oils derived from the leaves are also quite nice. One of the more interesting oils produced using juniper (specifically *J. oxycedrus,* the prickly juniper) is an extremely smokey one called *cade* or *juniper tar,* which is created by the destruction of the wood during the distillation process (*distillation per descensum*). It is one of the most often used treatments for hair loss and dandruff, as well as flaking skin conditions like eczema and psoriasis. Because it is a tar-like substance, it is diluted in oil before application to the skin.

Through a folkloric lens, juniper, no matter where it grows, is also spiritually significant to the cultures around it. Across the board, this tree is used to purify, bless, and exorcise a space, usually of the spirits of disincarnate entities (i.e., ghosts). Among the Navajo and Hopi of the American Southwest, there is an idea called "ghost sickness," which may occur after an encounter with a disincarnate spirit. It is characterized by feelings of lethargy, exhaustion, weakness of the body, nausea and dizziness, depression, nightmares, loss of appetite, and anxiety. There may also be the feeling of being hunted, of never feeling safe. One of the plants turned to as a cure to ghost sickness is juniper, with Pueblo peoples wearing necklaces or bracelets of juniper berries, or ghost beads, to ward off malicious witchcraft and the effects of ghost sickness. This echoes its apotropaic and spirit-strengthening uses across the globe. If I am making a preparation to exorcise and cleanse a space, juniper leaf and berry are generally the base to which other things are added.

Juniper tends to grow in areas that are mostly open, in homogenous stands of juniper as far as the eye can see, or among other conifers, such as fir, spruce, and pine. They can grow from extremely rocky soil or simply out of cliff faces and mountainous crags. They usually grow in twisting whorls of wood covered in long, thin strips of grayish bark. The only derivation from this pattern is the only non-medicinal juniper, *J. deppeana,* the alligator juniper, which grows bark in small, scale-like squares. The leaves are either small or needle-like, which is often the case for young growth across the junipers, becoming branched and scaled as they mature. A good rule of thumb for telling them apart from *Cedrus* species is that the leaves of *Juniperus* plants do not lie flat, whereas cedar leaves will.

Contrary to popular belief, juniper does not grow berries. It grows female cones that have fleshy, merged scales that present a berry-like appearance and take almost a full year to mature. One can see the young, green cones on the tree simultaneously with the mature purple cones. They also present with a very thin, waxy white coating, a naturally occurring yeast, which can be used in fermenting processes. The seeds found within the cone can remain viable in the soil for nearly sixty years, meaning a good fruiting season in one year can lead to a good sprouting season even decades in the future. This, of course, is one of the adaptations of this tree that leads to its ability to spread into areas quickly and profusely.

Foraging Uses

Juniper is one of my favorite plants to forage from. The flavor is wholly unique and lends itself to a number of dishes, particularly when it comes to gamey meats like bison, beef, and lamb. It can also be used to make a version of rejuvelac, a fermented beverage usually made with wheat berries for energy boosting and focus. The berries are the most often foraged part of the juniper, though the leaves can be eaten, as can the inner bark, the latter having been used by Pueblo peoples as a famine food.

Juniper Berry Compote

- 3 c. blackberries
- 1 oz. juniper berries
- 3 Tbsp. orange juice
- ⅛ tsp. clove powder
- ⅛ tsp. cinnamon powder
- 1 Tbsp. sugar or honey
- 1 pinch of salt

1. Grind or smash the juniper berries thoroughly before adding them and the blackberries, the sugar or honey, and the orange juice to a small saucepan. Bring this to a medium heat.
2. Once the liquid begins to simmer, begin to smash the berries together using a fruit masher or a spoon. Stir the mixture for about five to ten minutes or until it begins to thicken.
3. Remove the compote from the heat. Add your spices and the *tiniest* pinch of salt, stir together, then enjoy with anything from waffles and ice cream to lamb and pork dishes! This will keep in the fridge for 5–7 days.

Juniper Berry Rejuvelac

- ¼ c. juniper berries, crushed
- ¼ c. fenugreek seeds, whole
- 32 oz. filtered water
- Square of cloth
- Quart mason jar

1. In a quart jar, place your juniper berries, fenugreek seeds, and water. Do not seal the jar but screw the outer ring of the mason jar over the fabric square, allowing the rejuvelac to breathe.
2. Allow this to sit in a warm place for about 24 hours. It will be somewhat cloudy and a bit fizzy.
3. Decant and taste the liquid. It should be light and refreshing.
4. Pour another 32 ounces of water over the reserved berries and seeds to get a second batch, but toss or compost the mixture after this. Rejuvelac will keep in the fridge for about 5 days.

Remedial Applications

This is one of the plans I turn to fairly often for a number of issues. The only time it is truly contraindicated is in the case of kidney disease, as the volatile oils of juniper, which in other cases are useful, are quite harmful to the overall organ and can create further damage. Also, too much juniper in a short period can lead to irritation of the gut, intestine, and kidney, so it is best to use it in moderation, even when it is strongly indicated for a malady. That said, I use juniper for stomach complaints, sluggish digestion, urinary tract issues (such as UTIs and bladder infections), muscle tension, constipation, wound care, edema, and things like colds and flus. Three cups of tea per day or 30 drops of tincture twice per day should help to alleviate most of the above-mentioned issues within a few days to a few weeks, depending on severity.

The best way to make remedies with juniper is with aqueous infusions. A tea made with juniper berry and leaf is going to be endlessly helpful, whereas other preparations may be specific to certain maladies or conditions. It should be stated, though, that more than a pint of juniper infusion should not be taken in a 24-hour period. It is safe for infants and is useful for colic, though only in small amounts. Freeze juniper berry tea (you can also mix this with chamomile tea) and then make ice chips that your infant can suck on. To make the infusion, simply steep 1 teaspoon of crushed juniper berries in 1 cup of nearly boiled water for about 20 minutes.

Juniper Berry Arthritis Oil

- ½ oz. juniper berry, crushed
- ½ oz. mugwort leaf
- ½ oz. chamomile flower
- 1 c. sunflower or safflower oil

1. In a medium saucepan, mix your herbs and your oil together.
2. Bring this to a medium heat. You should be able to smell the herbs, but they shouldn't begin to smell nutty or "cooked."
3. Let this warm in the pan for about 10–15 minutes, then allow it to cool. Repeat this process once more if you'd like.
4. Strain the oil through a cloth into a jar. Use it as often as you'd like to ease arthritic pain, achy muscles, and general soreness.

Juniper Berry Paste For Wounds

- 2 oz. juniper berries, dried
- 1 oz. tamarisk leaves, dried
- 1 c. honey

1. Grind the berries and the leaves together, creating a green powder.
2. Mix this with your honey and apply it to wounds. Wash the wound and change out the paste every 4 hours.

Magical Applications

Juniper is my favorite herb for removing negative, malicious, and harmful energies from a space, as well as removing the spirits of the dead. It is also used in love magic and charms meant to increase masculine potency. As stated, juniper resonates with Jupiter, the Sun, and Mars. I think it is important to point out that the new growth, when it is still sharp and needle-like, is more resonant with Mars than the mature, scaly leaves, which resonate most with Jupiter. The berries are an equal mix of Solar and Jupiterian qualities. It is also worth noting that *J. deppeana,* the alligator juniper, is a solely Jupiterian plant, in my experience, whereas *J. communis* and *J. oxycedrus* are mostly Martial. The other *Juniperus* species tend to be more mutable in their planetary qualities, at least between these three luminaries.

Banishing and Exorcism Incense

- ½ oz. juniper leaf
- ½ oz. boneset leaf and flower
- ½ oz. rue leaf
- ½ oz. rosemary leaf
- ½ oz. garlic powder
- 1 oz. frankincense or other tree resin
- ¼ oz. salt

Mix all the ingredients together and use a coal tablet, which can be found in most smoke shops, to burn them in a thurible. Use your breath, a feather, a sprig of juniper, or just your hand to waft the smoke about the space you are cleansing. As you do so, pray or speak a spell that tells the smoke what to do and what you require of the spirits in the space. An example:

> *"By the virtues of this smoke, I do cleanse and exorcise this space. No spirit with malice toward me in its heart, no power that wishes me harm, no force that wishes to entrap and entangle me may enter this space. Those that are already present are expelled, pushed to the ends of the universe. So it is in all dimensions and facets of reality throughout the multiverse, infinitely, throughout all time, without limit or exception."*

Juniper Kyphi

Kyphi is one of the oldest known scent profiles used for beautification of the self and a burnt offering to the gods, a recipe that goes back to Ancient Egypt. There are actually several recipes and the following is my own version using some of the plants talked about in this book.

- 3 oz. juniper berries, fresh and pulverized
- 3 oz. Russian olive fruit, fresh and pulverized
- 1½ oz. sweet clover flowers, fresh and pulverized
- 1½ oz. vetiver root *or* 20 drops of essential oil
- 1¼ oz. myrrh or other tree resin
- ½ oz. cinnamon bark powder
- ½ oz. pine needles, fresh and pulverized
- 1 bottle of red wine, sweet
- 1 pound honey

1. Take your herbs and pound them together until they are a well-integrated mash. This can be done in a mortar or with a blender or food processor—it doesn't really matter.
2. Put these into a large mason jar and pour your wine over them. Let this sit for about a lunar month, from dark moon to dark moon.
3. Strain the herbs apart from the wine and put the liquid into a double boiler. Add your honey and heat up the mixture. Continue to heat it, making the mixture thicker over time.
4. When it is about the texture of thick molasses, pour it into a silicone pan or into a pan lined with parchment paper.
5. Place this in the oven at a very low setting, about 125°F, with the door cracked. You can also place this in a dehydrator if you have one. Remove all moisture from the preparation until it is a hardened, resin-like substance. Break this into smaller pieces and use a coal tablet to burn it.
6. You may also dissolve the chunks into a 190-proof alcohol to make a perfume.

Juniper Love Bath

- ½ oz. juniper berries, crushed
- ½ oz. coriander seed
- 32 oz. water

1. Simmer the herbs in water for about 13 minutes.
2. Add the liquid to a bath and bathe "up," meaning that you use purposeful motions to wash your body that moves from your feet toward your head, never away.
3. Sprinkle this water and the boiled herbs in your yard, strewing them toward the east to attract new love. Strew them toward the west while saying, *"NN, come back to me,"* to bring an old lover back into your life. Sprinkle this in the backyard to increase fidelity.

Jove Juice For Masculine Potency

- 1 oz. juniper berries, crushed
- ½ oz. saw palmetto berries, crushed
- ½ oz. hot cayenne, powdered
- 16 oz. whiskey of your choice

1. On a Tuesday in the hour of Mars, infuse the crushed berries of juniper and saw palmetto as well as the cayenne powder (the hottest you can find) into a whiskey for 1 month. Then, decant on a Thursday in the hour of Jupiter.
2. Take about 1 teaspoon a day for 8 days, starting on a Thursday and ending on a Thursday, to increase masculine potency, be that for virility and the masculine nature or to draw in masculine powers and as an offering to masculine entities.

KNAPWEED

(*CENTAUREA SPP.*) MERCURY—MARS (STAR THISTLES)—AIR—GEMINI

AKA: *Panicled knapweed, hurt sickle, hardhead, loggerheads, iron heads, horse knob, bull weed, bottleweed, bachelor's buttons, cornflower, star thistle, basketflower, matte felon, maude felone, boltsede, bluet, bluebottle, bluebow, blue cap, Good Robin's rags,* ripped hem**

Knapweed is native to Europe and the Mediterranean area, though it has become invasive in most other places through imported seed. *Centaurea* is a genus with a wide variety of morphologies and applications, so though this entry is a bit generalized, each species should be researched separately. Some are thistle-like, with sharp barbs beneath the flower head, as with yellow star thistle (*C. solstitialis*), purple star thistle (*C. calcitrapa*), and sulfur star thistle (*C. sulphurea*). Others are soft, like cornflower (*C. cyanus*) and spotted knapweed (*C. stoebe*). The flowers of most knapweeds are ragged, varying in shades of pink and purple, rarely white, and there are some species that are yellow. They erupt from a teardrop-shaped ampule of black-tipped bracts that look like a scaly basket (giving it one of its common names). Most have large leaves near the bottom of the plant that become smaller and more irregular toward the top. Almost all the species are considered invasive somewhere.

Knapweeds are first-stage successional plants and can grow very prolifically, creating thick mats of themselves that shade and crowd out other plants, but only temporarily. They tend to grow on compacted, barren soils that have been stripped bare, either by drought, mechanical degradation, or overgrazing. The star thistles, especially, form a protective covering for soils that need to heal, keeping people and animals at bay as they work their cycle of remediation. They will grow and die and feed the soil in the process. Knapweed creates several allelopathic chemicals that, rather than suppressing the growth of other plants, seem to restore microbial activity in the soil and help to draw nutrients out of it, making them available to the entire community that they *will* make way for. Some species, particularly yellow star thistle, also draw iron up to the surface from deeper layers of soil in the lots and fields they like to grow in, which are often low on free iron for plants to use. When they fall to the earth and rot, they also leave a deep hole in the ground where their long taproot grew, allowing water and bacteria to penetrate and work on deep, compacted layers of soil.

Their bodies are also hyperaccumulators of nickel, which can be a toxic element in areas like mining operations and cement plants, as well as copper, zinc, cadmium, and radiocesium 134, a product of nuclear fission. The latter is strongly held by clay soils and is difficult to move out of the soil, especially in woodlands, where trees and other plants uptake it and drop it back to the soil in their leaf litter in a long cycle. Plants that can draw out radioactive materials, such as knapweed, sunflower, and rice, can be removed and disposed of properly, helping to remediate and cleanse the soil of radioactive pollutants. They should be celebrated, not made the target of eradication efforts.

So, why are they considered invasive? Because they are considered noxious weeds in arable crops (read "economically useful" crops). They reduce the percentage of profitable yield, so they are considered a nuisance and are dealt with through herbicide use, which they are becoming more resistant to, and through nitrogen fertilization, which is hard on the Land. Yellow star-thistle and Russian knapweed can cause toxicity in horses who graze on the plant too much over about a month's time. They begin to develop "chewing disease," or *nigropallidal encephalomalacia,* a set of Parkinson's disease-like symptoms including jaw weakness and a protruding tongue coexisting in some cases with hypertonicity of the facial muscles, leading to odd facial expressions and baring of the teeth. Because of this, the plants have been studied for their benefit to things such as Parkinson's, and research shows promising results. *C. calcitrapa* is being studied for its efficacy against phyto- and human pathogenic strains of drug-resistant bacteria.

Even so, they are an important food for pollinators, including bees whose honey is made sweeter and in greater quantity when feeding on knapweed. Not to mention that some species of *Centaurea,* such as cornflower, produce volatile oils that attract parasitoid insects like carabid beetles that help to keep populations of crop pests like cabbage moths down without the use of insecticides.

Foraging Uses

Knapweeds are eaten for a variety of reasons, at least species like spotted knapweed and cornflower, which lack the toxicity of the star thistles and their barbs. Cornflower blossoms are used as a colorant for food, making a sort of blue-purple hue, and as a dye for fabrics, using alum as a mordant. They can also be made into fritters, like dandelion and black locust, or made into a veggie hash with other plants and herbs before being frittered. Spotted knapweed is relatively high in protein and makes for a good salad green, especially the leaves in the rosette stage before it flowers, though the flowers are also tasty.

Remedial Applications

The various members of the knapweed family have been used medicinally in many ways for a great long time. The uses are species dependent, though, and need to be described one at a time. I will list a few below and some of the ways they've each been used.

Black Knapweed *(Centaurea nigra):* This plant has been used to "stay fluxes," in the words of Culpeper, which means it helps to stop bleeding. A mouthwash made from the tea of this flower will help with dental bleeding and mouth sores. It clears up bruising, especially as a compress applied to the area. A decoction used as a wash can help to dry up weeping sores, blisters, pustules, and cysts. Make an oxymel with black knapweed and clove for sore throat. A decoction of the flower in water or wine helps to move mucus out of the lungs and a decoction of the root can be used as a diaphoretic (something that causes one to sweat) and a diuretic.

Cornflower *(Centaurea cyanus):* This flower is used to stimulate appetite, treat diarrhea, and as a hepatoprotective, similar to the uses of blessed thistle. It is used to alleviate bruises, inflammations, and wounding, especially in conjunction with plantain. It can be made into a blue ink infused in high-proof alcohol along with resin, such as gum arabic, and can be used to good effect in Jupiterian magic. The tough stems of cornflower give it the name *hurtsickle,* and of it is said, "Thou blunt'st the very reaper's sickle and so in life and death becom'st the farmer's foe." Use it as a protective ingredient against unknown dangers. It is also said that it is this flower that Chiron, the great healer, used to heal his own hoof.

Spotted Knapweed *(Centaurea stoebe):* Another wound healer, this plant has been used as a snake bite remedy, though I wouldn't put it to the test. Overall, it is used in the same way as black (greater) knapweed.

Yellow Star Thistle *(Caentaurea solstitialis):* The seeds of yellow star thistle have been powdered and taken as a hot aqueous infusion for kidney stones, as has the root. As with the other knapweeds, this plant has been used to dry up weeping wounds and infections. An aqueous infusion of the root and flower is used to treat ulcers. A star thistle head carried in a phylactery protects from malice and all that would disrupt the peace around you. Combined with comfrey and worn on the left side of the body, it can prevent accidents while traveling.

Magical Applications

Centaurea plants, in general, are useful aids to magic. They are like nets and caltrops, traps for spirits and people. It is a flower with energy like a patient spider in its web. The flower essence of knapweed helps to move energy through the body, upwards and inwards, in the way the Air element flows, which can bring inspiration and epiphany. The essence also helps to shore up personal energetic boundaries.

Caltrop Powder

Make this powder on a Tuesday in the hour of the Moon to bring nightmares, the hour of Mercury to hobble the target's words and thoughts, in the hour of Venus to bring romantic unrest, in the hour of the Sun to bring hopelessness, the hour of Mars to cause confusion and mental discomfort, the hour of Jupiter to bring money troubles, and in the hour of Saturn to bring great malady or illness.

- 1 oz. yellow star thistle tops
- 1 oz. puncture vine fruits
- 1 oz. poppy seed
- 1 Tbsp. iron filings
- 1 tsp. black pepper
- 3 dead flies, ethically gathered
- ½ tsp. graveyard dirt, paid for

Parlour Room Oil

I'm sure you've heard at least part of the poem this preparation is inspired by:

> *"Will you walk into my parlour?" said a spider to a fly;*
> *"'Tis the prettiest little parlour that ever you did spy.*
> *The way up to my parlour is up a winding stair,*
> *And I have many pretty things to shew when you are there."*[68]

I will include the entirety of the poem at the end of this book, as I think it makes a suitable incantation for enchanting this oil, which is meant to ensnare a person and bring them easily into your influence, garnering you victory.[69]

- Knapweed
- Dodder
- Spider web

---

68 "The Spider and the Fly" by Mary Howitt.

69 See Appendix C.

- Spider, ethically sourced (optional)
- 3 flies, ethically sourced (optional)
- Magnet
- Twine, enough to wrap the jar 8 times

1. Start this preparation on a full moon, the night of the huntress, preferably on a Saturday in the hour of Mars. All the better if Mars is in a detrimental aspect to Mercury, so your quarry won't see you coming. End it on the following dark moon, on a Tuesday in the hour of Saturn, to tie up the ends of the operation.
2. Purify each item and name its purpose in the spell. Place the jar you intend to use atop an enlivened Fourth Pentacle of Mars and invoke its power into the space. See the section "Using the Planetary Pentacles" on page 57 for instructions on this.
3. Add the knapweed, dodder, spider web, and the magnet to the oil. Also add the ephemera (spider and flies) if you've chosen to do so. Only use animals that have already passed away, which are usually easily found on windowsills or behind bookshelves. Cover it over with oil.
4. Seal the jar tightly and wrap it around the middle with the twine as a spider wraps its prey. As you do so, recite the poem "The Spider and the Fly," found in Appendix C, or whatever incantation you come up with.
5. Put the mother bottle away in a dark cabinet, only taking it out at night. Put a bit into an extremely beautiful bottle, which you keep under a cloth on your altar or in a cabinet with other magical items. Apply it to your fingertips, wrists, neck, and lips every time you need to apply a bit of cunning and influence to your words and actions, such as during job interviews, foreseen arguments, and even presentations.

KUDZU

(*Pueraria montana*) Moon—Venus—Water—Scorpio

AKA: *Japanese arrowroot, foot-a-night, the vine that ate the South, vine-by-the-foot,* violet dragon,* creeping wyrm,* teetotaler's tuber**

When I first started telling people about this book, kudzu was the most asked-about herb. "Are you going to talk about kudzu? It's such a bad plant." To try and shift the perspective on this maligned vine so that people stop thinking of it as bad, I decided to include it after all. It is a problematic plant, for certain, as it can overtake enormous swathes of Land very quickly. It grows about twelve inches per day! It can tear down structures, block roads, make farming nearly impossible, and can make an intolerable nuisance of itself. It absolutely needs better management because it can get out of control *very* quickly. All of that is true, but what does it do?

Kudzu is a climbing vine native to the Asian continent but was introduced to the US in the 1930s by the Civilian Conservation Corps (CCC) to help control soil erosion in the South, which it does a great job of. It very quickly covers bare soil and keeps the topsoil from exposure and degradation while simultaneously bringing nutrients (particularly nitrogen) to the upper layers and shading the soil microbes until they can establish healthy colonies. Not only that, but kudzu has been shown to clean petroleum from polluted soils, making it a huge benefit to remediation. It was also used by people in the South to create ornamental shade covers, as it offers heavy shade.

As part of the *Fabaceae,* the vine twines and twirls its way around everything in its path. They display average pea leaves, which are trifoliated with three leaflets. Kudzu's leaves are often oblong, shield-shaped or heart-shaped, and can be bigger than an adult's palm. The trunk of the vine can be extremely thick and woody, narrowing down into the thin, curling fingers of the vine that grab onto things. The flowers are a delightful variety of purple shades and are beautifully aromatic. They taste like grape flavoring, which I think is enjoyable, but others find distasteful. The flowers are a favorite of bees, too, and the honey they make from them takes on a deep purple color and a somewhat grape-like flavor, which I think is just the bee's knees.

Kudzu makes a great forage, as it is high in protein and tasty. Both humans and farm animals can benefit from eating it, and the whole plant can be utilized in this way. When it comes to gathering it as a feed, it yields less than a commercial farm may find useful, but our commercial farming practices in this country, especially when it comes to animals, are in need of a massive overhaul.

The root is called arrowroot (not to be confused with *Maranta arundinacea,* the actual arrowroot plant, or with cassava, zedoary, wahoo, or arrow arum, all of which are commonly and confusingly called arrowroot), and the powder of the root can be used to thicken soups, as an adjuvant for cosmetics, and, along with rice, a good filler for pillows meant to be heated for sore muscles and such.

The plant can also be used to make baskets, paper, high-yield compost, and it produces enough carbohydrates that it is a viable plant to make biofuel. In Japan, it is even processed into a fabric similar to silk. The problem isn't kudzu itself, obviously, but its mismanagement. We are underutilizing kudzu because we don't find it on market shelves, so we don't know better, but there are so many ways to use it. In the book *Beyond the War on Invasive Species,* Tao Orion imagines an entire community based around farming this single plant.

It can't be commercially farmed in the way crops like wheat, soy, and corn are, though, so it also can't be fully capitalized on, making it a prime target for the propaganda machine of industrial agriculture. It is so much easier to make people hate a plant and eradicate it for you, opening Land for crop farming, than it is to teach them to use it well and treat it as a good neighbor. Of course, that means free food, fuel, and equity for everyone, which is anathema to the agro-industrial philosophy. There's no such thing as a free lunch...unless you're eating weeds like kudzu!

FORAGING USES

As stated above, the entirety of the kudzu plant is edible. The roots can be eaten like potatoes or other tubers and can be made into tuber hash, fries, and fritas, or even mashed kudzu root. The starch from the root is used as a gluten and dairy-free thickener, to make noodles, and can even be used to make masa for tamales, which are a local staple here in New Mexico. The leaves can get furry as they age, so it is best to eat the younger leaves, which can be turned into chips in a dehydrator, cooked down like spinach, and eaten as a green.

The stalks and vines can be steamed, stir-fried, or eaten like any other vegetable. The flowers can be made into jelly, jam, or syrup, candied, frittered, turned into ice cream, and so much more. Because they contain anthocyanins, liquids made with the flowers change colors with the addition of acids and alkaline substances.

It truly is a versatile plant that needs to be better utilized and *can* be...for free! In 1977, a cookbook that is entirely devoted to kudzu was published, called *The Book of Kudzu: A Culinary and Healing Guide* by William Shurtleff and Akiko Aoyagi, and it is readily available online.

JUNE BUGZU

This is an alcoholic cocktail that changes color as you make it, which is a neat party trick that everyone enjoys. A variation on a June Bug, this drink is meant to be sweet and enjoyed responsibly with friends.

- ½ oz. kudzu flower
- ½ oz. butterfly pea flower
- 375 ml Malibu rum
- 1 oz. sweet and sour mix
- 2 oz. pineapple juice
- 1 wedge of lemon

1. Start by infusing the rum with the kudzu and butterfly pea flowers overnight. This will make a deep blue-purple liquor that is stunning on its own.
2. Pour about an ounce of this rum into a low-ball glass.

3. Add the sweet and sour, then the pineapple juice, and finally squeeze the lemon over it. Mix the drink between each new ingredient and watch it turn more and more pink as the pH lowers. Pour the result over ice and enjoy with a fun pineapple garnish.

REMEDIAL APPLICATIONS

Possibly the most important remedial quality of kudzu comes in its isoflavones, which are called puerarin, daidzein, and daidzin, which have been studied for their effects on alcohol consumption. Studies show that a daily dose of kudzu root tincture can reduce the amount of alcohol consumed in a week by up to 57%. The tincture I have found to be the best preparation is a 1:4 with 80% alcohol, then take 30 drops twice daily. About 12 grams of the flower can be used in a tea to help ease hangover issues. It is also used for cardiovascular disease, menopause, diabetes, diarrhea, cold and flu symptoms, and eye pain. It has astringent and anti-inflammatory properties, as well as estrogenic properties that combine well with things like vitex, raspberry leaf, and angelica.

MAGICAL APPLICATIONS

The magic of kudzu is linked mainly to its ability to grow so fast. It rapidly overtakes and tears down all sorts of things in its path and it can travel very far in little time. The flowers of the kudzu vine can also be added to the recipe for the clairvoyance preparation with purple loosestrife found on page 174 and to other scrying waters, as its Lunar resonance can be useful in that art.

KUDZU PAPER

Kudzu makes a useful, easy-to-make paper that can be used in the creation of *liber lamiae* (also called "books of shadows" or "grimoires"), petition papers, and ritual masks. The process of paper-making can be complicated, but it's worth the effort.

1. Collect about two pounds of kudzu vine and leaf; the younger and more tender, the better.
2. Chop your kudzu into small pieces, then put them in a pot and boil them for a few hours until they are very mushy.

3. Strain them and toss them into a blender along with wastepaper (old newspapers or magazines, old forms, and bills, whatever paper you were going to throw away anyhow) until the blender is about halfway full.
4. Fill the blender to the top with water and blend it all into a pulp.
5. Prepare a separate amount of "thickened water," which is simply water with a thickener in it. Some people use glue, others use okra, but for this, you can use kudzu starch from the root. Thicken it until it is the consistency of a syrup.
6. You will then need an equal amount of clean water in a large basin. Mix it with the pulp and the thickened water so the basin is about ¾ full.
7. Hog the water, meaning use your hand to mix the pulp through the other liquid until the whole basin is cloudy, then use a deckle[70] to scoop a thin layer of the pulp out of the basin. Very gently press it with a wooden spatula to get it to lay flat.
8. Do this as many times as you can while still getting an even covering of pulp on the screen. Once it seems to thin, stop.
9. Allow these to set for about 10 minutes as you prepare moistened sheets of either felt or canvas, just slightly bigger than the perimeter of your deckle. These can simply be moistened in the basin and wrung out so they remain damp but not sopping.
10. Place these over your paper sheet and flip the deckle over, transferring the wet paper pulp to the canvas or felt. These can be stacked, but the uppermost one needs to be covered with another sheet.
11. The next step is to press the sheets, which is to lay a piece of wood or stone about the size of the sheets over the stack, then place a heavy weight on top of it, hopefully evenly distributing weight.

---

70 A deckle is a wooden frame with a screen, often used in paper making and screen printing. It allows for water to drain from the pulp and keep the shape of a thin, rectangular sheet of paper.

12. Allow these to dry completely, which may take a few days, or you can use a heater or dry them in the sun. *Very* carefully remove the paper from the fabric, and you'll have a piece of paper you can write on!

If you'd rather use the pulp to make papier-mâché, I suggest making what is called papier-mâché clay, a product invented by the artist Jonni Good.[71]

1. Instead of the whole basin process, you simply mix about 1¼ cups of your pulp (out of which you press most of the water until it falls apart easily but isn't dripping) with 1 cup drywall joint compound (which is just a gypsum mud you can get at most hardware stores), ¾ cup craft glue, and ½ cup flour of your choice.
2. Mix these together until they are a thick-yet-spreadable paste, and use them to thinly cover over an armature with about ⅛ inch of the stuff. Once it dries, it will be solidly hard and durable.
3. If you want to add fine details, allow the first coat to dry, and then add a bit more flour to the clay so it becomes doughier. Use this to sculpt things like feathers, textures, bumps, and lumps.
4. When it is done correctly, you can make very smooth, beautiful sculptures and masks that you can paint however you'd like and will last for years.

Galloping Powder

If you want a spell to work fast, a boost from something like galloping powder isn't a bad idea. This can be added to pokes, sprinkled over spell candles, and spread over petition papers before they are burned. For operations performed using this powder, consider placing a horseshoe

71 The recipe can also be found online at www.ultimatepapermache.com/paper-mache-clay. Her recipe calls for moistened toilet paper, but you can use plant pulp.

around your candle or passing your poke through a number of times meaningful to your spell.

- 1 oz. kudzu vine and flower, dried and powdered
- 1 oz. horseweed, dried and powdered
- 1 oz. chilé flakes, dried and powdered
- ½ oz. kudzu root, dried and powdered
- ¼ oz. iron filings
- A pinch of dirt from a racetrack
- A bit of horsehair

You may recite the first verse from "Rain and Wind"[72] by Madison Julius Cawein (1865-1914) while you mix the powder or whatever spell you'd like to.

"I hear the hoofs of horses
galloping over the hill,
galloping on and galloping on,
when all the night is shrill
with wind and rain that beats the panes
and my soul with awe is still."

72 See Cawein's poem on allpoetry.com/Rain-And-Wind.

PLANTAIN

(*PLANTAGO MAJOR*) MARS—VENUS—WATER—CAPRICORN

AKA: *White man's footprint, broadleaf plantain, rippleleaf plantain, waybread, waybroad, wandering maiden, mother of plants, snakeweed, ripplegrass, cuckoo's bread, leaf of Patrick, Patrick's dock, St. Patrick's leaf, soldierswort, ribwort, cat grass, backbite,* chill touch,* Hermes' delight,* road opener**

A humble herb growing along roadsides and often directly under feet, plantain has a long history of being highly valued by many cultures, even those into which it has invaded. It grows very close to the ground, basically being just a rosette of leaves that are deeply and evenly ribbed from base to tip. This is how it spends most of its lifetime, until it shoots up long, spear-shaped stalks tipped in a spike of fluffy white flowers that turn to something that resembles a very long ear swab full of tiny seeds. It is not unfair to call it a "cute" plant, though Culpeper's allotment of *Plantago* to Mars makes a lot of sense, given its spear-shaped flower stalks and the orderliness of the lengthwise ribs that give this plant many of its common names.

Plantago is a storied plant that may have existed for nearly 4,000 years, evolving alongside humanity and the fields we till. It is one of the Anglo-Saxon "nine sacred herbs," probably because of its incredible tenacity. It can be trampled, eaten, poisoned, burned, and still thrive despite it all, making it a symbol of absolute resiliency.

A myth about *Plantago* in Greece concerns Demeter, the goddess of the cycles of life and death. She happened upon a young maiden crying at the edge of the road, a girl whose lover had left her behind to travel abroad, so she went and waited for his return every day at the roadside. Demeter asked the girl, "If you miss him so, why do you not go and find him?" at which point she turned the girl into a plantain plant. The goddess commanded that the girl travel every road in the world until she found her lover, which the girl still does to this day, never giving up and always remaining loyal to both her love, her search, and the command of the goddess. Because of this lore, plantain can also be attributed to Venus, which also tracks with its uses as skin aide and moisturizing soother of bodily tissues.

Plantain is a rapid seeder and a very adept and rapidly spreading first-stage succession plant (i.e., invader). There are about thirty-four species of *Plantago* across the globe, each adapting rapidly to new environments. It is now considered invasive across the entirety of the US and has been spreading since the initial contact with European colonizers. So much so, in fact, that the common name among Native American peoples means "white man's foot" because the plant seemed to follow wherever their feet fell. The name *Plantago* comes from the Latin *planta,* which means "sole of the foot," indicating that plantain has always had the connotation of following the footsteps of humanity and being resilient enough to spring back after being trampled.

An important thing to remember about plantain is that it is one of the only plants that *can* grow in some of the most severely disturbed sites, places where other plants simply cannot survive. It is also one of the most powerful soil remediators amongst the invasives and is capable of leeching numerous toxins from the Land. It can remove nitrogen dioxide and sulfur dioxide, can thrive even in soils deeply polluted by oil and other industrial waste, and can stabilize heavy metals such as copper in its root structure. The remediation capabilities of plantain have not been fully researched, but we can guess that it is doing an amazing job.

Not only that, because plantain grows in severely disturbed areas, it is one of the primary plants that stabilizes the soil in areas where it has been massively destabilized. It holds the topsoil together and revitalizes the Land, making the way for future plants to root and begin to build a new ecosystem. Their seed is a favorite food of small birds and mammals, such as chipmunks, and their nectar and pollen are important food crops for pollinators and insects, such as ants, which harvest the pollen from the flowers. The larvae of butterflies and moths will also preferentially choose to eat the leaves of plantain, meaning it is also important to the generational cycle of pollinators.

FORAGING USES

Plantain has a thick, fibrous leaf, but it is actually quite delicious and makes a readily edible green, though it can be cooked into dishes along with other greens, like spinach, or baked into nutrient-dense crackers. The young leaves, though still somewhat tough, can be eaten raw in salads and used as a green in sandwiches. They also make a pleasant addition to pesto and other green sauces.

PLANTAIN CRACKERS

- 8 oz. plantain leaf
- 4 oz. horseweed
- 4 oz. dandelion leaf
- ½ c. pumpkin seeds
- ½ c. sunflower seeds, hulled
- ¼ c. hemp seeds
- ¼ c. chia seeds
- 1½ c. water
- 1 tsp. salt
- 1 tsp. sumac powder
- 1 tsp. white pepper powder
- 1 tsp. oregano leaf

1. Toast your pumpkin seeds in the oven at about 275°F for about 10 minutes. Lightly salt them afterward and mix them with your other seeds.
2. Wash your greens, mix them with your water, and let them sit for about 5 minutes, then blend them together until they become a gel-like paste.

3. Mix the green liquid with the seeds and add your spices. Stir this until everything is thoroughly integrated into a dough-like paste.
4. On a baking sheet, place a piece of parchment paper that is twice as long as the tray so that it can be folded over the paste, then sprinkle your mixture with flour (gluten-free if you need) and press your mixture between the sheets. Roll it out with a pin until it is about ⅛ inch thick.
5. Remove the top layer of parchment, then use a pizza cutter to score the mixture into squares, as this will make it easier to break the final product into cracker shapes.
6. Place the cooking sheet into the oven at about 200°F and allow them to bake for about 20 minutes. Check them every 5 minutes to make sure they are not burning, but they should become crisp and hard (like a cracker). If they need more than 20 minutes, allow them to bake until they are crisp.
7. Once they are done, remove them from the oven and allow them to cool completely. Once they are, have fun snapping them apart and eating them! These go well with tzatziki sauce as a dip, a recipe for which can be found in the Horseweed section on page 127.

Remedial Applications

Plantago is one of the remedial powerhouses in the herbalist's repertoire. It can do so much and grows *everywhere.* It is most often used to cool and soothe red, hot, inflamed conditions, making it perfect for rashes, bug bites, stings, and bites. A simple spit poultice (chewing the leaves and then placing the wad on an inflamed area) works incredibly well, especially if you get bitten or stung in the field. In fact, its common name of "snakeweed" comes from the lore around its efficacy against venomous bites. It cannot act as an antivenom, of course, and it should *definitely* not be used as such in that kind of serious situation. Think of plantain more as a universal coolant, removing heat, redness, and pain both externally and internally.

Simply taking plantain as a tea can have profound effects on the digestive system, including better digestion, easing of pain, and helping with symptoms related to IBS and other syndromes of that sort. If you experience heat and tightness in the intestines, particularly with a dropping feeling in the stomach, a tea of plantain and Russian olive leaf will help ease you back toward comfort. Plantain can also help with heartburn, particularly if it comes with a sensation of fire in the lower abdomen. This is especially true if your heartburn is worse when you have spikes in anxiety or after experiencing embarrassment. If your heartburn is worse after getting angry, add *Viola odorata* flower to your tea.

Plantain is also a great tissue repairer. It works well with ulcerations, both internally and topically. Russian olive was earlier mentioned as a good companion to plantain, which holds true here. A wash made with plantain leaf and Russian olive fruits and leaves can help speed the recovery of a wound while simultaneously helping to keep it clean and ease pain around the site. It would also work well with a wash made from purple loosestrife.

Plantain Oxymel

This is a delicious way to help your digestion and heal your GI tract while simultaneously cooling your internal organs.

- 16 oz. apple cider vinegar
- 2 c. honey
- 2 oz. plantain leaf, fresh and chopped

1. Finely chop about 2 ounces of plantain leaf, then mix it with your vinegar. If you have access to a blender, simply mix the vinegar and plantain in the upper part of the blender and turn it on a medium setting for about 3 minutes.
2. Allow this to sit for 2–4 weeks in a warm, dark place.
3. Strain the resulting liquid, which should be somewhat greenish, and measure that. Whatever amount you have left over after straining, add the same amount of honey, so it becomes a 1:1 mix. Put this in the refrigerator and use as needed.
4. Shake vigorously each time you want to use it. Take 1–2 teaspoons before and after meals to aid digestion, or take 1 teaspoon to ease a hot, upset stomach. You can also use this as a mouthwash to heal canker sores and ulcerations of the mouth and throat.

Plantain Burn Salve

It is important to note with a remedy like this that it should not be applied immediately to a burn. Wait until the heat is mostly out of the area and the throbbing subsides. A salve will help to heal the burn, but if it is applied too quickly, it can keep heat in and make the burn worse.

- 16 oz. oil of your choice
- 1 oz. plantain leaf, dried
- ½ oz. lavender flower, dried
- ½ oz. calendula flower, dried
- 2 oz. beeswax

1. Put your herbs into a saucepan, then pour your oil over them. Bring this to a low heat.
2. Allow it to sit on the heat until you begin to notice bubbles forming in the oil. Turn the heat down and allow it to cool.
3. Let the mixture sit in the pan, covered, for about 3–6 hours, then strain it from the herbs.
4. In a double boiler, mix the oil and the beeswax. Remember, the perfect ratio is 1 cup of oil to 1 ounce of beeswax. Melt these together, then pour the liquid into a vessel. Allow this to cool, then use your salve as you will.

Magical Applications

One of my favorite magical uses for plantain is as a remedy for treating injuries incurred in the Spirit World. These can be extremely damaging and deleterious over time, so it is important to maintain proper spiritual hygiene and cleanse yourself after transvection, particularly if you had a rough go of it.

Astral Remediator Mixture

This mix can be used in multiple ways to heal the Astral body after a rough time over the hedge. It can be mixed with clay or soil, honey, and water to create a sort of mask, it can be made into a wash, it can be used as an incense or smoke bath, and it can be used as a strewing herb for a ritual fire used to burn away spiritual hitchhikers (spirits that cling to your Astral body in a parasitical way). If you can think of other ways to use it, please do so!

- 1 oz. plantain leaf, dry
- ½ oz. tamarisk leaf, dry
- ½ oz. spike verbena, dry
- ½ oz. rose petals, dry
- ½ oz. pine needles, dry

Waybroad Protection Charm

It is said that simply hanging the leaves of plantain in your home can avert all manner of troubles, particularly spiritual intrusions and bad dreams. If you suffer from attacks by spirits, especially at night, or are prone to nightmares, take five leaves of plantain, splay them out in a fan, and tie them together with red thread. Hang these over your bed, as directly over where your head rests as possible. Change this charm out every full moon. These fans are best made on the Summer Solstice, so make enough to last the year on that day.

Travelers' Trinket

This is a charm to protect you while you travel. It is a simple charm to be worn on your person as you travel the many roads that plantain knows so well.

- 11 large plantain leaves, fresh
- 7 juniper berries
- 1 pinch comfrey root, powdered
- 1 pinch comfrey leaf
- 1 pinch dirt from 7 different roads that travel in different directions
- 1 pinch cascarilla (eggshell powder)
- Vectors of the traveler(s)
- 1 red pouch
- 1 heart-length green twine
- 1 iron nail
- 1 white candle

1. Gather your materials, preferably on a Wednesday in a daylight hour of Mercury or Jupiter. For the dirt from 7 roads, try to get it from roads that are somewhat distant from each other, that run North to South, East to West, but also at diagonals, that make loops, that dead end. Get creative and try to think of all the roads a traveler may run into, trying to make sure all of them are represented in the 7 samples.
2. On a Wednesday in the first hour of Mercury, place all of your ingredients in the red pouch. As you do so, chant:

   "Goosey, goosey gander, wither shall I wander?
   West, North, East, South? In an angel's hands or a serpent's mouth?
   By the spirits of the seven roads and the maid of the waybroad,
   May my path be safely laid; may all harm be ever stayed."

3. Tie the bag closed with your green twine and knot the iron nail into it, thus sealing the magic in. As you do so, say this:

   "By the Green Mother's thread, stop all dread,
   Tie a knot in the adder's tail, still it with an iron nail."

4. Carve this symbol into the white candle using a scribe of your choice

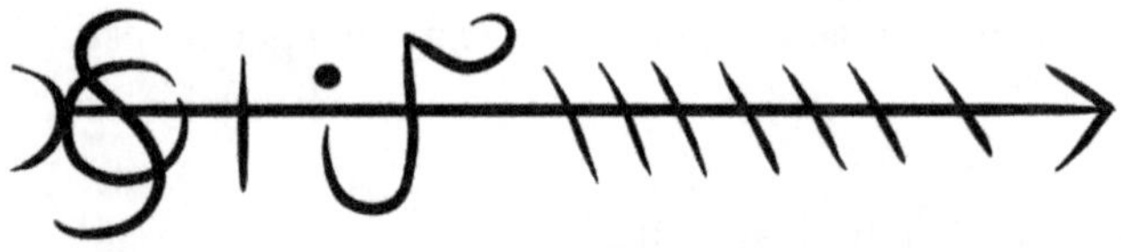

5. Draw a circle on a piece of paper or somewhere in your working space, then place the candle in a fire-safe holder and in a safe place with the pouch laid out in front of it. Allow the candle to burn all the way down, saying whichever prayers over your pouch you'd like to say.
6. Carry the pouch with you as you travel.

Way Opener Mixture

There are certain spells meant to open roads and pathways to better opportunities or to break through oppositions and blockages that hold you back. Plantain is an excellent addition to most of those spells, especially to help smooth out the edges and make the path that is opened easier to traverse. The following recipe should be prepared as a powder that can be burned, strewn, infused, or rolled onto the surface of a candle.

If you want to infuse it as an anointing oil, use the stove top method as usual. You can also add essential oils like orange, lemon, or eucalyptus to help clear the obstructions you've broken down out of your way.

- 1 oz. plantain leaf, dried
- ½ oz. hoarhound, dried
- ½ oz. American or English ivy, dried
- ½ oz. boneset, dried
- ½ oz. dandelion root, dried
- ½ oz. scotch broom twigs and flowers, dried
- ½ oz. of benzoin resin powder
- 1 tsp. salt

PRICKLY WILD LETTUCE

(*LACTUCA SERRIOLA*) MERCURY—WATER—GEMINI—PISCES

AKA: *Compass plant, compass lettuce, opium lettuce, milk lettuce, prickly endive, milk thistle, milk weed, horse thistle, scarole, Devil's milk,* bittertit**

This common weed has had a remedial and magical relationship with humans going as far back as Ancient Egypt, where it was used as an aphrodisiac, a sedative, and a pain reliever. It has fallen out of favor in recent years, with many people considering it too weak to act as an effective pain reliever, though I think it is quite strong when prepared correctly. People often expect it to be a very strong narcotic because of its common name, "opium lettuce." It does not have opium or any related chemicals in it, however. It creates a milky exudate called lactucarium, which, when it is dried, turns a reddish brown and resembles the opium derived from *Papver somniferum.* It has even been used as an adulterant in the creation of opium and heroin, though it is nowhere near as strong. It can be smoked on its own, though, and also taken internally as a sedative and pain reliever, with no risk of addiction.

Wild lettuce is native to the Mediterranean region, though it now grows in the US in disturbed soils, from country roadsides to sidewalks and lawns. It sometimes grows a bit taller than six feet tall as one long stalk with leaves that basally grasp the stem. The leaves are deeply toothed, similar to dandelion, though the edges appear more ragged and spiked. The midribs of the leaves, which can sometimes grow up to eighteen inches long, are lined by small prickles, the feature that gives this plant its common name. The base of the stem may also be covered in spines, though they are not prone to pricking through the skin.

The flowers grow from the branching top of the plant, each one appearing like very small dandelion flowers. They are almost always yellow in color, though white and blue are rarely seen. These give way to seeds with white hair, again very similar to dandelion, though wild lettuce is more clustered and fluffier looking. These make wind-driven dispersal of the seeds very easy, and one plant may make up to one million seeds over the course of a single season.

Prickly lettuce, though hated as a weed that takes water from crops and whose sap may clog farm equipment, is a plant that serves important roles in ecosystems. As a plant with a deep taproot, wild lettuce brings up nutrients from deep within the soil, which aids the growth of more shallowly rooted natives it often grows with. It is also a prolific flowerer early in the season, providing early food for pollinators, such as butterflies and moths, as well as other insects, hummingbirds, and flower-reliant feeders. The seeds are food for various birds and small mammals, as the leaves are a source of nutrients for a wide variety of animals.

Foraging Uses

The young leaves of prickly lettuce are edible, though bitter. I think they make a great addition to salads, especially when mixed with other greens and vegetables that have less bitterness. One of my favorites is a mix of arugula and radish with a lemon oil dressing, sometimes with lamb's quarters if it's growing well in my yard. If the bitterness is too much, the leaves can be boiled for 1–2 minutes in three changes of water and added to other greens like spinach, bok choi, and tatsoi. Older leaves must have the midrib removed, as the prickles become harder and less palatable as they age. Younger leaves are definitely more delicious, so it is best to stick to eating those.

The flowers of wild lettuce are also edible and can be fried like dandelion fritters, though much smaller. They can also be eaten raw in salads and impart a bittersweet flavor that is quite delightful. They should be prepared or eaten immediately after harvesting, as they will go to seed very quickly after they are picked.

Wild Lettuce and Dandelion Capers

- 1 c. of dandelion and wild lettuce buds
- 3 garlic cloves, diced
- ¼ onion, diced
- 1 oz. grated ginger root, sliced
- 2 sprigs of horseweed
- ½ c. of apple cider vinegar
- ½ c. water
- 1 Tbsp. sea salt

1. Fill a small mason jar with your dandelion and wild lettuce buds, herbs, and veggies. Make sure your buds are tightly closed, the ones that have never opened. This will ensure that they don't go to seed in your menstruum.
2. Heat the water and vinegar until it begins to boil, then remove it from the heat.
3. Dissolve the salt in the vinegar and water solution, then pour it over the buds. Place a piece of waxed paper over the mouth of the jar before tightening the lid. Allow the jar to sit out on the counter for about a week, tasting it every 2 days. After this, put the jar in the fridge to finish pickling for about 3 weeks.

Wild Lettuce Cookies
(Adapted from a recipe by Mei Wong)[73]

- ¼ c. wild lettuce flowers, open
- ⅓ c. butter, room temperature
- 1¼ c. flour, sifted
- ⅓ c. sugar
- 2 eggs
- 1 tsp. baking soda
- 1 pinch of salt

---

73 From her recipe article "Dandelion Cookies and Pickled Buds" published on medium.com.

1. Preheat your oven to 350°F.
2. Gently rinse your flowers to remove dirt, bugs, and other debris, then dry them gently between towels.
3. You do not need to separate the petals from the calyx, but you may. I like the bitterness of the green bits.
4. Cream the butter and sugar together, then beat in the eggs and salt until they are thoroughly incorporated.
5. Add the flour to this mixture, about ⅓ cup at a time, and mix until it becomes dough. Toss in your wild lettuce flowers and mix them well into the dough.
6. Roll the dough into small balls and place them on parchment on a cookie sheet. Use a fork to press them down, leaving four distinct marks on the cookie. Otherwise, use a mold of your choice to make them into whatever shape you like.
7. Bake them for about 10 minutes, and enjoy with black tea!

Remedial Applications

Wild lettuce is a wonderful sedative and pain reliever that is not given the credence it deserves. There are various ways to take advantage of its medicine, including tea, tincture, smoke, and the extraction of lactucarium from the plant, which can be used as a moderate to strong remedy. One of the easiest ways to use this plant for its sedative properties and to ease insomnia is to smoke the dry leaf, either by itself or with other herbs like lavender. The smoke is bitter but does its job well. Tea made with the leaves is weaker than an extracted lactucarium, but it works well in conjunction with spike verbena and other nervine sedatives. It is also a very mild laxative and can be added to Siberian elm to help with bowel movement as well as a mild expectorant that works well with herbs like grindelia and marshmallow. Similarly, the tincture is not as strong as the extract but still has some effect on easing pain and bringing sleep.

Lactucarium

- 1 part wild lettuce leaf, dry
- 5 parts 190-proof alcohol
- 5 parts water
- Heatproof dish, ramekin
- Blender

1. Collect an amount of wild lettuce leaf that you would like to work with and dry it thoroughly. It is best to do this indoors or, if you live in a humid climate, with a dehydrator.
2. Place your dry plant matter into a blender and break it down well without powdering it.
3. Weight the plant matter to get an exact weight. Write this down. Whatever that number is, multiply it by 5 and prepare that amount of 190-proof alcohol in fluid ounces. Write this number down, too.
4. In a separate vessel, combine your alcohol and dry herb. Allow this to extract for about 1 week.
5. After this period, pour your tincture into a medium-sized pot, something large enough to hold double the volume of fluid, because you will now add the same amount of water to the mixture as you did alcohol.
6. Put this over a low heat, never allowing the temperature of the mixture to get above 180°F. Allow the liquid to evaporate by about half, then strain it through a cloth. Squeeze out as much of the liquid as you possibly can.
7. Pour this back into a clean pot, then put it over low heat again, still not allowing it to get above 180°F. As this evaporates, you will see it get thicker and darker. Allow this to continue until it becomes a thick paste. This can be kept in the refrigerator almost indefinitely.
8. If you'd like to make this into a thick tar, place this paste into a dehydrator or place it on waxed paper and allow it to air dry until it becomes a thick, resinous solid that can be stored in a jar. This can be taken in very small bites, about the size of a matchstick head.
9. The resin can be dissolved in vodka at a 1:2 ratio if you'd prefer a liquid. Take 1 dropper full per day, either in the morning or at night, to ease anxiety, help with sleep, better digestion, and increase erotic libido.

Magical Applications

Wild lettuce is one of the best herbs to add to teas or washes meant to aid in divination or to bless divination tools. A tisane made with either the leaves or with a small bit of lactucarium dissolved in hot water can be used to wash the eyes before engaging in scrying, to wash the hands before handling things like dowsing rods and pendulums, or to bless tools like curiomancy or bone reading sets and tarot decks. The tisane can also be used as part of your tasseomancy practice, as it may help you to find your way. This can be mixed with the fluid condenser mentioned in the purple loosestrife section on page 174, as well. Wild lettuce can also be prepped as a smoke, as an asperging water, and used as an addition to sacred drinks imbibed before undertaking divinatory practices.

This plant resonates strongly with every planet, which makes its astrological associations hard to pin down. It helps us dream and get in touch with our subconscious and has a milky exudate (Lunar); it has effects on respiration and is used in magic to find lost things (Mercurial); it has been used as an aphrodisiac (Venusian); it is used in divinatory practices and even follows the path of the Sun in the sky (Solar); it is prickly and bitter and helps with digestive motility (Martial); it increases joy and brings prosperity (Jupiter); and it grows directly from the round as a rosette and has some effects on connective tissue in the body (Saturn). Because of this, I simply give it to Mercury, the planet that balances the rest. Others give it firmly to the Moon, which I can agree with on most counts, but I feel that doesn't speak to the wholeness of this plant. When it comes to this one, do what makes sense to you and do what works.

Prickly Lettuce Divination Incense

- 1 oz. wild lettuce leaf and flower, dry
- ½ oz. mugwort leaves, dry
- ½ oz. calendula petals, dry
- ½ oz. purple loosestrife flowers, dry
- ½ oz. dandelion root, powdered
- Honey

1. On a Sunday or Monday in the hour of the Sun, prepare your dry herbs by grinding them together, not to powder, but finely.

2. In a bowl, mix enough honey into the herbs to give them the consistency of kinetic sand, meaning it will hold its shape but will also crumble easily.
3. Allow this to sit in a sealed container for about 2 weeks.
4. Press incense into molds or roll it into spheres, then allow it to dry in the open air for another 2 weeks or until it is completely dry.
5. Use a charcoal in a thurible to burn the incense and bathe yourself and your divination tools in the smoke before divining.

Lactuca Kykeon Rejuvelac

Kykeon is a historical drink sacred to Demeter, Persephone, and the other gods associated with the Eleusinian Rites. Preparing it the way it is historically described makes a thick, chunky, soup-like drink that tastes…well, terrible. Thus, the rejuvelac version! This drink is a panoply of flavors and still not the most enjoyable thing (it's not your mee-maw's sweet tea, certainly), but in the context of sacredness, absolutely drinkable.

- 4 c. distilled water
- 1 c. barley
- 2 charges, ½ oz. of wild lettuce leaves, fresh
- 2 charges, ½ oz. pennyroyal or peppermint, fresh
- 2 Tbsp. honey
- 1 Tbsp. Greek yogurt
- Red wine, dry and bitter

1. Wash your barley seeds, removing any floating seeds and debris. Afterward, mix your distilled water and your washed barley seeds together in a wide-mouth mason jar.
2. Muddle ½ an ounce each of your wild lettuce and pennyroyal/peppermint leaves together, then lay them gently on top of the barley water in your jar.
3. Place a bit of cheesecloth or other thin fabric over the mouth and screw down the lid, as the liquid needs to "breathe."
4. Place the jar in a warm spot.

5. The next morning, muddle another ½ ounce each of wild lettuce and penny royal or peppermint leaves and change the charge on top of your kykeon rejuvelac. If some has sunk down, don't worry about it.
6. After 2 days, strain your kykeon rejuvelac. Set aside the seeds to make a second batch, if you'd like, or compost them. They also make a good salad dressing ingredient! Add red wine vinegar, olive oil, and salt to the barley seeds (sumac is a nice addition, too) and put them through a food processor, then pour the result over salads!
7. Mix your Greek yogurt and your honey together, then place about a tablespoon at the bottom of a glass (the fancier, the better!).
8. Pour the kykeon rejuvelac over the top of the yogurt, sprinkle with a bit of lemon juice, and garnish with a bit of mint or wild lettuce flowers. Enjoy this drink as part of various rituals or simply as a fun cocktail option!

Prickly Lettuce Blessing Oil

This is an oil meant to aid you in your divination practice, to help open doors, clarify visions, and amplify your natural abilities. Another herb that I often add that can be harder to come by is Syrian rue, a hallucinogenic plant that is considered invasive in some areas. Another possibility is blue lotus. The only necessary items, however, are the prickly lettuce and the oil of your choice.

1 oz. wild lettuce leaves, dry
1 c. oil or your choice

1. Simply heat your oil over medium heat in a saucepan, then add your lettuce leaves, making sure they do not burn.
2. After about 10 minutes, remove the oil from the heat and allow it to cool.
3. Strain the oil through a cloth and into an appropriate bottle, such as amber or cobalt.
4. Use this oil to bless items or to rub over your body before divination.

PURPLE LOOSESTRIFE

(*Lythrum salicaria*) Venus—Water—Cancer

AKA: *Rainbow weed, purple Lhythrum, willowwort, willowweed, willow herb, bouquet violet, flowering Sally, purple grass, brighteyes,* witchsight,* purple pure,* water witch**

Loosestrife has possibly the most metal nickname of all the invasives: *The Purple Plague*. Since the 1800s, it has become prolific and widespread. It grows along roadways and other disturbed, heavily trafficked areas, but also tends to populate in waterways and wetlands, making it a particularly hated invasive plant that finds it very easy to get around. The seed of loosestrife found its way to the Americas from Europe and Asia via ship ballast, detritus in sheep wool and the fur of livestock, and animal feed and bedding, while the mature plant was planted as a medicinal, ornamental, and as a crop for beekeepers.

Loosestrife is particularly tannic, giving it a distinctly bitter flavor. This indicates to the savvy forager and survivalist that this plant can be used in hide tanning. Tannins make leather products more absorbent and breathable and help to maintain the overall cellular structure of the tanned hide, making them more comfortable to wear and longer lasting.

Purple loosestrife is native to Eurasia. It began to naturalize in the US around the Great Lakes and has spread across the country, where it is now found in a range of wetland habitats. Plants usually grow two to six feet tall, exhibiting inflorescences of purple-red flowers.

Purple loosestrife is a powerful remediator of wetland soils, as it uptakes phosphorus, nitrogen, and heavy metals that can pollute wetland water supplies while simultaneously acting to bring up nutrients for the plants around it. Loosestrife also acts to aerate wetland soils, increasing microbiota and balancing overall soil health. Its widely branching root system also helps to avoid soil erosion in wetlands. This plant also provides ample food for pollinators where it grows, being a preferred food plant for many insects, which in turn increases the available food for other animals that rely on insect populations for sustenance.

Foraging Uses

Loosestrife has a significant number of tannins, so it is not very palatable. Tannins are a plant's defense against being eaten before they are ready, and they create a drying, coating, and unpleasant mouth feel when eaten. Even so, the young shoots and the young leaves can be eaten in small quantities but may still lead to stomach upset and metabolic issues. This is not a plant I would suggest eating, really.

The best way to use loosestrife for food is to build beehives near a field of it. The nectar of loosestrife is particularly sweet and the honey made from it is exquisite. The plant is, of course, an important source of food for many pollinators in the areas where it lives, which is proven by the general "buzz" around loosestrife patches, even in years that are low on insect activity.

Remedial Applications

On the remedial side of things, though, purple loosestrife is a wonder! Its astringency is healing to tissues and helps keep wounds clean. It helps with redness and itchiness in the eye, helps ease diarrhea and related stomach issues, stops bleeding, helps the liver perform better, and has some effect against cold and flu. It has also been used as a remedy for dry, itchy eyes and as a wash to better eyesight.

The best preparation for loosestrife for any of these uses is an *aqueous infusion* (tisane) of the aerial parts. It is best not to exceed 16 ounces in a day, as the tannins may cause stomach upset. When taking the tea internally, it is also best to drink the tea about fifteen minutes before eating so it has a chance to astringe through your system. If using the tea for an eye wash, make sure all the sediment is thoroughly cleared from the liquid. For use with diarrhea, 2 ounces of the root can be decocted in about 16 ounces of water for about fifteen minutes, and 2 ounces of the liquid are taken up to 3 times daily or until symptoms abate. Either the root decoction or the aqueous infusion of the aerial parts can be used to stop bleeding, clean wounds, and help achieve a rapid recovery.

Magical Applications

The Latin name *lhythrum* comes from the word *luthron,* meaning "gore," a call to the plant's purple-red flowers. This plays into the possibilities for its magical uses, of course, as loosestrife can be used to either ease or antagonize strife. A simple way to achieve peace in the home using loosestrife is to simply hang a bouquet of loosestrife flowers in the room in which the family spends the most time. It can also be dried and used as a suffumigating incense to influence peace or wrath.

Purple loosestrife can also be used to banish various spirits, especially those that cause issues between lovers or cause psychic distress through dreams and intrusive thoughts, by hanging a bundle of the flowers over the head of the bed, by bathing in the smoke of the plant, or by taking a bath in water infused with purple loosestrife.

Purple Khernips

Khernips is an Ancient Greek way of preparing "holy water" for the purgation of miasma, the negative energy that separates a person from the divine. This is a preparation to add to bath water, thus helping to alleviate bad dreams, intrusive thoughts, weakened magical ability, and overall psychic disruptions.

- 1 oz. purple loosestrife flowers
- 1 sprig of juniper leaf, dry
- 1 Tbsp. sea salt
- 32 oz. water
- 1 match or lighter

1. Heat your water and infuse the purple flowers of loosestrife into it by steeping them for about 15 minutes. Allow the water to cool.

2. Place the water into a bowl. Bless it in whichever way you prefer, an example being:

   "Creature of Water, I do summon, stir, and conjure the. Awake and hear me. You are blessed and purified, unto the end of ages. Awake, awake, awake!"

3. Bless the salt in the same way as a "creature of Earth." Once it is blessed, mix it into the water until all of the salt is dissolved.
4. Light the sprig of dry juniper on fire and allow it to smolder as you bless it as a "creature of Fire."
5. Blow it out and bless the smoke as a "creature of Air." Put the sprig into the bowl of water, thus mixing all four Elements together.
6. Hold your hands over the bowl and say:

   "Creatures of the Elements, I bring you into unity, complete and whole, that you may work with me and purify me and cleanse me and bring me into my own wholeness that I may walk amongst the gods. So it is."

7. Use a bit of this water to wash your hands, to pour over your head, or as an additive to bath water that will help to cleanse your subtle bodies and bring you into greater wholeness and power.

Floor Wash to Dispel Strife in the Home

- 1 oz. purple loosestrife aerial parts
- 1 oz. saltcedar leaf tips
- 1 Tbsp. sea salt
- 1 gallon water

8. Begin by at least picking up your house. No need for a deep clean, but a good once-over of your living space will help energy move through the space more easily.
9. To make this preparation, simply boil the herbs in a gallon of water and add your salt. This will be added to your mop water. Use this to mop your floors while you say,

   "Green salt and willow herb, good increase. Push out anger, bring in peace."

Powder to Bring Strife to an Enemy

- 1 oz. purple loosestrife
- ¼ oz. cayenne
- ¼ oz. nettle leaf
- 1 small steak

1. Begin heating a pan on the stove. Wait until it is searing hot.
2. Place a photo of the target or their name written five times on a piece of paper into the pan and allow it to burn.
3. Sprinkle the herbs into the pan and allow them to burn.
4. Place the steak in the pan and let it blacken. I tend to use an icon of the goddess Brimo, which I bathe in the smoke of the "burnt offering" as I intone an incantation along the lines of:

   "Brimo, Strong One, Mother of Pain, she of the Mouth Filled with Swords, I do summon, stir, and conjure you to bring all pain, strife, and violence upon this enemy, NN. May they never know another night's peace and may their blood flow freely, that you may sate your hunger, Queen of Pain."

Fluid Condenser for Clairvoyance

- 1 oz. purple loosestrife flowers
- 1 piece 18k rose gold *or* 1 piece 24k gold *and* 1 piece copper
- 16 oz. distilled water
- Saucepan

1. On a Monday in the hour of the Sun, pour your water into an appropriate saucepan, then place your rose gold or your gold and copper into the water. Bring this to a simmer for about 30 minutes or until the water content is about halved.
2. Pour into a heat-safe vessel and allow it to cool for about 10 minutes.
3. Steep your loosestrife flowers in the slightly cooled water for about 20 minutes.
4. This fluid can be applied to the eyelids to increase psychic ability and clairvoyance, but it may also help you to "overlook" a person or place a hex by virtue of your gaze.

RUSSIAN OLIVE

(*Eleagnus angustifolia*) Sun—Fire—Leo

AKA: *Autumn olive, silverberry, silverthorn, oleaster, wild olive, Jerusalem willow, Persian olive, wilde ölbaum, l'olivier de Bohéme, arbre d'argent, pins-n-needles,* seamripper,* Apollowood,* Hekate's rod**

Russian olive has served an important role in its native habitat, being an important food crop, an item of commerce, and even for cosmetics. This tree has been a large part of the cultures that have surrounded it, their fruit even being a part of traditional dishes such as the Afghani *haft mēwa* served at Norwuz. They are an important part of the wild landscape, but have also been domesticated and farmed for food, medicine, and ritual for millennia. It has also been used for tanning leather, as a dark brown to black dye, for chewing gum, musical instruments, and carpentry projects, such as the submerged legs of bridges. The tree has also been an important cosmetic ingredient, mainly for hair care but also for skin health.

There are also a number of taboos about *E. angustifolia,* mostly having to do with harming the tree or befouling it. In Turkistan, there are stories of branches having fallen near holy sites and blood gushing from the trunks of Russian olive, followed by screams of pain, so there are prescriptions against cutting them down or harming them in any way. It is also considered unacceptable to bury people or livestock underneath them, to relieve oneself against them, or even to let chickens roost in the branches.

Ecology

Every summer, the riparian area of Albuquerque, called the Bosque, is scented with the four-petaled, buttery yellow flowers of this tree. It is one of the most beautiful scents I have ever smelled, and we are lucky enough that an entire area of our city benefits from it for weeks and weeks in summer. The leaves of the tree are also fragrant, very much like olive leaves, though they are silvery and somewhat furry on both sides, light green, and long. The word *eleagnus* comes from the Greek words *eleia,* "olive tree," and *agnos,* "chaste, pure, innocent, sacred," where *angustifolia* means "narrow-leaved." The new bark is a gorgeous red with a honey-golden sheen that matures to almost black in older trees, and the long, frond-like twigs are lined with vicious spines.

In the Autumn, Russian olive produces lovely, small fruits that ripen after the first frost of the year, which is usually mid-October here in New Mexico. Once they turn from a light-yellow color to a reddish brown, they are ready to harvest. The flesh is thinly spread over a large pit, but they can be separated by a simple winnowing process. They can also simply be ground into a fatty flour that can be added to baked goods or used to make dumplings and the like.

Russian olive saplings are easy to mistake for something else, as they often look like fleshy, hairy-leaved forbs, not young trees. They tend to look a lot like flowerless globemallow or even a mutated mullein, slowly growing woodier and more like what it will be as an adult. They are shapeshifters, transforming from one thing into another, becoming more themselves over time.

Native to Europe, the Middle East, and Asia, this tree made its way to the Americas in the early to mid-1800s and has made itself quite at home in the areas along Western river systems. It takes advantage of the disturbed areas along riversides, particularly those that have lower water flow due to our water use practices and reliance on dams and, therefore, are not subject to flood occurrences. Not only this, but their roots are nitrogen fixers, meaning they can live in a very wide variety of environments, from partial shade and nutrient poor soil to high sun and rich soil. They really aren't very picky.

They can dominate an area very easily and have become one of the most populous woody plants found in riverine ecosystems, causing issues for native plants. They are particularly problematic for things like native cottonwoods in that they overshade saplings that are sunlight-dependent. It is worth noting, though, that the same saplings are also floodplain dependent, and it is our doing that their native habitats have been so greatly altered as to no longer flood. Therefore, it is not the Russian olive who is to blame for the poor health of native plants in riparian areas, but, yet again…humans.

Foraging Uses

Russian olive is one of my favorite plants to forage from, not only because the fruits of the tree are sweet, tangy, and delightful but because they are packed with phytonutrients. The flowers, leaves, and bark are all edible, as well, making this an extremely useful tree. It has been considered so for millennia in its native landscape and proves itself so today, even in the areas where it has become "invasive."

One of the easiest ways to forage from Russian olive is to collect the fruits, dry them in the shade or in a dehydrator, then grind the whole fruit into a flour. It becomes a reddish-brown powder that can be added to all sorts of baked goods, like cookies and muffins, or even to dough for noodles and dumplings. The dried flesh can also be separated from the seed by rubbing the fruits over a rough surface, such as a screen. It powders easily from the kernel and can be used in the same way as the whole fruit flour, though I prefer the latter. The seed is chock full of fatty acids, minerals, and vitamins and makes for a nutrient-dense addition to anything that is made with flour. The fresh fruits can be boiled down while they are still soft to make jam, jelly, and even fruit leather.

The leaves make a lovely aqueous infusion that tastes a bit like green tea but also like olive leaf. It has an energizing quality and is also useful for boosting immunity and helping people get through illness or ease arthritic pain; a true example of "food as medicine." The flowers of the tree are deliciously fragrant and make a beautiful, floral jelly that can be enjoyed with bread and butter, other baked goods, or with more savory dishes like pork and chicken. The bark is also a nice tea, though more astringent than the leaves. Water made by boiling the ripe fruits can be added to it to make it a bit more palatable.

Oleaster Flower Jelly

- 1½ loose c. Russian olive flowers, removed from green calyx
- 2 c. boiling water
- 3 c. white sugar or turbinado
- 1 pack powdered pectin
- 3–4 Tbsp. lemon juice

1. You will want to sterilize whichever jars you're going to use to can your jelly to avoid spoilage. This can be done with a quick rinse under cold water, then a rub down inside and out with a little bit of rubbing alcohol, then a dip in boiling water. Make sure the jars stay hot because *hot* jelly should not poured into *cold* glass.
2. In a medium to large bowl, mix your Russian olive flowers with your 2 cups of boiling hot water. Allow this to steep for about 15 minutes. The water will turn a yellowish color and smell like Russian olive flowers.
3. Using an immersion blender (or an emulsifying blender, whichever you have handy), mix the Russian olive flowers into the water until it is mostly smooth and well-integrated.
4. Strain this through a very tight cloth filter, such as a nut milk bag. There should be *no* particulate in the water you filter, just yellow, Russian olive goodness. If necessary (it probably will be), add hot water until you have 2 cups again.
5. Transfer that liquid into a saucepan over high heat, add your pectin, and bring to a boil for about 1 minute.
6. Add your sugar and allow to boil for another minute, then mix in your lemon juice and remove from the heat.
7. Pour your jelly into the jars and put the lids on immediately. Allow the jars to chill to room temperature before putting them in the fridge. Jelly can take days to weeks to fully set, but if it's spreadable, enjoy it on whatever foods you'd like to. This should keep indefinitely if you follow a full canning process, but it will keep up to 2 months if kept in the fridge.

OLEASTER CHICKEN BECHAMEL

This is a sweet and savory dish for the lover of all things delicious.

- 2–3 boneless chicken breasts

Marinade

- 1 c. of white wine *or* apple cider vinegar
- ½ oz. horseweed, dried
- ½ oz. oregano, dried
- 2 garlic cloves, smashed
- ¼ c. lemon juice

Breading

- 4 large eggs
- ¼ c. milk *or* cream
- 4 Tbsp. cotija cheese
- 4 Tbsp. flour of your choice
- 4 Tbsp. Russian olive fruit flour
- 2 tsp. salt
- 2 tsp. garlic powder
- 1 tsp. ginger powder
- ¼ tsp. black pepper, crushed

Bechamel Sauce

- 2 Tbsp. butter
- 1 Tbsp. onion, finely chopped
- ¼ c. flour of your choice
- 24 oz. milk
- ½ tsp. salt
- ½ tsp. white pepper, crushed
- 1 pinch nutmeg
- 1 pinch clove

Later Sauce Additions

- 13 cloves garlic, half-smashed
- ½ c. diced onion
- 1¼ c. bone broth or other stock of your choice

1. First, you will make your marinade by mixing together the wine or vinegar, horseweed, oregano, smashed garlic cloves, and lemon juice. Whisk them together thoroughly and pour into a plastic baggy. Put your chicken breasts in the marinade and make sure they are thoroughly coated with it. Seal the bag and let them sit in the marinade for about 48 hours. This can also be done in a small bowl.
2. While you wait, you can make your bechamel sauce.
3. Melt your 4 tablespoons of butter into a saucepan and sauté your 1 tablespoon of onion in it until they are soft but not browned.
4. Add a ½ cup of flour, mix it in, and let it cook until the flour just begins to become golden.
5. In a separate pan, heat your milk until it is very warm but not boiling. Add this about ⅓ at a time into your flour and onion mixture just as the flour begins to turn golden. Vigorously whisk it together with your salt, pepper, and other spices.
6. Bring the temperature to a low-medium heat and cook this for about 30 minutes, stirring frequently, until the volume is reduced by about ⅓. You should be left with about 16 ounces of bechamel sauce, which can be used in various projects, not just this one. If you put it in a clean mason jar, it will keep for about a week in the fridge.
7. When your chicken is marinated and your bechamel is made, you will start this dish by making your breading. In a bowl, mix the chosen flour, cotija, garlic powder, ginger powder, salt, and pepper. In another bowl, whisk your 4 eggs and your cream or milk together. Spread the fruit flour out on a plate.
8. Dredge your chicken breast in the flour mixture, thoroughly coating it. Then dip it into the egg wash, again making sure to get all parts of the breast. Then, bread it over with the fruit flour by patting it against the plate.
9. In a skillet, put 2–3 tablespoons of an oil of your choice and 1 tablespoon of butter over medium-high heat. Once the butter is melted, swirl the fats around to coat the entire pan.
10. Place your breaded chicken breasts into the pan and fry them for about 4–6 minutes per side, depending on how thick the breasts are, then move them to an oven-safe dish in the oven

at a low temperature with the door cracked, just to keep them warm.

11. Reduce the heat to low-medium heat and melt another pat of butter into the juices already there. Put your ½ cup of onions in and let sauté for about 2 minutes, stirring slowly, then place your 13 cloves of garlic in the pan. By half-crushing them in the pan, they will caramelize after about 3 minutes, and the sweetness of the garlic will come to the forefront.
12. Pour your bone broth over the sauteed garlic and onion mixture to deglaze the pan, mixing everything well.
13. Add 1¼ cups of bechamel sauce to this, bring it to a simmer, and stir slowly and consistently until everything is well integrated.
14. Add your chicken breasts back into the pan and let them simmer in the sauce for about 3–5 minutes more, gently spooning sauce over them. Serve the chicken on plates, spoon the remaining sauce over them, and serve with your choice of greens, such as the almyrikia found in the Tamarisk section on page 214, and a spoonful of Russian olive flower jelly.

Russian Olive Fruit Cookies

Everybody loves a good chocolate chip cookie. With Russian olive fruit flour, though, they can be made even better and much more nutritious.

- 3 c. flour of your choice
- ½ c. butter, salted and softened
- 1 c. granulated white sugar
- 1 c. dark brown sugar, packed
- 1 c. dark chocolate chips
- ½ c. Russian olive fruit flour
- ½ c. cherries, dried
- ½ c. cream cheese
- 2 tsp. vanilla *or* hazelnut *or* almond extract
- 1 tsp. baking soda
- 1 tsp. salt
- ½ tsp. baking powder
- 2 large eggs

1. Preheat your oven to 375°F.
2. Mix together your dry ingredients (flour, baking soda and powder, and salt), then set the mixture aside.
3. Cream together your softened butter, brown and white sugar, and your cream cheese.
4. Whip the eggs and your chosen extract into the butter mixture until it becomes light and fluffy.
5. Mix your dry ingredients into the butter mixture until it is completely combined, then mix in your chocolate chips and cherries until they are well dispersed. This is your dough!
6. Place a piece of parchment paper on a cooking sheet.
7. Roll about 3 tablespoons of cookie dough at a time into balls, then place them evenly in lines to fill your cookie sheet.
8. Bake them for about 10 minutes or until they are just about turning brown. Remove the pan and let the cookies sit on the hot pan for 2–3 minutes before removing them to cool. If you let them get fully golden in the oven, they will be less chewy and more crunchy (no judgment to the crunchy cookie people). Flatten them as soon as they come out of the oven with the back of a spatula.
9. Enjoy with a glass of Russian olive fruit tea and cream!

Watermelon and Oleaster Gazpacho

This is a sweet and savory soup that is meant to be served chilled. It is best served with a flavorful, crusty bread and a beverage that has a good tang or a bit of spice.

- 1 full watermelon, seeded and cubed (1 c. set aside)
- 3–4 heirloom tomatoes, large, sliced
- 2 cucumbers, peeled and seeded (1 additional cucumber, sliced thickly, quartered, set aside)
- 2 c. Russian olive fruits, fresh or dried
- ½ c. cantaloupe, seeded, cubed, and set aside
- ½ c. strawberries, sliced and set aside
- ⅓ c. mint leaves, well packed and bruised

- ½ onion, chopped
- 1 tsp. salt
- ½ tsp. black pepper, crushed
- ½ tsp. cumin
- ½ tsp. red chilé *or* Tajín, set aside for garnish
- 2–4 cloves garlic, crushed

1. To begin, boil your Russian olive fruits for about 5 minutes. The water will turn brown and thicken, becoming sweet, and the fruits will become soft. Allow this to cool in the pot, then strain the fruits out of the water, but keep the water and set it aside.
2. Once the fruits are cool, pour them into a blender along with the majority of your watermelon, tomatoes, 2 cucumbers, mint, onion, salt, pepper, cumin, and garlic. Add 1 cup of the water from your Russian olive fruits. Puree this all together into a thick paste, the consistency of spaghetti sauce.
3. Pour this into a bowl, then add the watermelon, cantaloupe, strawberries, and cucumber that you set aside. Mix them in to make the soup a bit more interesting.
4. Cover the bowl and chill this for at least an hour before serving. Garnish each bowl with mint or parsley and sprinkle it over with Tajín. Also serve each with a thick slice of crusty bread soaked in olive oil and herbs and a suitable beverage of your choice.
5. The rest of the water you set aside from your fruits can be added to drinks, taken as a beverage on its own, or reduced to make a syrup for use in other dishes.

Remedial Applications

Russian olive has so many remedial uses, from nourishing the skin to healing ulcers throughout the body to relieving skeletal pain and even fighting cancerous cells. It truly is a wonder that it is *still* the target of eradication efforts the nation over, and people gleefully poison it, rip it from the ground, and, in other ways, break all of the taboos against harming it.

PAIN RELIEF TEA

The fruits of the Russian olive act as a good pain reliever, particularly for rheumatic pains, skeletal muscle soreness, and issues with nervous system over-sensitivity.

- 32 oz. water
- 2 c. Russian olive fruit, fresh
- ½ oz. willow bark, dried or fresh
- ½ oz. cat's claw bark, dried
- ½ oz. meadowsweet, dried or fresh
- ½ oz. wild lettuce leaves, dried

1. Bring your 32 ounces of water to a near boil, where you begin to see bubbles forming at the bottom of your pot and streaming upward (the string of pearls).
2. Simmer your Russian olive fruits for about 5 minutes until the water is thickened and brownish.
3. Add the willow and cat's claw and simmer these with your fruits for about 5 more minutes.
4. Strain the water and use it to steep your meadowsweet and wild lettuce for about 10 minutes. Add hot water to bring the volume back to 32 ounces total.
5. Add a tablespoon of honey to the whole batch or add honey to taste. Drink about 4 ounces at a time throughout the day.

STOMACHACHE TEA

- 32 oz. water
- 1 c. fresh Russian olive fruit
- ½ c. Russian olive leaf, fresh
- ½ c. horseweed leaves, fresh

1. Decoct the fruits for about 15–20 minutes, then strain them.
2. Wait for about 10 minutes, then use the water you strained to steep the Russian olive and horseweed leaves for about 15 minutes.
3. Drink this as often as you'd like! You may also add honey and even a bit of mint to make the flavor more interesting.

Anti-arthritic Pain Salve

- ½ oz. Russian olive leaf and flower, dried and crushed
- ½ oz. prickly lettuce leaves, dried and crushed
- ½ oz. cayenne powder
- ½ oz. rosemary leaves
- 16 oz. of oil of choice
- 2 oz. beeswax

1. Prepare a stovetop infusion of oil using the above herbs.
2. Strain the herbs from your oil and measure the volume, which should be close to 16 ounces. Add oil back until it equals 16 ounces.
3. Put the oil into a double boiler and add the beeswax, melting the two together.
4. Pour the salve into one or more jars and use it whenever you please to ease the pain of arthritis and inflamed joints. Be cautious, as the cayenne will make touching mucosal membranes very uncomfortable!

Anti-microbial Salve

- 1 oz. of Russian olive leaf and flower
- 1 oz. tamarisk leaf and flower
- ½ oz. of Russian olive fruit, pulverized
- ½ oz. of sweet clover
- 12–16 oz. of oil of choice
- 2½–3 oz. beeswax

1. Place your oil into a skillet and bring it to a low heat.
2. Place your herbs into the oil and stir consistently until you can smell the herbs in the air.
3. Turn the skillet off and allow it to cool.
4. Bring this back to a low heat, stirring consistently.
5. Remove from heat and allow to cool, then strain.
6. For every cup of oil, add 1 ounce of beeswax and melt these together in a double boiler.
7. Pour your salve off into one or more jars. It should keep for quite a while.

Fever Reduction Tea

- ½ oz. Russian olive leaf and flower
- ½ oz. willow bark

1. Decoct the willow bark for 10–15 minutes, then use the resulting water to steep your Russian olive leaves and flowers for about 10 minutes.
2. Allow it to cool completely, then give the person with a fever 4-ounce doses once every hour until the fever breaks.

Magical Application

Russian olive is a tree with strong links to purification, cleansing, healing, and protection. Those are the best places to utilize its magic, whether in poppetry, ritual tool making, or as a suffumigant for smoke bathing. When it comes to the astrological associations for this plant, there are many varying opinions. I think it resonates most completely with Mercury, though, as it has some resonances with all of the major planets and acts as a pain reliever, most of which under the auspice of Mercury.

Poppet Pins

One of the most eye-catching characteristics of the Russian olive is the long, sharp, golden thorns that grow along the twigs. They can be useful in all sorts of magical pursuits, but I like them very much for poppetry. They can be used almost like acupuncture needles, piercing the poppet in areas that are painful for the person the poppet represents in order to treat them or poking into areas that may relieve energetic issues for that person. This is a type of healing magic that can be done remotely, so it is enormously useful and adaptable.

Russian olive thorns make very useful healing tools for this purpose, as the wood acts as a conduit for purifying and protective powers, so each one becomes a locus of healing. They can also be left in the poppet indefinitely without causing any pain to anyone. These can be blessed individually by running them through the smoke of burning oleaster bark, leaves, and flowers or through any other blessing or purifying incense you use.

Purifictory Smoke

The following recipe is to create a suffumigant that will help to purify your home. This is best done on a Sunday in the hour of Mercury.

- 1 oz. Russian olive leaves, dried
- 1 oz. juniper berries, dried
- ½ oz. garlic powder
- ½ oz. salt
- 1 small sprig of Russian olive, about a handspan long

After mixing together the first four ingredients, light a charcoal tab and place it in a small bowl filled with salt or sand. Sprinkle the charcoal over with these herbs and allow them to start billowing with smoke. Take the handspan length of Russian olive and use this to guide the smoke over the person or item or through the space you are purifying. Use a strong, commanding tone as you direct all entities, energies, and powers that cause disharmony and inquietude to leave.

Incense of Offering and Feeding

This can be used as an offering to deities, genius oikos and loci (spirits of home and place), familiars, ancestors, the dead, and any other spirit you work with. It can also be used as part of general house clearings and blessings or to replace energies removed during healing with more positive, beneficial ones.

- 1 qt. honey
- 1 bottle red wine (750 ml)
- 1 c. Russian olive fruit, dried and crushed
- ½ c. figs, dried and pulverized
- ½ c. chokecherries, dried and pulverized
- ½ oz. resin of your choice
- ½ oz. blue vervain, dried
- ½ oz. meadowsweet, dried
- ½ oz. sweet clover, dried
- ½ oz. cinnamon bark, dried
- ½ oz. nutmeg powder
- Essence of Gold (optional)

1. The easiest way to begin the first part of this preparation is to place your fruits, herbs, and wine in a blender on low for 1–2 minutes. This will break down your fruits almost completely and integrate all the parts together. Add a bit of pure gold if you want to add Essence of Gold to your preparation. You will pour this into a jar and allow it to sit for about 2 weeks.
2. After the wine is infused with the fruits and herbs, strain them from the wine using a cloth with a tight weave, such as a tea towel or a nut milk bag. Put the infused wine into a large jar (I usually use a gallon pickle jar).
3. Add the honey to your wine and mix them together. Put the jar in a large pot of water and bring it to a boil. You are looking to slowly evaporate the water content from the mixture, thickening it. This will take several hours. You're looking for a consistency slightly thicker than molasses.
4. Once it is properly dehydrated, pour it out into a bottle you like. When you want to burn it, light a coal, place that in a bowl of salt or sand, and put a lima bean-sized amount on top of that. It will bubble and splutter, then send up plenty of smoke to feed and honor the spirits you work with.

Home Protection Charm

This is a version of a witches' ladder to hang by the front door for protection. On a dark moon, gather 13 thorns of a Russian olive tree and a heart length of red twine. If you've got them, also include 13 feathers of a white hen (but any light-colored feather will do in a pinch). On the day of the Summer Solstice, you will knot one thorn and one feather together into the twine in 13 knots along the length of the twine while reciting a charm for each as you walk around the perimeter of your home:

> *"I do summon, stir, and conjure you, spirits of the Land on which I dwell, also the spirits of the house in which I live, and the ancestral spirits that guard me, and the guardian set over me when first my soul awoke beyond the Solar Gate. Roost upon this thorn and touch this feather with your breath. May they reflect your power and act as guardians at my door. May they protect my home and those within from all manner of intrusion, degradation, and malice, no matter the source. It is so."*

If you can, tie a piece of your home into the bottom of the ladder, something as simple as one screw from one of the hinges on the front door of your home or something similar. If that isn't possible, that's also fine. You'll also want to weigh down the ladder with something like a hag stone, a small mirror, or a heavy charm of some kind. When the charm is done, hand it by your front door in a place where the Sun will be able to impart its power to the charm.

Libation to Apollo

A libation is just a liquid poured out on the ground as an offering to a deity or other spirit, though it is traditionally a drink of some kind, such as whiskey, rum, or wine. This is a recipe for a sweet libation meant to honor Apollo and any other Solar deity you'd like to.

To make this preparation, simply boil a cup of Oleaster fruits, 6 bay leaves, and a pinch of lemon balm in about 4 cups of red wine. If you have access to it, snakeskin can be added to the mix, as can gold and any of the Solar stones, such as citrine or amber. Strain the infused wine and melt in about a cup of honey, then jar it up. Use about ¼ cup of this preparation per 16 ounces of water to pour as an offering during ritual. I'll note here that Russian olive also makes an appropriate addition to libations for Hermes or Mercury.

Ritum Ponere Requietibus

This returns us to one of the traditional uses of this plant, which was to remove illness and negative spiritual influences that may lead to it. This usually requires an animal sacrifice, but we have replaced the animal with a poppet of the person being healed. The way I've written this ritual also comes with a choice between burning the poppet or burying it, and you may choose which suits you better.

- 1 Russian olive branch, thin and about 2 feet long
- 12 rosehips, whole and fresh (dried is okay)
- 12 Russian olive fruits, whole and fresh (dried is okay)
- 12 juniper berries, whole and fresh (dried is okay)
- 1 poppet of the person in question
- 1 pt. of warmed blood (gotten from butcher) *or* warm red wine (optional, for burial)

- 1 pt. of warmed milk (optional, for burial)
- 1 c. of honey (optional, for burial)
- 3 iron nails (optional, for burial)
- Dry juniper and Russian olive wood to burn (optional, for burning)
- Incense of Offering and Feeding (optional, for burning)
- 2 bowls, purified
- Ritual dagger
- Incense made of Russian olive leaf and flower, juniper leaf and berry, wild lettuce leaf, rose petals, and a resin of your choice.

1. Prepare a sacred space and call up the Anemoi, the four winds (Eurus, Notus, Zephyrus, and Boreas). Give them offerings and ask them to be present for your rite. Prepare the space in whichever way you are used to doing, but bringing in the Anemoi and preparing a circle is an important step.
2. Have the person stand, if they are able, in the center of the space.
3. Use the longer branch of Russian olive to sweep their body, praying or chanting as you go. An example of something to say is:

   "Eurus, Notus, Zephyrus, Boreas, Lords of the Four Winds, I have conjured thee to this place. As you have passed through the leaves of this bough, so pass through NN and purify them. As you cleanse the Land and Air by the virtue of your breath, so cleanse NN. This holy branch, so used to the kisses of your great mouths, shall remove all negativity, malice, and ill intent from NN, throughout all aspects and dimensions of all reality throughout the multiverse, throughout all time, and without end. So it is."

4. Take your incense and burn it on a coal in an appropriate thurible. Suffumigate the person in question, from head to toe, and also suffumigate the room you are performing this ritual in. Use the smoke to create a ritual circle of protection in the room. You may also make a tea of Russian olive leaves and flowers and use a sprig of juniper to asperge it around the room.
5. Cleanse and bless your fruits in incense smoke, then put them in one of the bowls and place it to one side of the person. Take one fruit at a time and touch it to an area of the body

(rosehips for the midline, oleaster for the right side, juniper for the left) and recite a prayer that makes sense for your practice. The following is merely an example:

"Spirits of the Autumn, marching toward the Land of the Dead, I command you: HALT! By virtue of the power in this fruit and in me and in this person, NN, and granted by the spirits of the Land, the spirits of the winds, this house, the bloodline, the planets, stars, and forces around and about us, I do compel you: HALT AND TURN. By virtue of the power this person, NN, and I possess, I command you: RETREAT. The winds shall guide you back and away. Return to the place you have come from and leave this person, NN. Let NN be and leave them in good health, good standing, and with a happy mind for all time, throughout all aspects and dimensions of reality throughout the multiverse, without end. So it is."

6. The relevant parts of the body, which my mentor called *puntos vulnerables,* the vulnerable points, are listed here:

- between the eyebrows (glabella)
- at the top of the head directly between the ears (bregma)
- at the whorl of the hair (lambda)
- at the base of the skull, where it meets the spine
- at C7 where there is a bulge at the base of the neck
- directly in the middle of the right trapezius (shoulder)
- directly in the middle of the left trapezius
- at the place where the clavicles meet the manubrium, also called the jugular notch
- on the sternum just in front of the heart
- T7, just behind the heart
- at the solar plexus (between the lower ribcage and the navel)
- just below the navel
- the curve of the lower back
- at the pubis
- at the right antecubital fossa
- at the left antecubital fossa
- in the right palm
- in the left palm
- at the back of the right hand
- at the back of the left hand
- at the right hip

- at the left hip
- at the right patella
- at the left patella
- at the right popliteal fossa
- at the left popliteal fossa
- at the right lateral malleolus
- at the left lateral malleolus
- at the right medial malleolus
- at the left medial malleolus
- at the top of the right foot
- at the top of the left foot
- at the sole of the right foot
- at the sole of the left foot

7. As the prayer is said with each fruit, transfer the fruit to the empty bowl, which should be placed on the other side of the client from the bowl of unused fruit.
8. Once you've worked your way through the fruits, get the poppet, place it at the top of the head, and say,

   "I name this poppet NN, for it has the thoughts and consciousness of NN."

   Then, place it over their heart and say,

   "I name this poppet NN, for it has the feelings and emotions of NN."

   Then, place it between the person's feet and say,

   "I name this poppet NN, for it has walked the ways and miles of NN but stops here to lay the burdens of NN to rest as NN walks on without those burdens."

   Place the poppet just in front of the person in question.

9. Take your ritual dagger and rub it in a counterclockwise manner on all of the *puntos vulnerables* you had placed fruits against. Say a prayer at each one, such as:

   "I sever all energies and entities, all spirits and powers that cause all manner of malady, be it of body, mind, or spirit. They are removed from this person, NN, and transferred to NN, for all time, throughout all aspects and dimensions of the multiverse, without limit. It is so."

10. After *each* point, rub your dagger against the poppet to transfer the energy from the person to the doll. Once this is done, you may disperse your circle, the Anemoi, and the other spirits you've called in with appropriate thanks and offering. Prepare for the next phase.

Here is the *choice*. Now that the person is cleansed and the energies have been removed and transferred to the poppet, they need to be laid to rest. You can choose option A, which is to bury the poppet, or option B, which is to burn it. Whichever of those resonates with you and your practice most strongly is the one to go with, or if you have a third option you'd prefer, go with that one!

For Burial:

1. Get a pint of blood from the butcher, it doesn't matter which kind. Whatever they have will be fine. Warm it to about body temperature, so around 98°F. Also warm the milk to about that temperature.
2. Take these things, your cup of honey, the fruits you used to cleanse the person, the branch, and three iron nails to the place you intend to bury your poppet. Dig a hole about 1–2 feet deep, something that will fit your poppet nicely.
3. Pour the milk into the hole and say,

   "Spirits of the Earth, I propitiate you with this offering of milk. May you be made ready to accept the body of NN, who carries the burdens of NN."

   Lay the poppet in the hole.

4. In an aesthetically pleasing way, surround the poppet with the fruits you used to cleanse the person.

   "With the body of NN, I lay to rest their burdens and their strifes and all that keeps them from their greatest and most potent potential. May they become the fertile ground for the growth of NN, for the strength of NN, and for the joy of NN."

5. Now, pour the blood over the poppet and into the hole.

   "An offering I make to the spirits of the unquiet dead and the spirits who hunger, an offering of blood. Let it sate you. Leave NN to continue on their path without you, that they may find their peace and that you may find yours."

6. Pour the honey in the shape of a symbol with meaning to you in this context, something protective. A pentacle is always a good choice, but so is a hag's foot (six-pointed asterisk).

   "By virtue of this sign and symbol, may this rite be kindly sealed. May the path that extends before NN be made sweet and fruitful, and may their steps be guided toward their greatest potential. So it is."

7. Cover the poppet with dirt, filling the hole. Say whatever prayers are appropriate for you and your practice.
8. Just above the "grave," you will hammer your nails into the ground one at a time.

   With the first say, *"I lay your mind to rest, NN."*

   With the second say, *"I lay your heart to rest, NN."*

   With the third say, *"I lay your body to rest, NN."*

9. Lay the branch over the "grave" and say,

   "As this branch withers, so shall the connections between NN below and NN above. From this place, walk forth renewed and free, NN!"

10. The person, if they are present, will step over the grave, and both of you will leave the place *without turning around.* The rite is done at this point.

For Burning:

1. Prepare a ritual fire in a safe place and in the way you are used to. Bring the poppet, the branch, and the fruits to the fire. You may choose to bring the blood, milk, and honey as well, but they are not necessary.
2. Stand before the fire and say,

   "May this fire act as a gateway of transformation of NN. May their burdens and their strifes and all that keeps them from their greatest potential be sublimated and transformed into health, strength, and joy."

3. Cast the fruits into the fire, then the poppet, your chosen funerary herbs (be sure they are safe to burn), and, after cutting it into smaller pieces, also cast the Russian olive branch into the fire. Allow them to burn down to ash.
4. Once the fire has cooled, take a cup of the ash and sift it to remove any large chunks of wood or other matter. The ash may be further calcined (reduced to pure, white ash) or simply washed to gather the finest particulate. While you prepare the ash and wash it, say whichever prayers or incantations make sense to you. I will often call on various planetary agencies during this type of thing, drawing sigils in the ash or water to bond them with my preparation. Agiel, the Intelligence of Saturn, might make a good choice here, as this spirit can be a powerful protector.
5. To wash the ashes, place a tightly woven cloth in a ceramic dish that can be placed on the stovetop. Put the ashes in the cloth and pour a small amount (1 ounce) of water over them, just enough to fill the bottom of the dish. Filter the ash and water through the cloth so there is just a cloudy layer on the bottom.
6. Put this over very low heat to evaporate the water. You will be left with a thin, dry layer of fine ash. Scrape this up and place it in a locket, a small bottle, press it between glass, or in some other way make an amulet that can be worn. This will act as an apotropaic charm for the person. The rite is done at this point.

SIBERIAN ELM

(*Ulmus pumila*) Saturn—Water—Virgo

AKA: *Little leaf elm, dwarf elm, Asiatic elm, wafer elm,* coin-in-a-casket,* Ferryman's tree,* pay-the-toll**

Though it is native to central Asia, eastern Siberia, and Russia, as well as parts of China, India, and Korea, it has naturalized in many other places and is considered invasive throughout much of the US. Though this tree is one of the most hated trees in the States, it is also one of our greatest botanical heroes and one of our future saviors. The Siberian elm has been a great help in repairing the devastation experienced during the Dust Bowl, a period during the 1930s when drought combined with poor agricultural practices led to monstrous dust storms, massive loss of topsoil, and a barren landscape in a large portion of the Southern US.

Due to incentives from the government, such as the Homestead Act of 1862 and the Enlarged Homestead Act of 1909, along with the Nebraska-specific Kincaid Act of 1904, large numbers of people inexperienced with farming and impassioned by the philosophy of Manifest Destiny moved west onto the Great Plains, many into areas where irrigation was impossible. This was a major opportunity for many of these people, including freed slaves who were looking for a new start in a new frontier but one they were unprepared to deal with. They ripped out the deep-rooted prairie long grasses that had been there for millennia as part of the indigenous landscape and planted European wheat crops, which failed almost immediately due to drought.

Removing the prairie grasses, though necessary for farming, was a huge mistake, especially in areas distant from water sources. The native prairie grasses were not only holding the topsoil in place but were harboring carbon dioxide in their root systems, lowering overall temperatures in the Great Plains and allowing for greater rainfall. There is no way to measure it now, but I imagine that when they were ripped from the ground without a second thought, all that carbon dioxide was no longer vaulted away, and there was nowhere for more CO_2 to go, so the temperature went up.

With higher temperatures, rainfall declined, which brought drought, and the dry, exposed topsoil that was once a lush plain was simply swept away by great dust storms (called "black blizzards"), some of which reached all the way to New York to blanket the Statue of Liberty. In just one day, April 14th, 1935, later termed "Black Sunday," it is estimated that over three million tons of topsoil were swept east to the Atlantic Ocean from as far east as the Oklahoma panhandle. This event led to the Associated Press coining the term "Dust Bowl" for the affected areas, which included Texas, Colorado, Nebraska, Kansas, New Mexico, and Oklahoma. It stands as one of the largest ecological disasters of the twentieth century. One hundred sixty million acres of Land and topsoil were affected, thirty-five million of which became barren wasteland that not even grass could grow in for nearly a decade.

Enter *Ulmus pumila*, the Siberian elm. To hamper the dust storms and to try to remediate the situation, President Franklin D. Roosevelt began various programs to address the problems with the soil and the agricultural practices that led to the disaster. The Soil Conservation Service, now the Natural Resources Conservation Service, was established in 1935 to meet the issue as it unfolded. One of their solutions was to plant windbreaks of quickly growing, weather-hearty trees across the Great Plains, and the tree they chose as most suitable was Siberian elm. These were planted and quickly naturalized into the areas they were planted, leading to rapidly increasing populations of this tree. They helped to slow the rate of topsoil erosion and to break up dust storms, serving their purpose admirably.

At the same time, Dutch Elm Disease (DED) became a huge problem globally. An infection of the *Ophiostoma novo-ulmi* fungus carried by elm bark beetles leads to the disease, which is characterized by crown wasting and premature yellowing of leaves. The fungus dissolves the cell walls of the plant to feed on rich carbohydrates in the xylem layer, which causes the tree to produce gum plugs and tyloses (bladder-like extensions of the xylem cells) to try and protect itself. These plugs block fluid from traveling through the xylem, one of the primary vascular layers in the tree, which then starves the affected parts for water and nutrients, leading to eventual death. It was first discovered in 1910, and most strains discovered between then and the 1930s were mild, but a more virulent, contagious strain developed into the late 1960s. By the late 1980s, the majority of the world's elms had died, leaving the landscape greatly changed. It remains a huge problem and ongoing experiments to create resistant cultivars, which started in the 1930s and continue through today, return disappointing results. Some cultivars show promise, such as the Princeton and the Accolade, though they often take a lot of tending in the first decade to avoid DED. Some natural elm species have shown continued resistance, though, among them the Siberian elm.

Not only all of that, but the Siberian elm is also a species that seems capable of weathering the growing issues of climate change. Here in New Mexico, it will one day be one of the only shade trees left in our riparian areas and in our open spaces. It can handle drought and high heat better than most large tree species, as well as soil that has been alkalized due to agriculture and poor water use practices, which is a problem all over the US. Here in the high desert, we will have less and less water as the years proceed, so trees that can both withstand the water we have and the droughts to come are a blessing in any form. Still, because they are considered "invasive," they continue to be the target of eradication campaigns that fell tall, shade-providing trees, which in turn causes the temperature index to rise, especially around cities. When so many trees are dying or struggling across the country, and the temperatures continue to rise due to climate shift, why remove a plant that is succeeding?

As witches, we see a deeper value in this tree, to be sure, particularly in the lore of elms in general. The Siberian elm shares in the lore of its European and American cousins, which usually revolves around either the dead or the fairy folk. Depending on the story and the fairy, they could even be one and the same, as there are a great number of stories in which the spirits of the dead become fairies or take on a fairy-like existence, especially if they are unquiet and unrestful. Spirits like the Cauld Lad of Hylton, a banshee-like entity, and the Sluagh na marbh (the Host of the Dead) are said to be fairies that were once living mortals, for instance. There are many more stories like this, of course, such as the tales of the Dullahan, the headless horseman.

As with caves and caverns, the elm is also considered a sort of door between this world, the Underworld, and the Otherworld (Fairyland). The latter is often described as either an invisible, parallel world or as "under the hollow hills," where the fairies there are called the *aes sidhe* (the people of the hollow hills). This is another link between fairies and the Land of the Dead, as the "hollow hills" are understood to be the cairns and burial mounds of the Ancient Celts and the *aes sidhe* as the remainders of the *Tuatha Dé Danann*, who were defeated and chased away by the Milesians, said to be the ancestors of modern Irish folk.

In Greek mythology, one of the eight hamadryad sisters, Ptelea, is the nymph-goddess of the elm species, who is the very life of the elm. It was the music of Orpheus, however, as he led the shade of his wife, Eurydice, out of Hades and back toward life that caused the first grove of elms to sprout at the gate to the Underworld. Also, when Achilles killed Eetion at Troy, the mountain nymphs (oreads) planted elms upon his tomb. Stories such as this narratively link the elm to the dead and to the presence of souls. Elm was once one of the most common woods chosen for the making of coffins in Europe, as well, probably because it resists rotting underground and tends not to split when nailed together, but possibly also because of its association with tales of the dead and travel between the worlds. Because of its ability to open doors and lead us between worlds, meditation, and offerings left under elms, especially those for the dead or the fairy folk, are particularly potent and well-received.

I include here two more quick stories that I want to relate for the sake of interest. In 2010, the oldest surviving and tallest American elm in the US, a 217-year-old tree named Herbie, was felled after succumbing to DED. It had a circumference of over 20 feet, stood 110 feet tall, and had a crown spread of nearly 100 feet. It was a true giant! Its wood was used to make several items, including a coffin made in secret for the man who had tended Herbie for 50 years, a man named Frank Knight, who died at the age of 103 in 2012. They remain together to this day. It is also an American elm that stands as the Northern feature of the memorial for the Oklahoma City National Memorial, a memorial for the victims of the Oklahoma City bombing of 1995. The tree was badly damaged by the bomb but survived and is now called "The Survivor Tree." It is interesting to me that elm finds a way to continue being a symbol of life and death, even in places where the majority of its lore did not originate.

Grieve, in *A Modern Herbal,* also lists "keels and bilge planks, the blocks and dead eyes of rigging and ship's pumps…wheels, furniture, turned articles and general carpenter's work…the lining of carts, wagons, and wheelbarrows…the outer shell of sheds [and] most of existing farm buildings… Previous to the common employment of cast-iron, elm was very much in use for waterpipes."[74] Elm has been an essential part of human life and the history of our ingenuity and deserves a place of respect in our hearts, even the Siberian elm, which has been invaluable in so many of our efforts.

Siberian elm prefers nutrient-poor, well-drained soils, and direct, intense sunlight, making it perfect for the desert conditions it was introduced to. It has smaller leaves than most elms, each being about 1–2½ inches long, toothed along the edges, and pointed at the tip. They are dark green on top with deep, even venation and light green on bottom where the venation protrudes. The bark of the tree is gray and deeply furrowed once the tree is mature, and it produces a rounded crown of graceful branches. It flowers in spring in greenish, drooping clusters, which give way to lime-green seed pods called *samaras.* These are thin, wafer-like seed coatings that surround a single seed.

The Siberian elm is not as tall and stately as its cousins, the American and red (or slippery) elm, but it is still a lovely tree, despite what so many people say about it. Where European and American elm could reach upwards of 150 feet in height, the Siberian elm maxes out its growth potential at about 60–70 feet.

Susceptible to elm leaf beetles, scale, borers, cankers, and leaf spots, it also tends to drop boughs, but so do all elms and most other trees that harbor water in their trunks and limbs. We cannot fault Siberian elm for doing what its whole family does. Besides, dropped elm boughs are powerfully magical, considered a gift freely given by the spirit of the tree, and the wood is used to make potent items called "elm babies."

Siberian elm is also a good soil remediator, especially for soils toxified due to factory pollution and other heavy metal issues. They are moderate accumulators of aluminum, zinc, lead, nickel, chromium, and arsenic. Do not gather elm from around factories or other large commercial concerns, but in your neighborhood or in parks should be alright.

---

74 Grieve 282.

FORAGING USES

The inner bark of Siberian elm is edible and provides plenty of carbohydrates and calories to keep one going. The powder of the inner bark can be mixed with water to create a sort of gruel, into which other plants can be added to create a tolerable meal. The powder can also be used to thicken stews and as an additive to other flours while baking.

The *samaras* can be harvested in their dry, brown form and winnowed to remove the seed casing, freeing the dried seed. These can be powdered and used as a sort of flour that can be mixed in with others to make them more nutrient-dense. When they are fresh, the seeds are edible raw while they remain green and taste a bit like sweet, nutty citrus. They are mucilaginous, so they will become somewhat slimy as you chew, which is entirely the point and should not alarm you.

The twigs can be chewed on for their mucigenic property and to clean the teeth. The leaves are edible and can be eaten like a sort of salad green (they are also slimy). They have a very lightly bitter flavor but are mostly reminiscent of a tougher spinach. The leaves and fresh seeds of the Siberian elm are some of my favorite spring and summer treats along the trails.

INVASIVE GREENS PASTA

- 1 c. of flour, heaping
- 4–5 egg yolks
- 1 c. elm samaras *or* leaf tips *or* both
- 1 c. horseweed leaves
- 1 c. dandelion greens *or* garlic mustard *or* half of both
- 3 Tbsp . grass-fed butter
- ⅛ tsp. salt
- 1 tsp. minced garlic
- 1–3 Tbsp. goat cheese

1. Chop and steam the greens. They will need to be precooked before adding them to the flour and eggs. Strain the greens thoroughly and chop as finely as possible.
2. Dump the flour out onto a sizeable cutting board and make a crater in the middle. Place your greens and your egg yolks

inside the crater. Begin to mix the yolks, greens, and flour together with your hands.

3. Knead them together until they are a sticky, somewhat stiff dough. Wrap it in plastic wrap and let stand for about 1 hour, out of the fridge.
4. Roll the dough out into a thin sheet. Roll it lengthwise until it becomes a folded tube about 1½ inches wide.
5. Cut into thin strips starting at one end. This will make a hand-cut linguine that can be separated by tossing.
6. Boil the finished pasta for about 2–3 minutes, until they are cooked but a bit chewy (*al dente*).
7. Take about ½ cup of the water out, then strain the pasta.
8. Toss the butter into the pasta pot and sauté the minced garlic with it. Add the salt and your ½ cup of water, stir, then pass your pasta back in and toss together. This should be done quickly to avoid the pasta sticking to itself.
9. Place portions into bowls and add goat cheese on top with pepper (white or pink is best) to taste.

Remedial Applications

It is important to note that Siberian elm can be used in every way that slippery elm (*Ulmus rubra*) is used for. Though it is considered "of least concern," it is difficult to find mature slippery elm trees in the wild because they are susceptible to DED. Therefore, it is better to preferentially use Siberian elm, which will grow almost anywhere and stay healthy for years. Harvesting preferentially from this tree will also help to manage its growth and population, which is important when trying to maintain a balance between invasives and the ecosystem they are in.

Siberian elm inner bark is a light brown color and can be taken from the young branches of the tree by incising bark, which can then be easily decorticated. Use the blade of a knife to strip the inner bark from the outer, or place a strip of the fresh bark in a mortar and pound it until the inner bark separates from the rough, gray, outer bark. This can be stored as is or powdered for later use. This is used for a slew of health concerns, though it is most often used to treat sore throat and cough, bronchitis, upset stomach, and constipation. Elm of various species have also been used for arthritic complaints, wound care, worm and parasite infestation, and as astringents for GI ulcerations, IBS, and diarrhea.

Siberian Elm Slurry

For cough, sore throat, bronchitis, GI dryness, and constipation.

- 1 oz. of Siberian elm inner bark powder
- 1 fl. oz. of cold water
- 1 c. of hot (not boiled) water
- 1 Tbsp. of spices to taste
- 1½ c. dried oats (optional)

1. Mix the Siberian elm bark powder with the cold water until it becomes a slightly runny paste. Allow this to sit for about 10 minutes, and add more cold water to maintain the paste texture.
2. Pour about 1 cup of water that is on the hotter side of warm over the paste, mixing thoroughly.
3. Stir in your spices. Cinnamon, clove, fenugreek, nutmeg, and other aromatic cooking spices are often good choices for this. Drink 2–3 times daily until symptoms subside.
4. To make a sort of porridge, add 1½ cup of dried oats. This makes a particularly useful meal for those who have a hard time eating solids, including infants and the elderly.

Siberian Elm Enema for Worms or Diarrhea

Siberian elm makes a good ingredient in enemas to treat worm and parasite infestations as well as diarrhea.

- 1 oz. of elm bark
- 1 oz. Russian olive leaf
- 1 oz. oak bark

5. Simmer the herbs in about 16 ounces of water for fifteen minutes.
6. Allow to cool to room temperature. Use 8 ounces as an enema twice daily for about a week or until symptoms subside.

Siberian Elm Poultice for Healing Wounds

The bark can also be used to treat wounds, boils, abscesses, and sores, as well as burns, inflammation, and swollen glands.

- 1 oz. powdered Siberian elm bark
- 1 oz. powdered Oregon grape root
- 1 oz. powdered saltcedar leaf tips
- 1 Tbsp. activated charcoal

1. Mix the herbs with just enough hot water to make a paste.
2. Spread this thickly on a bit of gauze, a length of linen, or on a clean rag.
3. Apply directly to the wound, keeping it wet with added water as necessary for fresh wounds and burns, or allow it to dry completely to draw out infection and splinters. If the area is hairy, apply a little oil first to avoid ripping the hair out.

Siberian Elm Astringent Wash

The bark can also be simmered to make an astringent preparation to wash wounds with, to swish over canker sores, to help heal GI ulcerations, and to ease symptoms of IBS and other digestive complaints.

- 1 oz. of Siberian elm bark powder
- 1 qt. of water

1. Bring the water to a low boil and simmer the elm bark for about 20 minutes.
2. Strain and express the water from this, then put it back on the heat until there is only about 1 pint of liquid left. Use this as a wash for wounds and rashes.
3. Add about 1 ounce of this liquid to 1 cup of cold water or add 1 ounce to a tisane made with a mix of calendula, fennel, and caraway (use about 1 teaspoon of herbs for 1 cup of hot water, steep for 10 minutes) and drink 3–4 times daily to aid with GI issues.

SIBERIAN ELM FACE MASK

Elm bark also makes a great addition to face masks to help draw our blackheads, diminish acne, ease redness, and give your skin a luminous glow.

- 2 oz. Siberian elm bark powder
- Honey
- 1 egg white

1. Mix the elm bark with a bit of honey, 1 egg white, and a bit of warm water to make a thick paste.
2. Apply this to the face, avoiding the eyes and lips.
3. Allow to dry for 15–20 minutes, then wash off.

MAGICAL APPLICATIONS

DREAMING

Because of elm's association with travel between worlds, it makes a useful dreaming herb. One of the magical uses of elm I have read in numerous books is to pin one leaf under your pillow to enhance or gain control over your dreams or to dream of a future lover. This is safest when done with a safety pin, but the leaf can also be pinned directly to the mattress using a straight pin. I've had a few people try this, and all have come back with positive results for their desires.

SIBERIAN ELM DREAMING TEA

- 1 part Siberian elm leaves
- ½ part mugwort leaves
- ½ part prickly lettuce leaves
- ¼ part field bindweed flowers

Use about 1 teaspoon per 8 ounces of water and steep for 6–7 minutes. Drink this about 30 minutes to an hour before you plan to go to bed. While you're getting ready for sleep and drinking the tea, think of what you'd like your dreams to help you answer.

Necromancy

As we have mentioned, the elm is a tree of the cemetery, of death, and a favorite of the dead. Therefore, elms make appropriate sites for necromantic operations and offerings to the dead. Libations for the dead are often composed of milk, honey, coffee, fresh water, and things like rum or whiskey, though warm blood is also appropriate. The latter can be purchased from the butcher and warmed on the stove. These can be poured at the roots of a Siberian elm tree before calling on the dead to answer your questions or make pacts with or what have you.

Siberian Elm Necromancy Incense

- 1 part Siberian elm bark powder
- 1 part wormwood
- ½ part horseweed *or* oregano
- ¼ part arrowroot *or* other root starch
- ¼ part storax
- ¼ part blood meal
- ¼ part bone dust
- Honey

To make an incense, finely powder all of the above ingredients, using a sieve to sift out the chunks that resist powdering. You should have an almost talc-like texture. Add honey and mix it with the herbs until the overall consistency is like kinetic sand, meaning it will hold its shape when pressed but crumble apart with little effort. Put this in a jar or plastic bag and let it sit for two weeks. Then, it can be pressed into molds or rolled into small spheres and allowed to dry completely in the open air. Once it is dry, use a charcoal tab, such as a hookah coal, to burn your incense and off it to the spirits of the dead.

Wand of Insufflation

Insufflation is using the breath as part of a rite of exorcism, and elm is very useful here. To make this tool, take a small length of an elm branch, about 4–5 inches long, and use a drill bit to hollow it out. You will be left with a small tube. Anoint this with a suitable oil or tallow infused with something

like saltcedar leaves. Seal it with beeswax and polish the wood. This, you will take to a source of running water, such as a river or stream, on a Saturday in a nighttime hour of Mars, preferably when the Moon is waning or dark. Tie a bit of red thread around the tube and hold the other end, then allow the tube to rest gently in the river so that the water flows over and through it. As you do so, speak a prayer or spell you find suitable. Once the rite is done, take the tube, dry it, and keep it in a black bag between uses.

The Wand of Insufflation is used to breathe exorcising smoke through, to infuse the suffumigating smoke with the wand's virtue before it is used on the person to be cleansed. Between each application, speak an appropriate spell of cleansing. It can also be used to suck spirits out of a person in the process of animaphagy, but this should not be undertaken unless you are trained to do so, as the fallout can be dire. Each time you use this tool, wash it in a river or stream, preferably the one you made the wand in, repeating the initial enchantment.

Distance and Travel

Because of elm's association with travel, such as making carts and lining carriages and wheelbarrows, and because it has been used by peoples the world over to make fine bows, it is useful in creating strength and accuracy over a great distance or in travel magic. It can be a useful addition to most spells, but particularly those meant to affect multiple targets at once of distance and time or that are meant to aid your own travel, be that through the spirit realm or the physical world. Carrying a poke with elm leaves, a piece of sterling silver, three amber beads, and a button or bottle cap can protect you on long journeys.

Slander

Elm is often used in preparations to stop slander against you, such as "shut up" spells. The ashes of the wood used to mark your shoes with a protective symbol helps to avoid gossip and wagging tongues when you are in a large crowd, and elm twigs and stalks of garlic mustard tied in the shape of an "x" with black thread carried in a black poke will protect you from slanderers and keep away unwanted influences.

SWEET CLOVER

(*MELILOTUS OFFICINALIS*) MERCURY—AIR—ARIES

AKA: *Melilot, ribbed melilot, yellow melilot, yellow clover, hart's tree,* king's clover,* luzerne bâtarde, golden crown, sweet besom,* Lady's broom**

Living up to its name, this is a gentle, lovely little plant that grows along the margins of parking lots, along roadsides, and in meadows, particularly those that are often trafficked. They, like all clovers, are part of the *Fabaceae* family, and their pea-like flowers grow in spikes of small, yellow blossoms that smell a bit like vanilla. Their leaves alternate along the stem and end with three oval leaflets in a trident shape. They can grow very tall, especially the white variety called *M. officinalis alba,* sometimes nearly ten feet tall in the right conditions. In our Bosque area in Albuquerque, there is a narrow corridor where the sweet clover grows a few feet over my head, and I'm 6'2". It's a magical, beautiful-smelling path. Sweet clover contains coumarin, which makes it smell incredibly sweet and fragrant, like hay and vanilla, but makes it *taste* terribly bitter.

As with many of the plants we've discussed in this book, sweet clover is a nitrogen fixing soil remediator. It also draws water to the surface layers of the soil, helping the plants around it to stay well-hydrated. This is one of the reasons it is used in mainstay agriculture, to nutrify soil. It is then mowed down, dried well, and used as a forage crop for

livestock. It must be dried properly, though, because when it molds, the coumarin content within the plant degrades to dicoumarol, a massively powerful anti-coagulant and hemorrhagic used in rodenticides. Eating contaminated clover can lead to uncontrollable hemorrhaging and internal bleeding, which can be a major problem for livestock if sweet clover isn't properly dried and molders in the bale. It can also be a problem for humans who eat it, though we do not eat as much as cows, sheep, and goats and are less likely to see a problem from ingesting it.

Foraging Uses

This, as with all clovers, is an edible plant so long as it has not moldered, in which case it becomes a powerful poison. The well-dried blossoms make an excellent, fragrant, sweet jelly, while the fresh blossoms tend to make a slightly more bitter and green one. They can also be eaten fresh in salads for a bitter-sweet flavor among your greens. They can also be used in baking, as the flowers can be powdered and used as a flour additive to give your bread a bit of that hay-like flavor that goes well with honey.

Sweet Melilot Clover Rolls

- 2¼ tsp. dry active yeast
- 1 c. water, warm
- 2½ c. flour of your choice
- ½ c. powdered sweet clover blossoms
- 4 Tbsp. honey
- 3 Tbsp. butter, melted and cool
- 1 tsp. salt
- Olive oil
- 1 beaten egg, for wash
- Muffin pan

1. Put the warm water in the bowl you intend to mix in and sprinkle the yeast over it. Allow this to proof for about 8–10 minutes.
2. In a separate bowl, combine the flour and powdered sweet clover blossoms with the salt.

3. After the yeast is proofed, slowly mix in the honey and butter.
4. Once those are thoroughly mixed, begin to add in the dry ingredients, about a cup at a time. Mix until the dough becomes an easily managed ball. If it remains sticky, add a tablespoon of flour at a time until it isn't.
5. Grease a bowl and put the dough into it, cover it, then let it rise for about an hour.
6. Press the air from the dough and parcel it out into about 12 pieces or however many muffin cups your pan has. Tear those pieces into thirds and roll them into balls.
7. Grease your muffin cups and place a set of three dough balls in each cup. Cover the pan and let the dough rise again for about 30 minutes. Preheat your oven to about 425°F.
8. Once the dough has risen, beat your egg with a bit of water and use that to wash your dough balls before baking. This will make them nice and glossy. Sprinkle a bit of sweet clover blossom over the top, just to be cute.
9. Bake these for 8–12 minutes or until they are golden brown. Let them rest for about 5 minutes before serving with butter, sweet clover honey, and sweet clover jelly!

Remedial Applications

Coumarin, the primary constituent of sweet clover, is an anticoagulant. It is potentized and sold commercially by pharmaceutical companies as a blood thinner, though it merely stops the aggregation of platelets and prohibits the formation of thromboses (blood clots). Because of this, if you are on blood thinners, use caution when using this plant, as it can push a body toward internal bleeding if there is already thin blood in the veins.

The tea has been imbibed for headaches, especially those resulting from nerve impingements and stress, for stomach upset, as a diuretic, and to relieve muscle pain. It combines well with willow bark and meadowsweet for a pain-relieving tea. Topically, it is used to soften scar tissue, particularly as a compress, and it also helps to soften and beautify skin in general. It can also aid with arthritic pains and inflammations, varicosities, and to heal wounds, sores, and ulcers. Sweet clover has an antimicrobial action that also helps to keep wounds clean, making it a useful addition to things like tattoo salves. The flowers and leaves can be used to make a wash for tired, dry eyes.

Because it has blood-thinning and anticoagulant properties, it should be ingested with great caution if you are using any pharmaceuticals that do the same. Also, if you are pregnant or breastfeeding, this may be one to steer clear of.

Magical Applications

Sweet clover can be used as a replacement for sweetgrass (*Hierochloe odorata*), which is sacred to several indigenous groups between the US and Canada but has become overharvested due to its commercialization. In my experience, sweet clover does something very similar and works very well as an offering herb and as a smoke to draw in kind spirits. All you need to do is gather the herb, cut it to the size you want your suffumigation wand to be, dry it *very* well, and then tie the bits together with twine. This will make a very useful smoke stick for blessings and offerings.

TAMARISK

(*Tamarix ramosissima*) Saturn—Earth—Libra

AKA: *Saltcedar, fairy duster, pink cascade, western river willow, fern willow*

This may be one of the most hated plants in America while also being a prized, showy garden shrub. It has very graceful, red-barked fronds covered in feathery green leaves that are reminiscent of juniper, though it is not coniferous or even evergreen. The bark is striated with thin, gray indentations that make the whole branch look strongly jointed and serpentine. The flowers show up around mid-summer and form plumes of pink flowers that look like dusting rods. They smell sweet, scenting the air with a tinge of sugar and salt. The tree typically grows between 6–15 feet tall.

It tolerates very poor soil and prefers sandy environments, meaning it can quickly populate many riparian areas, in which it has become invasive in the US. In New Mexico, where I live, there is a stretch of the Rio Grande about two miles long that is almost uniformly populated by tamarisk, which demonstrates how well it can overtake an area once it is established there. However, seedlings of tamarisk do *not* outcompete most other shade-tolerant plants, and there is recent evidence showing that box elder (*Acer negundo*) may be able to overshade tamarisk and bring a better balance to the ecosystems in which it needs management.

In order to solve problems caused by erosion and sedimentation that clog dams, reducing power outputs and overall efficiency, tamarisk trees were purposefully planted upstream of various such watercourse structures. Their root systems very effectively harbor fine sediments, meaning that they act as natural filters for river water, thus aiding the dams further downstream. They also help to filter salt from river water, which has become a problem, as they have become about 53% saltier since the development of our modern agricultural methods and water use practices.

Tamarisk prolifically takes up salt, which gives it the common name "saltcedar." It is a valued garden shrub in seaside areas, as it can withstand very high levels of salt in soils. As I've mentioned, due to the methods of fertilization and irrigation used by the agricultural industry in the US, mining operations, and methods of natural gas extraction, waterways are becoming more and more salinated, which makes it hard for most native plants to thrive. Tamarisk is a plant that helps to *desalinate* water, meaning it is a powerful ally in the remediation of riparian soils. Now, part of its ecology is to uptake salt, move that to its leaves, and then drop them, potentially increasing surface salination in the soil through leaf litter. Research shows, however, that this is not a problem in areas that are allowed to flood, as the leaf litter is washed away during the spring. They also do not become overly invasive in those areas because their seed is washed away. Tamarisk most often becomes invasive in areas that have historically been flood plains but are no longer allowed to flood due to common water use practices and upriver damming, such as our Bosque de Albuquerque, where tamarisk is becoming more prolific.

Another point worth mentioning is the perceived amount of water that is "wasted" by tamarisk. Research that has since been discredited showed that tamarisk uptakes and evapotranspirates water at twice the rate of other plants. Better and more recent research shows that the tree is an intermediate user of water, whereas native cottonwoods, which are enormous, short-lived trees, are the highest users. In fact, observation after eradication efforts clearly shows that tamarisk does not lend to a reduction in water availability but rather the opposite. Also, in areas where tamarisk was widely destroyed, animal species fared worse, including some endangered bird species, water availability decreased, and salinity remained about the same, so we also know that tamarisk is not the villain that it has been made out to be. If they are kept in balance within an ecosystem, the environment will be truly better off for having tamarisk in it.

Foraging Uses

Tamarisk can be harvested as a green, which is a common use for it in the Mediterranean region. In Greece, it is called *almyrikia* and is one of the earliest warm-weather greens. The young leaves are supple and salty, making them a delicious, steamed veggie option. The flowers can be added to honey, making for a sweet, floral spread that can be used on pastries, toast, crackers, bread, and with cheese dishes.

Almyrikia with Baked Feta and Lemon Sauce

- 1 lb. tamarisk leaves
- 8 oz. feta cheese block, whole
- 1 c. cherry tomatoes, halved
- 1 c. bell pepper, sliced
- 1 c. red onion, diced
- 1 lemon
- Greek olive oil
- Salt, pepper, and oregano to taste

1. Begin by preheating your oven to 400°F and preparing a small, heat-safe dish, such as a ramekin. Put a thin layer of olive oil on the bottom of the dish, sprinkle in salt, pepper, and oregano, then your tomatoes, bell peppers, and onions. Toss all of this together.
2. Form a small well in the middle of your oiled veggies large enough for your cheese block and place it in the well. Place this in the oven for about 30 minutes.
3. After about 15 minutes have passed, bring a pot of water to a boil. Toss your tamarisk leaves in and allow them to boil for about 10 minutes or until they are tender.
4. While the leaves are boiling, cut and juice the lemons into a small bowl. Mix in about the same amount of olive oil, then sprinkle it with salt, pepper, and oregano to taste. Whisk these together briskly.
5. Once your leaves are tender, strain them from the water.
6. Take your cheese out of the oven. It should be lightly browned, and the veggies should be nicely baked and tender. Place the cheese on a serving dish or platter, placing the roasted veggies

around it. On top of the cheese, place your tamarisk leaves. Drizzle the whole thing with the lemon and oil sauce, then serve while it is still hot. This can be eaten by itself or with bread.

Remedial Applications

Of all the invasives I work with, I rely on tamarisk most often for wound care and keeping wounds clean. It is highly antimicrobial, partially on account of its high salt content, and makes an excellent tattoo salve. It is also useful as a styptic to treat intestinal issues and dental issues, to protect and heal the liver, and even to help manage diabetes.

Tamarisk Wound Salve

- 1 oz. tamarisk leaves
- ½ oz. Russian olive flower and leaf
- ½ oz. yarrow leaf and flower
- 32 oz. oil of choice
- 4 oz. beeswax

1. Put your oil into a saucepan and put over a medium heat.
2. Add the tamarisk, Russian olive, and yarrow, stirring frequently. Do not allow the oil to crisp the herbs. If they begin to cook, take the oil off of the heat. Repeat this step twice if you'd like.
3. Strain the oil from the herb using a cloth. Measure the amount of oil you still have, then add more to make it 32 ounces.
4. In a double boiler, melt together the herb-infused oil and 4 ounces. of beeswax (1 ounce. of beeswax per cup of oil).
5. Pour into jars of your choice, allow to cool, and apply as needed to cuts, burns, and other minor wounds.

Hepatoprotective Tamarisk Tincture (1:4)

- 2 oz. tamarisk leaves and flowers
- 1 oz. juniper berries, crushed
- ½ oz. burdock root
- ½ oz. barberry root
- 16 oz. vodka or other 40% abv liquor

1. Place your herbs and your liquor of choice into a blender. Allow to blend at a low speed for about 5 minutes. Decant this into a jar and let sit for 4–6 weeks.
2. Strain through a cloth and place into an amber or cobalt bottle, pouring off dosage bottles (droppers) as needed.
3. Dosage: 10–30 drops 3 times daily for 7 days. Take at least 3 days off. Do *not* use while pregnant or breastfeeding, if you have a concurrent eruption of measles, or if you are suffering a fever.

Magical Applications

Tamarisk is one of the most potent herbs I use for protection and purification. Its natural salt content makes it a perfect choice for these kinds of magic, not to mention healing spells and charms meant to halt or constrain illness. It also makes a powerful addition to preparations meant to draw on the powers of Saturn, particularly bindings on spiritual beings or bringing a close to spirit contracts, but also to bring resolve and straightforward, honest resolutions. One of the easiest ways to use tamarisk is the creation of *Green salt,* which is a preparation of powdered tamarisk leaves mixed with sea salt, though other protective herbs, such as nettle, can be added. Green salt is used to call on the energy of the Earth, the force called "the Green," and can be used as a protective and healing ingredient in various spells and charms.

Green Salt

To make Green salt, simply mix 2 parts tamarisk leaves with 1 part sea salt. Because of the Saturnine nature of this plant, prepare it in an earthen vessel on a Saturday, preferably at the mid-point of the day, during a waxing or full moon.

Green Chalk

Green chalk is a great way to prepare this salt for convenient use, particularly if you are using it to draw circles or glyphs on surfaces or to draw symbols around candle spells.

- 1 Tbsp. Green salt
- 1 Tbsp. eggshell powder (cascarilla)
- 1 tsp. all-purpose flour
- Water

1. Add your Green salt, eggshell, and flour to a bowl. Whisk them together thoroughly. You can also add egg *whites* if you have them, just to act as an extra binder.
2. Add just enough water to make a paste. You may add green food coloring if you want it to be *very* green.
3. Place this into a mold of your choice. I use water bottle ice cube trays, which make a nicely shaped piece of chalk.
4. Allow this to dry completely, which can take a few weeks. Pop the chalk out of your molds and use it as you will!

TAMARISK SCOURGE

This type of scourge is meant to whip the shadow of a person to remove ill-fortune, *mal ojo* (evil eye), and other pernicious and malevolent conditions. It may also be used to whip the air of a space to chase away unwanted spirits and entities, especially while you are suffumigating the space with juniper or sage smoke. The following charm requires three "heart lengths" of twine. To measure a heart length, hold the working end of your twine to your heart, then extend your arm fully to the side to get one heart length. In this case, you will do this once to the left and once to the right, thus getting two heart lengths for each color of twine that is called for.

- 13 tamarisk switches, defoliated
- 2 heart lengths red twine
- 2 heart lengths black twine
- 2 heart lengths white twine
- Blacking

1. Gather your tamarisk switches on a Saturday in the first hour of Saturn, usually sometime around 3 a.m. If this is too difficult or dangerous, choose a nighttime hour that works better for you.
2. In the following hour of the Sun, cleanse and purify your tamarisk switches and your lengths of twine by burning a bit

Green salt on a charcoal and bathing the fronds in the smoke. You may also use something like frankincense or another purifying smoke of your choice.

3. In the next hour of Saturn, tie your switches together using the black thread, saying:

   "Saturn, great binder of all things, bring for the black spirits and give this tool the authority to constrain all conditions, entities, and spirits who are put to its lash."

4. In the next hour of Mars, tie them with the red twine, saying:

   "Mars, fiery lord of all change and motion, bring forth the red spirits and give this tool the forceful nature to chase out and castigate all conditions, entities, and spirits brought under its strike."

5. In the next hour of the Moon, tie them with white thread, saying:

   "Moon, great mother and mistress of transitions, behold me with all your faces. Bring for the white spirits and give this tool the grace to remove all conditions, entities, and spirits from where they meet this whip to a place in better alignment to the wellbeing of all those involved in this rite."

6. In the third hour of Saturn, use a paintbrush or simply dip the tips of your scourge into the blacking, saying:

   "As this tool is marked by the black blood of Saturn, so shall the conditions, entities, and spirits that it touches be marked. Those who are marked must obey my command and be removed from this person/space in all aspects and dimensions of all realities throughout the multiverse, infinitely throughout all time. So it is."

7. Use this scourge to whip shadows and rooms to remove unwanted energies from your person or space. It can be stored until it is needed, then cleansed after use.

Tamarisk Spirit Trap

Sometimes pesky, mischievous spirits are hard to get rid of. They may only make visits to your space to cause a ruckus and not be present for various cleansings and they may even be able to figure out ways around wards and protective spells. This is a trap meant to be set for this type of entity.

- 6 tamarisk switches, defoliated
- Black twine
- Glass globe, fillable
- Seeds, colorful string, and various trinkets

1. Using three of your switches and some twine, create a triangle. To the base corners of this, tie two more switches to create another triangle pointing in the opposite direction. Bend these together so they are sitting at a forty-five-degree angle to each other, more or less. Use your sixth switch to tie between the apexes of these triangles, thus creating a three-dimensional object.
2. Fill the glass globe (craft Christmas ornaments work a treat for this) with birdseed, colorful pieces of thread and yarn, and other countable things like mustard seed, beans, or beads. If you can't find a glass globe, a cobalt blue bottle will also work.
3. Hang the seed-filled globe inside the triangular structure from its apex so it dangles inside when you hold it up.
4. From the structure, you may also hang interesting little baubles, toys, and other things that spirits find alluring. In the lore of various cultures, mischievous spirits often get wrapped up in counting things like seeds or playing with toys that are left out for them, so these act as good distractions.
5. Hang this in the space you need to protect or the room where the spirit causes the most trouble.
6. The point here is to distract the spirit in such a way that it becomes perpetually more interested in your trap rather than what you're doing. It becomes unable to leave the trap and can be cleansed from it via smoke or by leaving the trap in direct sunlight for about an hour.

TREE OF HEAVEN

(*AILANTHUS ALTISSIMA*) MARS—FIRE—SAGITTARIUS

AKA: *Skunk sumac, stink tree, varnish tree, Chinese sumac, paradise tree, copal tree, ghetto palm, angel's ladder,* tree of Hell, Horned King's steed,* conjurewood,* Simon-summon-up**

In Betty Smith's book *A Tree Grows in Brooklyn,* Tree of Heaven is a symbol of resiliency in the face of trauma and hardship, yet of all the plants I've written of in this book, this one is probably the *most* hated. It's hard to find even one kind word written about it, though it's one of my absolute favorite trees. Though many of its common names refer to it as a sumac, it is not one. Its foliage resembles the genus *Rhus,* even the red coloration of new growth. The leaves are long, sometimes up to three feet, with pairs of glossy, medium-to-dark green leaflets all the way down to the tip where a single leaflet usually protrudes. The leaf bud is a small, dome-shaped protrusion on the branch, and the leaf grows from underneath it. When the leaves fall, they leave a scar and the leaf bud behind, making a series of markings that look like angels up and down the bark.

Another diagnostic feature of this tree is the distinct smell of the leaves and flowers, which has been described as peanut-like, cashew-like, or rotting nuts. I rather like the smell, but it is most often called "foul" or "offensive." The bark itself is a bronzish-red when it is young, becoming gray to brown and textured very much like a rough cantaloupe. The older wood of this tree is very soft and light, though it becomes rather sturdy after drying, and the twigs and smaller branches are filled with a spongey, brown pith that grows harder over time.

Tree of Heaven is dioecious, meaning that a tree is either male or female. In the early summer, male trees produce greenish, yellow flowers that look like bursts of fireworks. The females will later produce pendulous clusters of seed pods, each a single seed in a twisting samara. The twist gives the seedpod spin when it falls, aiding in wind-dispersed reproduction. Tree of Heaven, however, tends to grow in clonal colonies through very aggressive suckering. These sprouts can grow up to fifty feet from the mother tree and become *more* aggressive if the mother tree is felled. In fact, it is almost impossible to kill an *A. altissima,* as it will sprout dozens of saplings from a single stump and sucker in every direction, which is part of the reason for the vitriol thrown at it. It is the fastest-growing tree in North America, and it can rapidly take over gaps of sunlight.

The tree prefers full sun and is very shade-intolerant, so it will do its best to dominate a nice, shady spot. It is also tolerant of a multitude of soil types and pH levels, preferring loamy soil with a high limestone content. It can tolerate a variety of water conditions, though it prefers moderate water, and it does not enjoy flooding or having very wet roots. Cold and wintery conditions (temperatures below 46°F) will cause it to die off until the spring, when it will explode from the earth with a million saplings growing from its roots. They grow mostly in (you guessed it!) disturbed areas or highly modified areas, such as along rail tracks, near mining operations, and along field margins.

It may also enter undisturbed areas, which is an indicator that the ecosystem is more modified than it may appear. The soil is probably low in phosphorus due to dry soil conditions, fertilizer and herbicide injury, soil compaction, and other issues. There may also be high salinity, again because of our fertilization and irrigation practices and our water use practices that restrict water flow and do not allow historic flooding areas to flood (which would naturally maintain *Ailanthus*). There is likely an excessive number of air-borne pollutants, such as carbon dioxide and sulfur dioxide,[75] which Tree of Heaven is very efficient at harboring in its leaves, as well as dust and car exhaust. Native plants, most of which are less tolerant to heightened

75 Sulfur dioxide is an extremely toxic gas that has proliferated through our air via the burning of fossil fuels and through the copper extraction processes essential to the electronics trade.

Solar intensity because of ozone depletion, may not be able to live in the areas that Tree of Heaven can, as it tolerates fairly intense Sun. The tissues of Ailanthus have also been shown to accumulate mercury, meaning it also cleans the damaged soil it colonizes, which seems like a good thing to me.

Trees of this species are the preferred food for the ailanthus silk moth (*Samia cynthia*), which hosts its eggs and larvae exclusively on *A. altissima*. It feeds on other plants, such as castor beans, but prefers Tree of Heaven. Though it is not as important to silk production as the silk moth, it still has an economic and cultural importance that makes the importance of Tree of Heaven worth consideration, not to mention the other members of the Lepidoptera family, including the Indian moon moth, and over forty other species that rely on this tree.

Another insect that prefers the Tree of Heaven as a habitat is the spotted lanternfly. For the amount of hatred these bugs get, you would think they were particularly dangerous, though evidence shows they are merely a nuisance. They can't bite humans or animals, there is no substantial evidence that they are toxic to pets, and they feed mainly on agricultural crops such as grapes and fruit trees, leaving most natives and other trees alone. They produce honeydew, which is a sticky excretion from the anus of the insect that has a sugary taste beloved by wasps, bees, and ants (which are also often considered pest species). The honeydew may host sooty mold, which can be problematic for plants, as it inhibits their ability to photosynthesize and can lead to death. However, there are many other insects that produce this substance and cause the same issue, so it isn't only the lantern fly that is to blame.

They *are* foreign, though, and damaging to cash crops and profit margins, as well as simply bothersome, so they have become a believable target of the propaganda of invasive biology. Because of their tight associations, management of Tree of Heaven will help to manage spotted lanternfly populations, not perfectly but to some degree. Though it is hearty and difficult to manage, it can be thinned through mechanical removal, which is much easier before the tree is established. The chemical suggestion is glyphosate applied directly to a fresh stump, but even that isn't enough to ensure the tree will die. I think it is better to tend to the trees that have established, keep them happy to avoid extreme suckering, and remove saplings as they sprout in areas that are undesirable. We should always be solution-minded, not eradication minded.

Besides, we brought them west as an ornamental. During the mid-late seventeenth-century *chinoiserie,* the replication, emulation, and appropriation

of Chinese and other Asiatic art forms and gardening styles was all the rage. *Ailanthus* was imported as a handsome addition to ornamental gardens, with its lovely red foliage, its shiny bark, and its bursts of yellow flowers. Of course, no one had studied them long enough to know about their suckering habits, their smell, and their prolific seeding, so they fell out of style, but not before they became established and now exist on every continent except Antarctica. I guess the joke was on the *chinoiserie* enthusiasts.

Foraging Uses

There are no reasons to eat this tree, so instead, I will mention here that it is a very useful tree for starting fires, from kindling to wood. It drops an enormity of biomass and the leaves are quick to catch fire. Because they are somewhat spongey and porous, the twigs make great kindling that burns quickly. The wood from older parts of the tree is hard but flexible, meaning it will burn slowly and well and doesn't tend to smell fetid as it does so. This means it's a great wood to explore for camp and cooking fires.

It is also one of the only leafy trees that can support itself in some environments, and it harbors water in its roots, so water can be gathered from the tree. Dig at the roots and you will find a good amount of water bound into the soil, or adhere a plastic bag around a well-leafed twig and wait. The tree will release water through the leaves as it breathes, and though it isn't much, it *will* collect in your bag. It is better to use multiple bags on multiple trees to get enough water for a day, as each twig will probably afford you enough for a swig or two after a whole day of evaporating. Because of the rapidity of its growth, its rate of metabolism, and how well leaved Tree of Heaven is, it makes a perfect choice for this process.

Remedial Applications

This is a plant that must be used with caution and in small doses. Larger doses will cause vomiting, dizziness, stomach upset, and body weakness. If you are on blood pressure medication, this is not the plant for you to use internally. Tree of Heaven has a long history of use in herbalism, particularly in traditional Chinese medicine, where it is used as an anti-malarial and a drying astringent to ease diarrhea and dysentery. The root bark is considered the most efficacious part of the plant and is made into a tincture. Only 5–20 drops are given at a time to avoid stomach upset. An aqueous infusion (decoction) may also be made using a third of an ounce for 16 ounces of water. Include things like licorice root (if you don't have hypertension), peppermint, chamomile, or spearmint in conjunction with this one to further mitigate possible stomach issues.

Heavenly Activated Charcoal For Diarrhea

- Medium fire, outside or in the hearth (Always have a fire extinguisher on hand)
- 1 pot with vented lid *or* a kettle
- 1 colander for washing the charcoal
- 1 large dish for mixing
- Enough bark and root bark of *A. altissima* to fill the pot
- ⅓ c. Calcium chloride solution *or* lemon juice

1. You will need to build a medium fire, either outside or in your home fireplace. Adhere to all fire safety concerns and have a fire extinguisher on hand. The fire should be large and hot enough to burn wood inside of a pot or kettle.
2. The pot you choose for this should have a vented lid, like a camping pot, or have a spout like a kettle where gasses can escape. It *must* have a lid, though, and must be mostly enclosed. I've also used a cookie tin with holes punched in the top for making charcoal, which works fine.
3. The wood you use should be bark from a Tree of Heaven—twig, branch, and root. If you can't get enough to fill the pot, you can add in coconut shell or other edible hardwoods that will char up nicely. Make sure it is as dry as possible before you begin. Place the wood in your pot loosely but firmly. You don't need to pack it full.
4. Roast the wood in the pot for 3–5 hours until steam and gas stop emitting from the vent. Let it go for about 30 more minutes, then pull it off of the fire, open the pot, and allow it to cool completely.
5. Once the charcoal is cool enough to touch, place it into your colander. Wash away all the ash and debris that have accumulated on it so that you are left with only black chunks.
6. Grind it to a fine powder. You can use a mortar and pestle, coffee grinder, or blender. I will often use a combo, starting

with a blender, then sifting the charcoal through a sieve, then putting the small chunks that are left in a coffee grinder, sifting it again, and finally grinding the smallest bits in a mortar. Any pieces that don't powder down finely can be tossed away or composted. Barring all of that, you can also put it in a bag and smash it with a hammer, which is always fun.

7. Allow the powder to dry completely, which takes about 24 hours. Touch the powder to make sure.
8. Now comes the chemistry. To make a calcium chloride ($CaCl_2$) solution, you will need 100 grams of calcium chloride powder and 1.3 ounces of water. Mix these together, but be *very* cautious as this mixture will get *very* hot and can cause burns. If you can't get the $CaCl_2$, then you can use 1.3 cups of lemon juice instead. It's also a bit safer and equally useful.
9. Put your charcoal powder in a large mixing bowl. Stir your $CaCl_2$ solution or lemon juice into the charcoal a little bit at a time, mixing it thoroughly until it becomes a black paste. Once this happens, stop adding the solution of juice, cover the bowl, and wait for 24 hours.
10. Drain any remaining liquid from the bowl so the charcoal remains damp, but not swimming.
11. Transfer the charcoal to a heat-safe pot with a lid (you may use the same pot you used for roasting) and put it back over a fire or a medium-high heat on your stove for about 3 hours.
12. For diarrhea, drink 4 ounces of water, then mix a teaspoon of your activated charcoal into 8 ounces of water and drink that. Follow with another 4 ounces of fresh water. Do that up to 3 times a day until the diarrhea stops.
13. Activated charcoal can also be used as a filter to clean air and water as well, so it's a handy thing to have around.

Magical Applications

Of all the woods that grow in my region, it is *Ailanthus* that I consider most potent for the command of spirits and for conducting them from one place to the other. The angel marks along the branch harken back to Jacob's Ladder, the vision of angels traveling to and from Heaven, and the wood makes an excellent tool for calling spirits to a sacred space. My stang is a triple-tined Tree of Heaven trunk, and it has served me well for many years. Thin Tree of Heaven twigs and branches marked with leaf scars make useful additions to spirit vessels, as well.

Familiar Spirit Tree (of Heaven) House

- 1 glass bottle
- 1 handful of graveyard dirt (paid for)
- 3 Tree of Heaven twigs, marked with leaf scars, angel heads upwards
- Personal effects and sympathetic representation
- Herbs and other additions to make the vessel comfortable

1. Bless all of your items in a purificatory and blessing smoke, such as Russian olive or rosemary. Make sure to get inside the bottle.
2. Pour in your graveyard dirt.

   "Let this soil be a place of stability, a place of comfort, a place to anchor you here upon the material plane on your sojourn from the spirit world."

3. Place the twigs of the Tree of Heaven in the jar.

   "This twig is a bridge for your soul. This twig is a bridge for your spirit. This twig is a bridge for your body. May you be fully present here within the vessel, so we may make conversation between us."

4. Add in your symbolic representations of your familiar or sympathetic links. Your familiar, if you have one, will likely lead you through choosing these items or provide them, but you can also use things like raven feathers, toad skin, eggshells, cat fur, or anything else that speaks to the form your familiar takes while it is here.
5. Add things your familiar likes or herbs of comfort like lemon balm, damiana, Russian olive fruits, blue vervain, or chamomile.

VELVETWEED

(*Oenothera curtiflora*) Venus—Water—Aquarius

AKA: *Lizard tail gaura, scarlet gaura, velvet gaura. Clockweed, Gaura parviflora, Devil's whip,* Lady's tongue,* speak-it-true**

Velvetweed is a stately plant, usually being about three to four feet tall but sometimes growing to over eight feet tall. They prefer soils that are not nutrient-dense and can withstand high salinity in soils, making them excellent additions to riparian areas that suffer from salination. The leaves of this plant alternate in pairs, spiraling around the stalk, and are the softest I've ever felt on a plant, the quality that gives them their common name. The leaves are also always noticeably cold to the touch, which is an interesting sensation on a hot day. The stalk ends in a long, trailing spike of white-to-pink flowers that whip about in the breeze like a lizard's tail, thus its *other* common name. Each flower is a tiny, perfect example of what evening primrose flowers ought to look like. It is a truly beautiful plant that is such a pleasure to deal with.

O. curtiflora is actually native to North America but has become an invasive due to human-driven ecosystem shifts, much like juniper. They are fast spreaders because their tail-like flower spikes fling seeds far away from the mother plant, strewing them in all directions. When I was a child, these were very sparse in the mountains I grew up in. My aunt had them on her property and my mother loved the curling, pink flowers so much that my aunt dug one up and planted it on my mother's land for her birthday one year. Within a few years after that, it became ubiquitous around my childhood home and spread all across the mesa, filling the landscape with waving tails of pink and white. It would probably have done this anyway, so no harm done, really.

Velvetweed does not pose a threat to environments in any way other than being a prolific seeder and, therefore, a possible contender for nutrients and water availability. However, because of its ability to clean salt from water and soil, it is more often a help than a hindrance to other plants in an area.

Foraging Uses

There is very little information on the edibility of this species, but it *can* be eaten, as all the *Oenothera* family plants are edible, and this one is no exception. The flowers are more edible than the leaves, as the latter are covered in soft hair. The root has been eaten like a roasted vegetable, often added to stews or mixed with meat. I have not eaten it myself, so I cannot report on its taste.

Remedial Applications

This plant's medicine most often has to do with snake bites, much like echinacea. A decoction of the root is prepared and given to the victims of snake bites or, in the case of the Zuni people, the root is chewed by a person before they suck on a snake bite to remove the venom, and a poultice of the root is applied to the bite. Another use is found in its leaves, which are consistently cold to the touch, likely because of the way the plant evaporates salt from its cells. They are used to ease fever by placing them against the forehead and to provide relief from inflammation, particularly of delicate or tender tissues, by using them in a poultice applied directly to the area in question. Infusing the aerial parts into oil creates a useful remedy for sunburn and other hot surface inflammations of the skin.

Magical Applications

One of the ways this plant is used magically is to help promote sleep and good dreams simply by placing the leaves in one's pillowcase, a practice of the Western Keres people. Because of its association with lizards, it has also been used as a charm for strength, health, and grace. Lizards are also considered lucky and clever, so this plant makes a good addition to gambling oils or charms meant to increase acuity, speed up thought, and sharpen wit. Some cultures also associate them with death, so velvetweed can also be used as a funerary or necrosophic plant and added into necromantic formulas for moving and compelling the dead.

VELVETWEED SLEEP CHARM

For this, take seven mature leaves and either place them directly in the pillowcase or sew them into a sachet with lavender and one Siberian elm leaf before placing it under the pillow. This charm should be changed out frequently.

VELVETWEED STRENGTH CHARM

- 1 velvetweed root
- 1 red pouch
- 1 length of red thread
- Vectors of target

1. The root of the plant can be used in magic to bring strength, resiliency, surety, and power to a person. Various Plains peoples have sewn the umbilical cord of little boys into bags that resemble lizards or are beaded to look like one. For us, we need only tie the vectors (personal effects) of the target to a velvetweed root with red thread and then tie it into a red pouch. While you tie the vectors to the root and the charm into the bag, sing:

   "Lizard, hurry, hurry,
   as you scurry!
   If you lose your tail,
   Grow another without fail.
   North is always true,
   South forever sure, for you."

2. Once the bag is completed, carry it with you when you need a boost of strength or confidence. Reenchant the charm on Solar holidays, such as solstices and equinoxes.

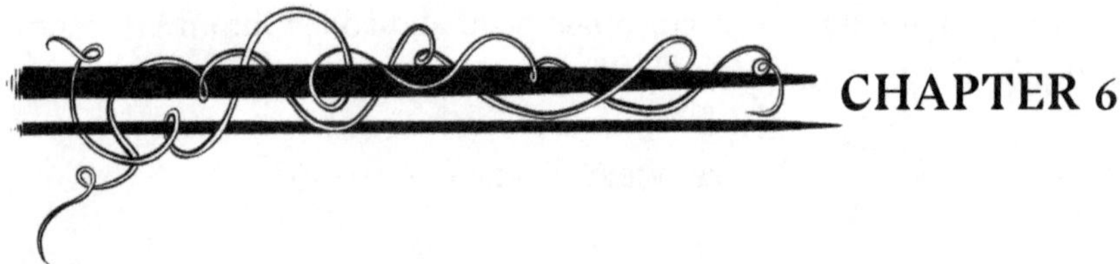

CHAPTER 6

Honor-herbal Mentions

I WISH I COULD WRITE ABOUT EVERY INVASIVE PLANT I can think of or have been asked about over the years, but there isn't enough time and space to do so in this book. So, instead of giving them larger sections, I've decided to say just a few interesting things about the plants that I didn't have time to write about, have been written on by many others, or didn't make the initial cut and still deserve a little limelight. Perhaps I'll write more in-depth entries for them in later works.

CHEATGRASS

(*Bromus tectorum*) Mercury—Air—Gemini

AKA: *Smoke grass,* hide-me-now grass,* downy brome, bronco grass, downy chess, dropping brome, June grass, early chess, military chess, thatch grass*

There are few plants I find hard to like, but this one took a while for me to find a reason. It is one of the invasive grasses that truly causes more problems than it solves, but it does have its uses. In forests that were traditionally managed with low-intensity fires, this grass may help to turn around some of the degradation caused by current mismanagement through burning it. It can act as a food plant, and the seeds can be made into a gruel, though not a very palatable one. The seeds can also be roasted and winnowed to make a sort of nutty-tasting food. I most like this plant for magical purposes. When it is pollinating, a stand of cheatgrass almost looks as if it is already on fire, as the surroundings will be hazy as if with smoke. This is why I call it "smoke grass" and use it in preparations meant for invisibility and obfuscation, sometimes to instill fear. The seeds and dried heads also make a tolerable smoking herb. It can also be added to incense meant to help give form to spirits, used in preparations for renewal and rebirth, and for protection.

DANDELION

(*TARAXACUM OFFICINALE*) SUN—JUPITER—EARTH—LEO

AKA: *Fairy clock, piss-a-bed, dente de leon, lion's tooth, cankerwort, Irish daisy, monk's head, priest's crown, puffball, blowball, earth nail, witch's gown, make-a-wish, wishball, Hekate's key**

Though it is often plucked and tossed at the first sign of its growth, dandelion is one of the earliest food sources for pollinators. It also acts as a powerful nitrogen fixer, aerates the soil with its long tap root, increases water permeability, and adds a good amount of biomass back into the Land when they die. The entire plant is edible, even the seeds, once they are separated from the pappus (white fluff). If you know how to make ice cream, try a green tea and dandelion leaf flavor, which is very tasty! The root also makes delightful, bitter pickles, and the blossoms are used in dandelion wine.

The root is useful for the colon and liver, reducing overall heat and stagnation body-wide. If there is generalized inflammation, especially with heat or deep aches and pain, dandelion root is indicated. The leaf is useful for the kidney, helping the organ to get rid of what is unnecessary while retaining vital nutrients and balancing hydration, as it is full of sodium and potassium. It works very well with hibiscus and citrus. Both the leaf and root are used in the case of gall and kidney stones as well as gall bladder disorders. The blossom is a lymphagogue and helps move surface fluids through the body, easing inflammation and fluid retention in connective tissue and helping with general immune system cleanup. Picked fresh and wilted, the blossoms make a very effective infused oil to ease the pain of sore, inflamed breast tissue. It is, overall, an opening and lifting herb that dives down into the deepest tissues to bring them light, movement, and nourishment.

I call this plant "Hekate's key" because its root reaches so deep into the earth that it must enter the Underworld at some point! I use the root in incense blends and hashes meant to provide protection and guidance on Underworld journeys and to help open doors that may be closed to me otherwise. Dandelion root can also make a very serviceable type of protective *alraun,* especially if you are not privy to having thick, fresh mandrake roots. They can also be used in love magic, according to Corrinne Boyer, and I think they can be put to good use in the ancient graveyard rites for bringing love. The leaves are used in love magic and to bring prophetic dreams. The whole plant can be used in magic to aid in divination.

The blossoms are Solar emblems, bringing joy and courage. They can also help to proffer Solar strengths to a persona and go well in Solar formulas. Perhaps the most lore is built around the seed head, as it is used to tell the age at which one might marry or die, the number of children one might have, the first letter of the name of one's true love, the direction of treasure, and even the time in Fairyland. They have also been used to send messages by facing the direction in which you believe a loved one to be, speaking a message, and then blowing on the seed head as hard as you can. If they all come off, the message will be received.

HOARHOUND

(*MARRUBIUM VULGARE*) MERCURY—AIR—GEMINI—LIBRA

AKA: *Bonhomme, houndsbane, herbe aux crocs, horehound bull's blood, hag's skin**

Another soil remediator, this is often one of the first plants to colonize barren areas of soil. Here in Albuquerque, it grows along the sandy edges of hiking trails and is dispersed throughout dry, arid areas covered in native sagebrush, chamisa, and saltbush. It is incredibly bitter and does not make for a decent forage, though it has been made into a traditional candy used for digestion and as a lozenge. It has also been used to make a soft drink that tastes somewhere between ginger ale and root beer, but hoarhound can also be used in brewing as a decent bittering agent in alcoholic beers.

One of the best and most often used herbs for sore throat and persistent cough accompanied by viscid mucus, this bitter plant can be a real lifesaver. When it feels like your lungs are full of thick, intractable slime, hoarhound can help to expel it and get your respiratory tissues back in shape, at which point you can switch to a moistening expectorant like marshmallow. If you are already dry or are prone to dry, asthmatic conditions, this may not be the herb for you, as it may worsen these conditions. However, herbalists such as Dara Seville, David Hoffman, and Michael Moore use it in cases of childhood asthma to very great effect, particularly with herbs such as licorice and marshmallow.

Large quantities of this herb will act as a laxative and as a liver and uterine stimulant, so it should be avoided during pregnancy. It also has effects on the heart, easing dysrhythmia, and because of its warming and astringent properties, it helps remove excess liquid from the body, particularly in the case of urinary hesitancy. Protracted use can also lead to hypertension, particularly in elderly people, so it should not be taken daily or for periods longer than seven to ten days. Topically, it is useful for dry, itchy skin, rashes, psoriasis, and shingles and it makes for a useful ally to lemon balm, wormwood, and Oregon grape.

Magically, hoarhound is one of the ultimate road-opening herbs, in my experience. When used with ivy and black pepper, it can be used as a powerful protection against unseen and psychic forces, particularly when there are physical manifestations of the attack. A sponge bath in horehound water mixed with a bit of garlic, sulfur, and salt will get rid of most persistent, spiritual clingers-on. In my work, I've used it along with tobacco and juniper to get rid of many infestations of spiritual parasites. If you suffer from frequent sleep paralysis and believe it to be some sort of energetic attack, keep a poke of horehound, harebell, and iron near your bed at all times, as this will protect you against magical attack and visitation. Because of these qualities, though, it can also be used to blast through the protections of another and set spirits on them.

JOHNSON GRASS

(*Sorghum halepense*) Mercury—Air—Libra

AKA: *Aleppo grass, milletgrass, devil's grass, dolly grass**

I include this plant here because many of my farmer friends, most of whom run organic operations and find it to be an intense nuisance, asked me to give a kinder perspective on this invasive grass. It is a native of the Mediterranean, Europe, and Africa but has been introduced everywhere but Antarctica. It creates very wide, dense stands of itself and propagates both through seed and rhizomatous growth, meaning it is nigh impossible to get rid of. The roots tend to break apart as they are torn from the ground, and the grass can grow from even a small piece left in the soil. The presence of even one plant has been shown to reduce yields of crop plants by up to 10%.

It is used to stop soil erosion, particularly after forest fire, and as a useful, nutritious forage once it is fully grown. When it is young and green or when it is in the presence of high levels of nitrogen (as with traditionally fertilized crops), it begins to accumulate enough hydrogen cyanide to become poisonous when eaten in quantity. As a pioneer species, it is a rapid colonizer of disturbed soils and brings nitrogen to the surface, particularly as it uses that element to create cyanide compounds as it first begins to grow. The seeds are edible, though, and can be toasted, winnowed, and eaten for their protein content. They can be used similarly to millet, rice, and other sorghum species to make flour.

The seeds can be used as a demulcent diuretic, and they make a useful addition to teas that include dandelion, uva ursi, and marshmallow. It is not very strong on its own, but it can be a good companion herb to help balance the work of the kidneys. The leaves can be mashed into a paste and turned into paper or used as a cooling poultice for burns. Magically, it can be useful for prosperity charms, and dollies made from the long leaves can act as protectors when hung near the front door.

KNOTWEED

(*Polygonum cuspidatum*) Saturn—Water—Capricorn

AKA: *Follopia japonica, Reynoutria japonica, Japanese knotweed, Asian knotweed, donkey rhubarb, bamboo, knuckle grass,* knucklebone,* finger of death**

This is a frequent colonizer of riparian areas, which makes it an easy target to hate. It also invades roadside and other wayside places, including abandoned lots and waste places, creating thick stands of nearly impenetrable growth that crowds out other species. Its roots can also tear structures down, meaning that the property it's on substantially decreases in value. It is one of the first-stage succession plants that can withstand high salinity, drought conditions, fluctuating soil pH, and soil types, making it incredibly flexible. Its root can survive temperatures under freezing and can extend up to twenty-three feet wide and ten feet deep, making its removal a gargantuan task that requires large machinery. If any root is missed…it will be back.

Of course, as we know, it remediates soil very well, cleaning out heavy metals, salts, and replenishing nutrients through its biomass and ability to fix nitrogen better than most other plants. This is also key to its cycle of life, as it will eventually go dormant and die off, leaving mid- and late-stage successional plants with better soil to establish new ecosystems on. The flowers are a useful food for pollinators of all varieties, various insects call it home, and it is eaten by animals, including humans.

The knotweed is also a tasty edible, having a sour, lemony flavor. The young shoots, which somewhat resemble nubby asparagus, need to be peeled before being eaten, but can then be eaten raw, grilled, sauteed, pickles, candied, fried, and any other way you can think of. It is used as a substitute for rhubarb in some recipes and can be made into pastries of various kinds. Blackberry knotweed pie is a must-have! Though, like rhubarb, too much can cause stomach upset, cramping, and diarrhea.

The constituent most studied in the plant is the antioxidant resveratrol, which helps to support blood vessel and heart health, eye health, and brain health. It makes a good companion to things like garlic and onion in the diet. Knotweed also contains the bowel-regulating chemical emodin, so it has been used as a mild laxative for a long time. Stephen H. Buhner, a New Mexican herbalist, also has studied its uses in treating Lyme disease. Like teasel, it makes spirochetes more susceptible to antimicrobial drugs.

Knotweed is used in binding magic of various sorts. It makes a good addition to love and fidelity spells but also for drawing spirits out of a person and binding them in the stalk through insufflation (see Siberian elm). The spirit is drawn into the stalk, sealed in with resin or wax, and tossed into a fire or a running body of water to be taken far away. It can also be used to heal, to tie up illness, and to make it wither as the stalk you bind it to withers.

LONDON ROCKET

(*SISYMBRIUM IRIO*) MARS—FIRE—ARIES

AKA: *Rocket mustard, tumble mustard, pamita, hedge mustard, desert mustard, winter mustard*

Also called wild yellow mustard, this immigrant from the Middle East first colonized Britain in the mid-1600s. It is currently considered an invasive pest in the US, though it is greatly useful. Like most short-lived annual weeds, it fixes nitrogen and nutrifies the soil it grows in, which is usually in the barren soil at the edges of structures. Its seed can be used like other mustards to make plasters and poultices for sore muscles and rheumatic pain, and it can be used to help clear mucus and open the lungs. The leaves and flowers make for delectable salad greens and can be smoked as a tobacco substitute. Try fermenting them for a bit before smoking them to give them a deeper flavor. Its seeds can be used in prosperity magic and it makes a good addition to things like galloping powder.

MIMOSA

(*Mimosa julibrissin*) Moon—Water—Cancer

AKA: *Silk tree, silky acacia, happiness tree, heartbreak tree, powder puff tree, fairy duster**

This tree seems like it belongs in a fairytale instead of alleyways, but that seems to be where it likes to grow. Its fluffy, pink flower puffs are a source of food for bees, butterflies, moths, and hummingbirds, as well as insects. The leaves make a protein-rich forage for animals, too. Like most invasive species, it harbors nitrogen in its roots and nutrifies soils but also draws phosphorus to itself, which is an enormously important mineral for photosynthesis. It is considered an early-mid successional plant and can withstand very shoddy soil.

The flowers and leaves are edible by humans, but the seeds are toxic. The beautifully fragrant flowers make a jelly that is out of this world. One of its folk names is "happiness tree," as it is commonly used as an aid for grief, anxiety, and heartbreak. I make a blend called "golden heart," which is mimosa flower and bark, motherwort, lemon balm, milky oat, and borage flower that really helps to uplift my perspective. It is also used for insomnia and has a regulating effect on the hypothalamic-pituitary-adrenal axis.

A flower essence made from this tree helps to key one into one's natural abilities with psychism and magic and also helps to alleviate feelings of loneliness. The flowers can be used in love spells, especially to make someone "sweet on you" and for making glamour perfumes meant to ensnare. The flowers can also be used to soothe and bring peace, making them good allies of loosestrife and plantain. They can also be used in dream sachets and pillow sprays. Snail shells can be tied to a mimosa stick and shaken like a rattle to call in lovers. The leaves can be used in protection and fidelity magic.

PUNCTURE VINE

(*Tribulus terrestris*) Mars—Water—Scorpio

AKA: *Goat head, caltrop, hobble seed, cat's head, Devil's thorn, Devil's eyelashes, Devil's jacks,* tackweed, crow's foot, sandbur, sticker weed, gokshura, Old Man's jest**

This is the bane of many New Mexican's lives. Stepping on a goat head is one of the most painful experiences in the world: searing, sharp, and lasting. Still, it is a powerful plant ally that I enjoy gathering. This plant is native to Eurasia and Africa but has been introduced to every other landmass and has been called an invasive "menace to people, pets, livestock, and bike tires." It propagates in loose, sandy, eroded, windblown soils at the edges of fields and parking lots and acts as one of the first plants to keep soil in place as it forms mats of prostrate leaves. Its yellow flowers become five-lobed fruits that dry down to the painfully pokey "goat heads."

Considered a famine food, *Tribulus* can be eaten as a green, particularly cooked down as a pot vegetable. The fruits can also be eaten when they are green and have a pleasant flavor, though when they are dry, they can be ground into a flour and eaten as a porridge or added to baked goods and soups. I've read that the flour can also be steamed into cakes, though I've never tried to do so myself. Remedially, *Tribulus* fruit has effects on blood pressure, immunity, inflammation, and blood sugar balance and helps with kidney-related issues through diuretic action. Though studies have shown that it does not increase testosterone, there is some evidence to show that its use increases sexual desire and helps with erection.

Goat head can be used in incenses meant to honor the Horned King, particularly in his role as the Devil. It also makes for a good addition to malefic charms meant to stop an enemy in their tracks, to cross an enemy, and makes an interesting ingredient in war water.

Crossing Powder

1. Powders added in the following order:

- Iron filings (magnetized)
- Hoarhound
- Graveyard dirt
- Goat heads
- Bindweed

2. Make this on a Tuesday in the hour of Saturn, preferably during the Moon's waning or when it is dark. Sprinkle it in the path of an enemy.

War Water of the Goat

- Stormwater
- 5 iron nails or a railroad spike
- Goat heads, at least 13
- Mud dauber nest

Make this on a Tuesday in the hour of Mars. Soak a red cloth in this and blood bought at the butcher's shop, then toss it over the house of an enemy to cross them. Cory Hutcheson mentions another method, which involves filling the hollowed-out shell of a black hen's egg over the house.[76] Catherine Yronwode suggests filling a glass bottle and hurling it at the doorstep of an enemy.[77] It can also be used on the tires of cars, poured across pathways, and used to anoint magical weapons of aggression.

---

76 Hutcheson, Blog 130.

77 Yronwode, Lucky Mojo "War Water."

RUSSIAN THISTLE

(*Kali tragus*) Mars—Air—Aquarius

AKA: *Tumbleweed, Russian cactus, glasswort, burning bush, saltwort, prickly glasswort, wind witch, get-thee-gone,* leap the field**

There may be no more iconic plant of the Southwest than the humble tumbleweed, the real star of all the Westerns and cowboy movies as it rolls across the silver screen. There are actually several plants, the dried skeletons of which are called tumbleweed, but the most recognizable are those of the Russian thistle, now *Kali tragus*. Russian thistle found its way to North America in the flaxseed of Eastern European immigrants in the 1870s. Since then, it has split into several genera and hybrids.

It is one of the first things to colonize soil, again bringing nutriment to the soil. An interesting quality of the Russian thistle is that it harbors no mycorrhizal partnerships but is susceptible to mycorrhizal colonization, which kills the plant. This allows for the mycorrhizae to consume the roots of the thistle and then spread to other plants nearby, most of which benefit from the colonization in the soil. They are, therefore, a powerful remediator of the soil and an important first-stage colonizer of soils. Where there is a stand of Russian thistle, there is currently no mycorrhizae…but there probably will be soon. They reproduce by seed, which is widely distributed as the weeds are blown about. Once they produce their seeds, the plant dries down to a woody ball of prickles that easily detaches from the root node, and then they begin their wind-born journey.

Because there are so many of them, they can aggregate into enormous clumps and become a bit of a nuisance. In 2014, they entirely engulfed the New Mexican town of Clovis. They buried houses from floor to roof and clogged the streets completely. Clovis isn't the only town this has happened to, though, as there are stories from all over the Southwest of towns being swallowed.

Russian thistle can be eaten when it is young and before it gets its prickles. The shoots look like tiny, green octopuses wriggling from the sandy soil. Some taste a bit like baking soda, and others taste like citrus. As they age, they gain more and more oxalic acid, which, in large amounts, can cause kidney stoning and cause the calcium to leech from bones. The young shoots can be eaten safely, though, and can be added to stewed or steamed veggies or eaten raw. Remedially, the shoots can be used like plantain to ease bug bites and the ash of the plant has been used on sores and wounds to help them heal.

The tumbleweed can be used in magic to get people to leave a place. Take cayenne, black pepper, and graveyard dirt, sprinkle them over a tumbleweed, stuff a picture of the person or their name into it, then burn it all to ash. Sprinkle this in front of their door or the path they walk to get them to tumble out of your way. It can also be used in conjunction with the war water recipe in the puncture vine section on page 244. Tumbleweed ash can also make a powerful protective agent, surrounding you in the prickly arms of the thistle's skeletonized body.

TEASEL

(*Dipsacus fullonum*) Saturn—Earth—Libra

AKA: *Cameleon, Devil's bit, Lady's Comb, Hera's Comb, Venus's basin, Venus's Bath, Venus's lips, Mary's basin, Our Lady's basin, Devil's spindle, Hekate's spindle, witch's spindle, card teasel, Devil's card, brushes and combs*

Looking like a tall, prickly ear swab and growing in the waysides and waste places of the world, teasel might be one of the coolest plants on the planet. It is part of the honeysuckle family, the *Caprifoliaceae.* It remediates soil in the same way most deeply tap-rooted invasives do but also creates thick stands of itself that shade soil for microbial proliferation, protects topsoil, and offers large amounts of biomass for nutrification. Teasel is possibly a protocarnivorous plant with sessile leaves that make a sort of cup around the stem. These fill with water when it rains or collect morning dew, thus leading to little drowning pools that catch insects and slugs, which break down and may feed the plant. Studies are still being done to determine if this is true. The basins may simply be evolved to prevent sap suckers from climbing the stem.

The young leaves of teasel can be used as a green, but the whole plant is covered in spines that make it no fun to eat. It is powerfully medicinal, though, and the root tincture is one of the only herbal preparations that shows effects against Lyme disease. It makes the spirochete more susceptible to conventional treatment, meaning that it must be used as an adjunct treatment, not on its own. Teasel root is mainly used as a kidney tonic and as an aid in repairing skeletal and connective tissue problems. It is also useful in managing an enlarged prostate, making it useful in conjunction with ocotillo and to help avoid miscarriage.

The dried heads of teasel have historically been used as a kind of drop spindle and to raise the nap on wool fabric, giving it a strong link to the magic and lore of spinning and weaving. The plant lends itself very easily to protective magic and banishment, though it is also a symbol of hardship and strife. Teasel can be used ritually as a symbol of the willing sacrifice, the ruler who gives their life for the Land, the sacrificial stag that brings new life through spilling its blood. It is associated with rejuvenation, youthfulness, and reinvigoration. It is also a very useful addition to baths and washes meant to break hexes and untangle jinxes.

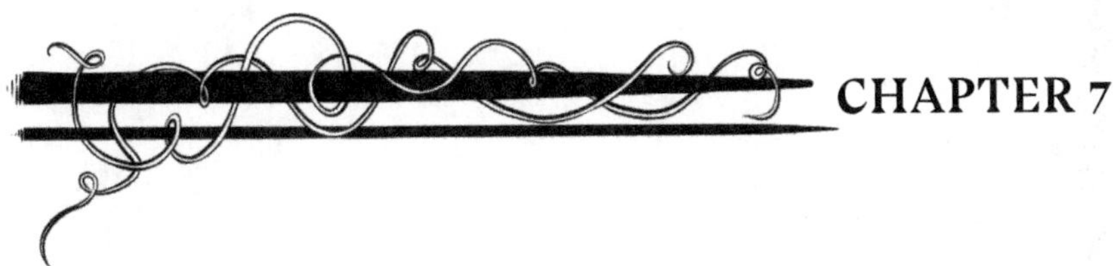

CHAPTER 7

May All Our Weeds Be Wildflowers

So, we come to the end of it...well, of this book at least. Though they are often maligned and blamed, and we are given heaping amounts of reasons not to see invasive species as essential partners in the coming shifts, I hope you can see through the falsity of much of that propaganda more clearly. I also hope that, in some small way, this book pushes the hands of the clock a little further from midnight, at least for a while. My dearest hope, though, is that in having read this book, in whatever fashion you did so, you feel a little more at home with these lovely plants and that you can harbor them in your heart like friends rather than enemies.

Instead of reiterating what is in this book or leaving you dire warnings, which I feel I've sprinkled liberally throughout the text, I will leave you with some words of beauty to think on. May the winds be gentle on your skin, may the sunlight warm your days, may the rains wash clean your heart, and may all your weeds be wildflowers.

WEEDS

BY WILLIAM HERBERT CARRUTH

Poor, homely, unloved things beside the way,
That strive in voiceless ignominy, still
Undaunted though downtrodden, to fulfill
Your appointed purpose! Patient the long day
Ye take the buffetings of scornful clay,
Sustained by that small portion of God's dew
Which thick-strewn dust permits to fall on you.
And live where finer herbs must wilt away.
Have ye too, dreams of better things to be?
Of worlds in which the crooked shall be straight,
Where all that are in bondage shall be free,
And lifted up all those of low estate?
Where, to the thought that knows the potent seeds,
Weeds shall be e'en as flowers, flowers as weeds.

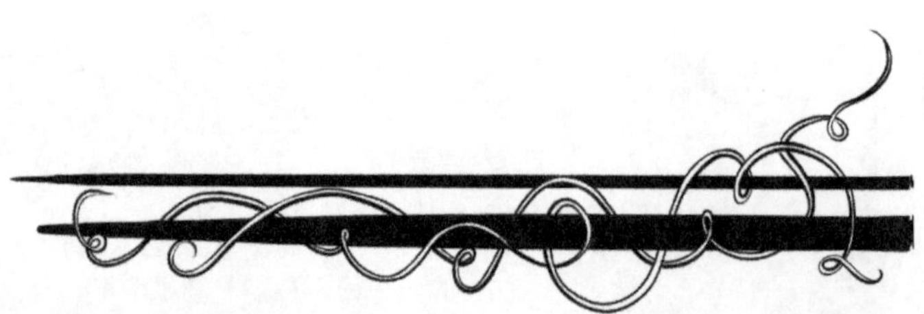

WEEDS

By Edna St. Vincent Millay

White with daisies and red with sorrel
And empty, empty under the sky!—
Life is a quest and love a quarrel—
Here is a place for me to lie.

Daisies spring from damnèd seeds,
And this red fire that here I see
Is a worthless crop of crimson weeds,
Cursed by farmers thriftily.

But here, unhated for an hour,
The sorrel runs in ragged flame,
The daisy stands, a bastard flower,
Like flowers that bear an honest name.

And here a while, where no wind brings
The baying of a pack athirst,
May sleep the sleep of blessèd things,
The blood too bright, the brow accurst.

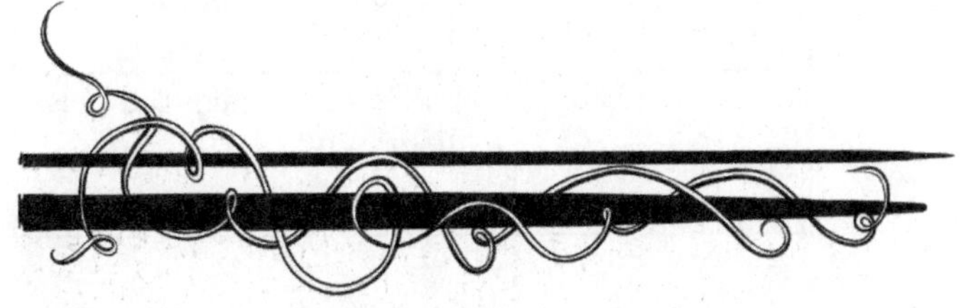

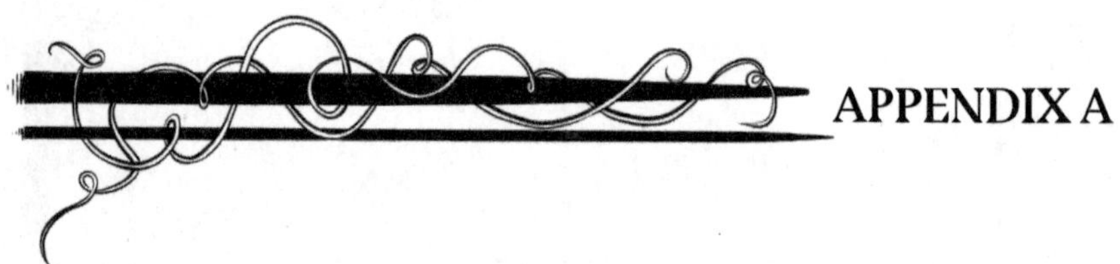

APPENDIX A

Invasive Plant Magic at a Glance

* Caution Necessary
** TOXIC

Plant	Planet	Element	Zodiac	Edible	Magical Uses
Acacia	Sun	Air	Sagittarius	Seeds, Flowers	Protection, Conjure, Necromancy
Bindweed*	Saturn	Earth	Virgo	Young Shoots, Leaves	Binding, Prosperity, Success, Fae work
Blackberry	Mars	Water	Cancer	Berries, Leaves, Stalks	Protection
Black Locust*	Mercury	Air	Gemini	Flowers	Protection, Blasting, Turning
Bull Thistle	Mars	Fire	Sagittarius	Flowers, Seed	Protection, Jinxing, Crossing
Burning Bush**	Mars	Fire	Leo	TOXIC	Jinx and Curse Removal, Apotropaic

Plant	Planet	Element	Zodiac	Edible	Magical Uses
Butterfly Bush	Mercury	Air	Virgo	Flowers	Communication, Messages, Cleansing
Canadian Thistle	Mars	Fire	Sagittarius	Seed, Flower, Leaves	Protection, Prosperity, Crossing
Cheatgrass	Venus	Air	Gemini	Seeds	Protection, Hiding, Jinx
Cheeseweed	Moon	Water	Libra	Whole Plant	Love, Fidelity, Psychic Power
Cogon Grass	Mercury	Air	Taurus	Young Flowers and Shoots, Root	Communication, Clearing, Purifying
Dalmatian Toadflax	Mars	Earth	Aquarius	TOXIC	Skin Turning, Protection
Dandelion	Sun, Jupiter	Earth	Leo	Whole Plant	Prosperity, Divination
Daylily	Venus, Moon	Water	Cancer	Flower, Root, Young Shoots	Happiness, Union, Marriage, Breaking Curses
Dodder	Saturn	Air	Libra	Depends on Host*	Binding, Crossing, Turning/Taking
English Ivy**	Saturn	Water	Aquarius	TOXIC	Protection, Luck, Fertility, Breaking
Eurasian Watermilfoil*	Mercury, Venus	Water	Aries	Root	Psychic Powers, Dreaming, Creativity

Plant	Planet	Element	Zodiac	Edible	Magical Uses
Garlic Mustard	Jupiter, Mars	Fire	Leo	Leaves, Flowers, Shoots	Prosperity, Protection, Amplification
Giant Cane	Jupiter	Earth	Virgo	Seeds, Young Shoots	Prosperity, Dominion, Growth
Giant Hogweed**	Saturn, Mercury	Air	Gemini	Seeds, Young Shoots,* Unopened Flowers*	Luck, Jinxing, Crossing, Prosperity
Golden Bamboo	Saturn	Air	Leo	Young Shoots	Divination, Psychic Powers, Blessing
Groundsel**	Mars	Water, Earth	Scorpio	TOXIC	Offering, Divination
Hoarhound	Mercury	Air	Libra	Aerial Parts	Road Opening, Psychic Protection, Purification
Honey Locust*	Mars	Air	Taurus	Flowers, Pith	Protection, Cursing, Blasting
Honeysuckle*	Jupiter	Earth	Pisces	Flowers	Prosperity, Luck
Horseweed	Mars	Fire	Virgo	Aerial Parts	Transvection, Virility, Attraction
Japanese Barberry	Mars	Earth	Aries, Scorpio	Flowers, Berries	Prosperity, Gambling, Protection
Johnson Grass	Mercury	Air	Libra	Seed	Poppetry, Prosperity
Juniper	Sun	Fire	Gemini	Leaf, Berries	Exorcism, Prosperity, Protection

Plant	Planet	Element	Zodiac	Edible	Magical Uses
Knapweed	Mercury, Mars	Air	Gemini	Flowers, Seeds	Inspiration, Protection, Jinx
Knotweed	Saturn	Water	Capricorn	Stalk	Cleansing, Binding
Kochia	Moon	Water	Pisces	Seed	Dreaming, Psychic Powers
Kudzu	Moon, Venus	Water	Scorpio	Whole Plant	Clairvoyance, Protection, Crossing
Leafy Spurge**	Saturn	Water	Capricorn	TOXIC	Strength, Empowerment, Force, Command
Lily of the Valley**	Mercury	Air	Gemini	TOXIC	Calmness, Peace, Joy
London Rocket	Mars	Fire	Aries	Whole Plant	Prosperity, Protection, Amplification
Mimosa	Moon	Water	Cancer	Flowers, Leaves	Happiness, Luck, Psychic Power, Love
Mulberry	Mercury	Air	Gemini	Leaves, Berries, Bark	Luck, Prosperity, Command
Musk Thistle	Mars	Air	Sagittarius	Seed, Flower	Protection, Glamour, Attraction
Parrotfeather	Venus	Water	Pisces	Young Tips	Prosperity, Dreaming, Revelation
Pennyroyal	Mars	Fire	Aries	Aerial Parts*	Purification, Sanctification, Initiation

Plant	Planet	Element	Zodiac	Edible	Magical Uses
Pepperweed	Mars	Fire	Leo	Flower, Seed	Amplification, Strength, Quickening
Plantain	Mars, Venus	Water	Capricorn	Whole Plant	Travel, Road Opening, Protection
Prickly Wild Lettuce	Mercury	Water	Gemini, Pisces	Flowers, Leaves	Divination, Psychic Powers, Inspiration
Purple Loosestrife	Venus	Water	Cancer	Flowers, Leaves, Roots	Psychic Powers, Purification, Dreaming
Quackgrass	Mercury	Air	Libra	Whole Plant	Happiness, Lust, Love, Exorcism
Reed Canary Grass**	Mercury	Air, Water	Cancer	Seeds	Communication, Necromancy
Russian Olive	Sun	Fire	Leo	Flowers, Fruits, Leaves	Divination, Poppetry, Cleansing
Russian Thistle	Mars	Air	Aquarius	Young Shoots	Jinxing, Crossing, Protection
St. John's Wort	Sun	Fire	Leo	Aerial Parts (Dried)	Joy, Inspiration, Divination, Visions
Scotch Broom*	Mars	Air	Aries, Scorpio	Flower Buds*	Exorcism, Divination, Clairvoyance
Siberian Elm	Saturn	Water	Virgo	Whole Plant	Protection, Necromancy, Anti-Slander

Plant	Planet	Element	Zodiac	Edible	Magical Uses
Sweet Clover	Mercury	Air	Aries	Flowers, Seeds	Blessing, Communication
Syrian Rue**	Mars, Moon	Air	Scorpio	TOXIC	Visions, Blessing
Tamarisk	Saturn	Earth	Libra	Young Leaves, Flowers	Exorcism, Trapping, Purification
Teasel	Saturn	Earth	Libra	Young Leaves	Probability Warping, Protection, Energy Direction
Tree of Heaven	Mars	Fire	Sagittarius	-	Spirit Conjure, Vessels, Energy Direction
Velvetweed	Venus	Water	Aquarius	Leaves, Root, Flowers	Strength, Protection, Courage
Wisteria**	Mercury	Water	Cancer	Flowers	Prosperity, Psychic Powers, Glamoury

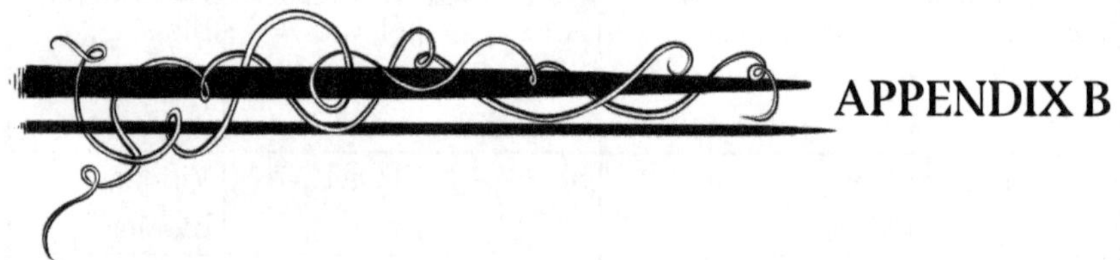

APPENDIX B

Invasive Plant Actions and Uses at a Glance

* Caution necessary
** TOXIC

Acacia
Flower: Anti-inflammatory, Antimicrobial
Sap: Anticholesterol

Bindweed*
Root: Laxative
Leaf/Stem and Flower: Urinary Tract Issues, Blood Pressure

Bittersweet**
Leaf/Stem and Flower: Topical—Psoriasis, Rash; Internal—Diuretic, Purgative

Blackberry
Leaf/Stem: Nutritive, Astringent, Diuretic, Vulnerary
Berries/Fruit: Nutritive, Laxative

Black Locust*
Flower: Febrifuge, Antispasmodic, Diuretic, Laxative
Seed: Cholagogue* (Cooked)

Bull Thistle
Leaf/Stem and Flower: Hemorrhoids, Varicosity, Neuralgia, Astringent

Burning Bush**
Leaf/Stem: Digestive Disorders, Vermifuge, Genitourinary Disorders

Butterfly Bush
Leaf/Stem: Diuretic, Analgesic, Anti-microbial, Eye Remedy, Anti-inflammatory, Antifungal, Antiseptic

Canadian Thistle
Leaf/Stem and Flower: Diuretic, Antidiarrheal, Astringent, Analgesic

Cheatgrass
Seed: Anti-catarrhal, Analgesic

Cheeseweed
Root, Leaf/Stem, Flower: Demulcent, Emollient, Expectorant, Dandruff Aid

Cogon Grass
Seed: Nephritis, Febrifuge, Antihypertensive, Dyspnea, Hepatoprotective, Anticholesterol

Dalmatian Toadflax
Leaf/Stem, Flower: Digestive, Urinary Tract Issues, Diaphoretic

Daylily
Root: Antimicrobial, Vermifuge, Tuberculostatic
Flower: Diuretic, Febrifuge, Laxative, Anodyne, Antispasmodic, Sedative

Dodder
Leaf/Stem: Urinary Tract Issues, Hepatoprotective, Eczema
Flower: Depression

English Ivy**
Leaf/Stem, Flower: Antioxidant, Anti-inflammatory, Antitussive

Eurasian Watermilfoil*
Leaf/Stem: Demulcent, Febrifuge

Garlic Mustard
Leaf/Stem, Flower: Antiseptic, Vulnerary, Expectorant, Anti-inflammatory, Decongestant, Diaphoretic, Urinary Issues

Giant Cane
Leaf/Stem: Diaphoretic, Diuretic, Emollient, Galactagogue, Pro-menstrual

Giant Hogweed**
Root: Hepatoprotective
Leaf/Stem: Digestion, Flatulence, Diarrhea, Bladder Infection, Kidney Stones, Dysmenorrhea, Warts
Seed: Hepatoprotective, Flatulence, Kidney Stones, Dysmenorrhea

Golden Bamboo
Root, Leaf/Stem: Antioxidation, Anti-inflammatory, Hepatoprotective

Groundsel**
Leaf/Stem, Flower: Vermifuge, Stomach Upset, Styptic

Honey Locust*
Berries/Fruit: Antibacterial, Antifungal, Expectorant, Vermifuge (Pith)

Honeysuckle*
Leaf/Stem, Flower: Digestive, Antibacterial, Urinary Issues, Headache, Anti-inflammatory

Horseweed
Leaf/Stem, Flower: Diarrhea, IBS, Styptic, Febrifuge, Expectorant, Anti-inflammatory

Japanese Barberry
Root: Blood Sugar Balance, Hepatoprotective, Gall Bladder Issues, Digestive, Urinary Issues, Antiamoeba

Juniper

Leaf/Stem: Digestion, Stomach Upset, Appetite, Carminative, Antispasmodic, Vermifuge, Antacid

Berries/Fruit: Digestion, Stomach Upset, Appetite, Carminative, Antispasmodic, Vermifuge, Antacid

Knapweed

Leaf/Stem, Flower: Vulnerary, Sore Throat, Anti-inflammatory, Expectorant

Knotweed

Leaf/Stem, Flower: Expectorant, Antitussive, Sore Throat, Diuretic, Bronchial Anti-inflammatory, Lyme Disease

Kochia

Leaf/Stem, Flower, Seed: Skin Eruptions and Rashes, Blood Sugar Balance

Kudzu

Root: Alcoholism, Anticholesterol, Menopausal Symptoms, Blood Sugar Balance, Antimicrobial

Leaf/Stem, Flower: Anticholesterol, Menopausal Symptoms, Blood Sugar Balance, Antimicrobial

Leafy Spurge**

All: TOXIC—Sap possibly good for warts but deeply irritating to skin and may cause blindness.

Lily of the Valley**

Leaf/Stem, Flower: Severe Cardiac Issue; TOXIC—may be lethal in wrong doses.

London Rocket

Leaf/Stem, Flower, Seed: Cough, Chest Congestion, Antiarthritic, Hepatoprotective, Vulnerary, Antimicrobial

MIMOSA
Leaf/Stem, Flower: Anxiety, Insomnia, Infection, Grief, Heartbreak, Depression (Bark and Flower)

MULBERRY
Leaf/Stem: Anticholesterol, Cardiovascular Disease
Berries/Fruit: Anti-inflammatory, Antioxidant, Brain Health

MUSK THISTLE
Leaf/Stem, Flower: Hemorrhoids, Varicosity, Neuralgia, Astringent

PARROTFEATHER
Leaf/Stem: Demulcent, Febrifuge

PENNYROYAL
Leaf/Stem, Flower: Carminative, Headache, Dizziness, Diaphoretic, Emmenagogue, Stimulant, Abortifacient

PEPPERWEED
Leaf/Stem, Flower, Seed: Antiasthmatic, Antitussive, Diuretic, Headache, Carminative, Digestive

PLANTAIN
Leaf/Stem, Flower: Cough, Bronchitis, Anti-inflammatory, Coolant, Diarrhea, Vulnerary, Anticholesterol, Ulceration, Dermatitis

PRICKLY WILD LETTUCE
Leaf/Stem, Flower: Anxiety, Muscle Soreness, Insomnia, Cough, Menstrual Pain, Aphrodisiac
Seed: Atherosclerosis

PURPLE LOOSESTRIFE
Leaf/Stem, Flower: Diarrhea, Hemorrhoid, Eczema, Vulnerary, Varicosity, Astringent, Eye Health, Antioxidant, Sore Throat, Hepatoprotective

QUACKGRASS
Leaf/Stem, Flower: Laxative, Anti-inflammatory, Hypertension, Kidney Stoning, Cough, Diuretic

Reed Canary Grass**

Leaf/Stem, Flower, Seed: Psychoactive (N, N-DMT & 5-MeO-DMT); Also contains gramine, which may cause severe nausea and vomiting.

Russian Olive

Leaf/Stem, Flower: Astringent, Kidney Stoning, Anti-inflammatory, Antimicrobial, Pain Relieving, Febrifuge

Berries/Fruit: Pain Relief, Analgesic, Anti-inflammatory, Antimicrobial, Antioxidant, Astringent

Russian Thistle

Leaf/Stem, Flower: Vulnerary, Diuretic, Stimulant, Emmenagogue, Laxative

St. John's Wort*

All: Reacts very strongly to MAOIs and SSRIs. *Do not mix them.*

Leaf/Stem, Flower: Depression, Anxiety, Menopausal Symptoms, ADHD, Burns, Vulnerary, Anti-inflammatory

Scotch Broom*

Leaf/Stem, Flower: Diuretic, Circulatory, Hypotension, Dysrhythmia

Siberian Elm

Leaf/Stem, Flower, Seed: Laxative, Expectorant, Nutritive, Digestive Issues, Skin Issues, Sore Throat, Febrifuge

Sweet Clover

Leaf/Stem, Flower: Blood Thinner, Neuralgia, Headache, Dysuria, Digestive, Sore Muscles, Anti-Inflammatory, Antimicrobial, Varicosity, Circulation, Vulnerary

Syrian Rue*

Leaf/Stem, Flower, Seed: Psychoactive (Harmaline alkaloids), Arthritic Pain, Menstrual Pain, Antioxidant, Anxiety, Depression

Tamarisk

Leaf/Stem, Flower: Antiseptic, Antimicrobial, Vulnerary, GI Issues, Diuretic, Skin Issues

Teasel

Root, Leaf/Stem, Flower: Lyme Disease, Diaphoretic, Diuretic, Stomachic, Hepatoprotective

Tree of Heaven

Root: Anti-malarial, Purgative, Diarrhea, Asthma, Genitourinary Issues, Vermifuge

Leaf/Stem, Flower: Purgative, Genitourinary Issues, Asthma

Velvetweed

Root: Snakebite,* Febrifuge, Burns, Anti-inflammatory

Wisteria**

Flower: Antioxidant

Seed: Cardiac Issues, Vermifuge, Abortifacient (TOXIC)

APPENDIX C

Miscellany

THE SPIDER AND THE FLY

Mary Howitt (1829)

I.

"Will you walk into my parlour?" said a spider to a fly;
"'Tis the prettiest little parlour that ever you did spy.
The way into my parlour is up a winding stair,
And I have many pretty things to shew when you are there."
"Oh no, no!" said the little fly, "to ask me is in vain,
For who goes up your winding stair can ne'er come down again."

II.

"I'm sure you must be weary, with soaring up so high,
Will you rest upon my little bed?" said the spider to the fly.
"There are pretty curtains drawn around, the sheets are fine and thin;
And if you like to rest awhile, I'll snugly tuck you in."
"Oh no, no!" said the little fly, "for I've often heard it said,
They never, never wake again, who sleep upon your bed!"

III.

Said the cunning spider to the fly, "Dear friend, what shall I do,
To prove the warm affection I've always felt for you?
I have, within my pantry, good store of all that's nice;

I'm sure you're very welcome—will you please to take a slice?"
"Oh no, no!" said the little fly, "kind sir, that cannot be,
I've heard what's in your pantry, and I do not wish to see."

IV.

"Sweet creature!" said the spider, "you're witty and you're wise.
How handsome are your gauzy wings, how brilliant are your eyes!
I have a little looking-glass upon my parlour shelf,
If you'll step in one moment, dear, you shall behold yourself."
"I thank you, gentle sir," she said, "for what you're pleased to say,
And bidding you good morning now, I'll call another day."

V.

The spider turned him round about, and went into his den,
For well he knew, the silly fly would soon come back again:
So he wove a subtle web, in a little corner, sly,
And set his table ready, to dine upon the fly.
Then he went out to his door again, and merrily did sing,
"Come hither, hither, pretty fly, with the pearl and silver wing;
Your robes are green and purple—there's a crest upon your head;
Your eyes are like the diamond bright, but mine are dull as lead."

VI.

Alas, alas! how very soon this silly little fly,
Hearing his wily, flattering words, came slowly flitting by;
With buzzing wings she hung aloft, then near and nearer drew,
Thinking only of her brilliant eyes, and green and purple hue:—
Thinking only of her crested head, poor foolish thing!—At last
Up jumped the cunning spider, and fiercely held her fast.

VII.

He dragged her up his winding stair, into his dismal den,
Within his little parlour—but she ne'er came out again!
—And now, dear little children, who may this story read,
To idle, silly, flattering words, I pray you ne'er give heed:
Unto an evil counsellor, close heart, and ear, and eye,
And take a lesson from this tale, of the Spider and the Fly.

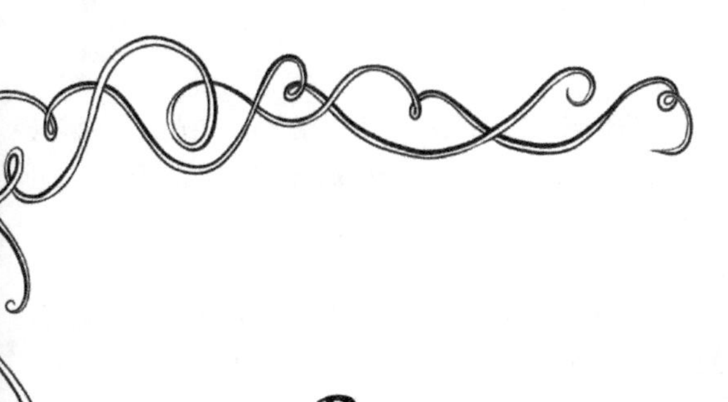

Bibliography

Books

Beyerl, Paul. *A Compendium of Herbal Magick*. Phoenix Publishing Inc., 1998.

—. *The Master Book of Herbalism*. Phoenix Publishing Inc., 1984.

Bjorn, Albert. *Icelandic Plant Magic: Folk Herbalism of the North*. Crossed Crow Books, 2023.

Boyer, Corrinne. *Under the Bramble Arch*. Troy Publishing, 2019.

Buhner, Stephen Harrod. *Plant Intelligence and the Imaginal Realm: Into the Dreaming of the Earth*. Bear & Co. Publishing, 2014.

—. *The Secret Teachings of Plants in the Direct Perception of Nature*. Bear & Co. Publishing, 2004.

Cornell, Kamden. *Ars Granorum: The Six Seed Arts of Witchcraft*. Acorn, 2020.

Culpeper, Nicholas. *Culpeper's Complete Herbal*. Edited by Steven Foster, Union Square & Co., 2019.

—. *Culpeper's Complete Astrology: The Lost Art of Astrological Medicine*. Microcosm Publishing, 2023.

Cunningham, Scott. *The Complete Book of Incense, Oils, and Brews*. Llewellyn Publications, 2003.

—. *Magical Herbalism: The Secret Craft of the Wise*. Llewellyn Publishing, 1991.

Curtin, L. S. M. *Healing Herbs of the Upper Rio Grande: Traditional Medicine of the Southwest*. Edited and revised by Michael Moore, Western Edge Press, 1997.

Davidow, Joie. *Infusions of Healing: A Treasury of Mexican-American Herbal Remedies*. Simon & Schuster, Inc., 1999.

Denning, Melita and Osborne Phillips. *The Magical Philosophy, Book IV: Planetary Magic*. Llewelyn Publications, 2020.

Diat, Louis. *Sauces: French and Famous*. Dover Publications, Inc., 1951

Dirr, Michael et al. *Manual of Woody Landscape Plants: Their Identification, Ornamental Characteristics, Culture, Propagation, and Uses.* 1975. Stipes Publishing, LLC., 2009.

Drew, A. J. *A Wiccan Formulary and Herbal.* New Page Books, 2005.

Dunmire, William W. and Gail D. Tierney. *Wild Plants and Native Peoples of the Four Corners.* Museum of New Mexico Press, 1997.

Edwards, Gail Faith. *Opening Our Hearts to the Healing Herbs.* Ash Tree Publishing, 2000.

Green, James. *The Male Herbal: Healthcare for Men and Boys.* The Crossing Press, 1991.

—. *The Herbal Medicine Maker's Handbook.* Crossing Press, 2000.

Greer, John Michael. *Natural Magic: Potions and Powers from the Magical Garden.* Llewellyn Publications, 2000.

Grieve, Mrs. M. *A Modern Herbal: The Medicinal, Culinary, Cosmetic, and Economic Properties, Cultivation, and Folk-Lore of Herbs, Grasses, Fungi, Shrubs, & Trees with Their Modern Scientific Uses, vol I & II.* Dover Publications, Inc., 1971.

Hashimoto, Shoji, et al. "Behavior of Radiocesium in the Forest." *Forest Radioecology in Fukushima: Radiocesium Dynamics, Impact, and Future.* Springer, 2022. pp. 21–46.

Hardin, Kiva Rose. *A Weedwife's Remedy: Folk Herbalism for the Hedgewise.* Plant Healer Press, ND.

Harrison, Karen. *The Herbal Alchemist's Handbook: A Grimoire of Philtres, Elixirs, Oils, Incense, and Formulas for Ritual Use.* Weiser Books, 2011.

Hesiod. *Homeric Hymns, Epic Cycle, Homerica.* Translated by H.G. Evelyn-White, Loeb Classical Library, 1914.

Hoffman, David. *The Herbal Handbook: A User's Guide to Medical Herbalism.* Healing Arts Press, 1988.

—. *The New Holistic Herbal.* Element Books Limited, 1990.

Hopman, Ellen Evert. *A Druid's Herbal of Sacred Tree Medicine.* Destiny Books, 2008.

—. *A Druid's Herbal for the Sacred Earth Year.* Destiny Books, 1995.

Hurley, Phillip. *Herbal Alchemy.* Lotus Publications, 1977.

Hutchens, Alma R. *A Handbook of Native American Herbs.* Shambala Press, 1992.

Jones, Evan John, and Robert Cochrane. *The Roebuck in the Thicket: An Anthology of the Robert Cochrane Witchcraft Tradition.* Capall Bann Publishing, 2001.

Junius, Manfred M. *Spagyrics: The Alchemical Preparation of Medicinal Essences, Tinctures, and Elixirs.* Healing Arts Press, 2007.

Kane, Charles W. *Medicinal Plants of the American Southwest.* Lincoln Town Press, 2016.

Keeler, Harriet. *Our Native Trees and How to Identify Them: A Popular Study of Their Habits and Their Peculiarities.* Charle's Scribner's Sons, 1910

Landels, John G. *Music in Ancient Greece & Rome.* Routledge, 1999.

Lavender, Susan and Anna Franklin. *Herb Craft: A Guide to the Shamanic Ritual Use of Herbs.* Capall Bann Publishing, 1996.

Lehner, Ernst and Johanna. *Folklore and Symbolism of Flowers, Plants, and Trees.* Dover Publications, 2003.

Mann, A. T. *The Round Art: The Astrology of Time and Space.* Mayflower Books, 1979.

Margulis, Lynn and Dorion Sagan. *Microcosmos: Four Billion Years of Evolution from Our Microbial Ancestors.* University of California Press, 1997.

Meyer, Felicia A. *Traditional Herbs de Nuevo Mexico: A Complete Booklet of Traditional Uses and Beliefs of New Mexican Herbs.* Rio Grande Herb Company, Inc., 1994.

Meyer, Joseph E. *The Herbalist.* Rand McNally & Company, 1960.

Moerman, Daniel E. *Native American Medicinal Plants: An Ethnobotanical Dictionary.* Timber Press, 2009.

Moore, Michael. *Medicinal Plants of the Mountain West: Revised and Expanded Edition.* Museum of New Mexico Press, 2003.

—. *Herbal Tinctures in Clinical Practice,* 3rd Ed. Southwest School of Botanical Medicine, 1996.

—. *Los Remedios: Traditional Herbal Remedies of the Southwest.* Red Crane Books, 1995.

—. *Principles and Practice of Constitutional Physiology for Herbalists.* Southwest School of Botanical Medicine, ND.

Muller-Eberling, Claudia, Christian Ratsch, and Wolf-Dieter Storl. *Witchcraft Medicine: Healing Arts, Shamanic Practices, and Forbidden Plants.* Inner Traditions, 1998.

Murray, Michael T., N.D. *The Healing Power of Herbs: The Enlightened Person's Guide to the Wonders of Medicinal Plants.* Prima Publishing, 1995.

Orion, Tao. *Beyond the War on Invasive Species: A Permaculture Approach to Ecosystem Restoration.* Chelsea Green Publishing, 2015.

Pearce, Fred. *The New Wild: Why Invasive Species Will Be Nature's Salvation.* Beacon Press, 2015.

Pearson, Nigel G. *The Devil's Plantation.* Troy Publishing, 2015.

—. *Wortcunning: A Folk Magic/Medicine Herbal.* Troy Publishing, 2019.

Pond, Barbara. *A Sampler of Wayside Herbs: Rediscovering Old Uses for Familiar Wild Plants.* The Chatham Press, Inc., 1974.

Popham, Sajah. *Evolutionary Herbalism: Science, Spirituality, and Medicine from the Heart of Nature.* North Atlantic Books, 2019.

Pursell, J. J. *The Herbal Apothecary.* Timber Press, 2015.

Rankin, David and Sorita d'Este. *Practical Planetary Magic: Working the Magic of the Classical Planets in the Western Mystery Tradition.* Avalonia Press, 2007

Ross, M. R. *Smoke Plants of North America: A Journey of Discovery.* MultiCultural Educational Publishing Company, 2002.

Sanchez Jr., Charlie. *Yerbas y Remedios: A Booklet of Herbs and Spices of the Southwest.* Rio Grande Herb Company, 1993.

Saville, Dara. *The Ecology of Herbal Medicine: A Guide to Plants and Living Landscapes of the American Southwest.* University of New Mexico Press, 2021.

Savinelli, Alfred. *Plants of Power.* Self-Published, Taos, 1997.

Scalzo, Richard and Michael Cronin. *Traditional Medicines from the Earth.* Herbal Research Publications, 2002.

Scott, Timothy Lee. *Invasive Plant Medicine: The Ecological Benefits and Healing Abilities of Invasives.* Healing Arts Press, 2010.

Scheidau, Lisa. *Botanical Folk Tales of Britain and Ireland.* The History Press, 2019.

Schulke, Daniel A. *Thirteen Pathways of Occult Herbalism.* Three Hands Press, 2017.

Shadow, Sirian. *Spirit Work: A Guide to Communicating & Forming Relationships with Spirits.* Self-Published, 2022.

Shurtleff, William and Akiko Aoyagi. *The Book of Kudzu: A Culinary & Healing Guide.* Autumn Press, 1977.

Slattery, John. *Southwest Foraging: 117 Wild and Flavorful Edibles from the Barrel Cactus to Wild Oregano.* Timber Press, 2016.

Smith, Steven R. *Wylundt's Book of Incense.* Samuel Weiser, Inc., 1989.

Tilgner, Sharol. *Herbal Medicine from the Heart of the Earth.* Wise Acres Press Inc., 1999.

Trismegistus, Hermes. *The Emerald Tablet of Hermes.* Merchant Books, 2022.

Wood, Matthew. *The Earthwise Herbal: A Complete Guide to Old World Medicinal Herbs.* North Atlantic Books, 2008.

Yronwode, Catherine. *Hoodoo Herb and Root Magic: A Materia Magica of African-American Conjure and Traditional Formulary Giving the Spiritual Uses of Natural Herbs, Roots, Minerals, and Zoological Curios.* The Lucky Mojo Curio Co., 2002.

Poetry

Carruth, William Herbert. "Weeds." ND.

Cawain, Madison Julius. "Wind and Rain." ND.

Howitt, Mary. "The Spider and the Fly," *The New Year's Gift and Juvenile Souvenir.* Longman, Reese, Orme, Brown, and Green, 1829.

Millay, Edna St. Vincent. "Weeds," *Second April.* Mitchell Kennerley, 1921.

Articles

Amiri Tehranizadeh, Zeinab, et al. "Russian olive (*Elaeagnus angustifolia*) as a herbal healer." *BioImpacts: BI,* vol. 6, no. 3, 2016, pp. 155–167, doi:10.15171/bi.2016.22

Babiker, Rasha, et al. "Effect of Gum Arabic (*Acacia Senegal*) supplementation on visceral adiposity index (VAI) and blood pressure in patients with type 2 diabetes mellitus as indicators of cardiovascular disease (CVD): a randomized and placebo-controlled clinical trial." *Lipids in Health and Disease,* vol. 1, no. 56, Mar. 2018, doi: 10.1186/s12944-018-0711-y

Berry, C. "Glyphosate and cancer: the importance of the whole picture." *Pest Manag Sci,* vol. 76, 2020, pp. 2874–2877. https://doi.org/10.1002/ps.5834. Accessed 21 Jan. 2024.

Costas-Ferreira, Carmen et al. "Toxic Effects of Glyphosate on the Nervous System: A Systematic Review." *International Journal of Molecular Sciences* vol. 23, no. 9, pp. 4605. 21 Apr. 2022. doi:10.3390/ijms23094605.

Dill GM, et al. "Glyphosate: Discovery, Development, Applications, and Properties." In: Glyphosate Resistance in Crops and Weeds: History, Development, and Management, edited by VK Nandula. John Wiley & Sons, Inc., 2010. John Wiley & Sons Website, https://media.johnwiley.com.au/product_data/excerpt/10/04704103/0470410310.pdf. Accessed 20 Jan. 2024.

Dimkić, Ivica, et al. "New perspectives of purple starthistle (*Centaurea calcitrapa*) leaf extracts: phtychemical analysis, cytotoxiscity, and antimicrobial activity." *AMB Express,* vol. 10, no. 183, 2020. doi:10.1186/s13568-020-01120-5

Hällzon, Patrick, et al. "Ethnobotany and Utilization Of the Oleaster, Elaeagnus angustifolia L. (fam. Elaeagnaceae), in Eastern Turkestan." *Orientalia Suecana,* vol. 71, 2022, pp. 38–61.

Knapp, Deborah W. "Detection of herbicides in the urine of pet dogs following home lawn chemical application." *Sci Total Environ.* vol. 456-457, 2013, 34–41. doi: 10.1016/j.scitotenv.2013.03.019. Accessed 20 Jan. 2024.

Lukas, Scott E., et al. "A Standardized Kudzu Extract (NPI-031) Reduces Alcohol Consumption in Nontreatment-seeking Male Heavy Drinkers." *Psychopharmacology (Berl)*, vol. 226, no. 1, Mar. 2013, pp. 65–73. National Library of Medicine, doi: 10.1007/s00213-012-2884-9

Mertens, Martha, et al. "Glyphosate, a chelating agent-relevant for ecological risk assessment?" *Environmental Science and Pollution Research International* vol. 25, no. 6, 2018, pp. 5298–5317. doi:10.1007/s11356-017-1080-1. Accessed 20 Jan. 2024.

Mohamed, Rima E., et al. "The Lowering Effect of Gum Arabic on Hyperlipidimia in Sudanese Patients." *Frontiers in Physiology*, vol. 6, art. 160, May 2015.

Rodgers, Vikki L. et al. "The invasive species Alliaria petiolata (garlic mustard) increases soil nutrient availability in northern hardwood-conifer forests." *Oecologia*, vol. 157, no. 3, Sep. 2008, pp. 459–471.

Sharma, Ajitha, et al. "Effect of ethanolic extract of *Acacia auriculiformis* leaves on learning and memory in rats." *Pharmacognosy Research*, vol. 6, no. 3, Jul.Sep. 2014, pp. 246–250, doi:10.4103/0974-8490.132605.

Uludag A, et al. "The effect of johnsongrass (Sorghum halepense (L.) Pers.) densities on cotton yield." *Pakistan Journal of Biological Sciences*, vol. 10, no. 3, Feb. 2007, pp. 523–525, doi: 10.3923/pjbs.2007.523.525.

Wright, Patrick Benjamin. "Accumulation of Heavy Metals in Conyza Canadensis and Implications for Phytoremediation." 2023. Christopher Newport U, MS thesis, https://www.proquest.com/openview/aaa1c433c2098d99b33eb466bd75eb62/1. Accessed 29 Jan. 2024.

Websites

Anderson, Michael. "Is Garlic Mustard an Invader or an Opportunist?" *American Scientist*, https://www.americanscientist.org/article/is-garlic-mustard-an-invader-or-an-opportunist. Accessed 22 July 2023.

Arkadian, Aerik. "What is a Fluid Condenser? (Part 1: Liquid Condensers)." 29 June 2023, https://aerikarkadian.com/2023/06/29/what-is-a-fluid-condenser-part-1/. Accessed 1 Aug. 2023.

"Black Locust Uses: A historic to modern guide." *Black Locust Lumber*, 17 Nov. 2020, https://www.blacklocustlumber.com/black-locust-uses-a-historic-to-modern-guide/. Accessed 28 Oct. 2023.

Charles, Dan. "Busted: EPA Discovers DOW Weedkiller Claim, Wants It Off the Market." NPR, 25 Nov. 2015, https://www.npr.org/sections/thesalt/2015/11/25/457393114/busted-epa-discovers-dow-weedkiller-claim-wants-it-off-the-market. Accessed 20 Jan. 2024.

Dobb, Edwin. "New Life in a Death Trap." *Discover*, 30 Nov. 2000, https://www.discovermagazine.com/environment/new-life-in-a-death-trap. Accessed 21 Jan. 2024.

"Elm." *The Goddess Tree,* http://www.thegoddesstree.com/trees/Elm.htm. Accessed 19 July 2023.

"Elm mythology and folklore," https://treesforlife.org.uk/into-the-forest/trees-plants-animals/trees/elm/elm-mythology-and-folklore/.Accessed 19 Jul. 2023.

Fay, Richard H. "The Connection Between Fairies and the Dead." *Classically Educated.* https://classicallyeducated.wordpress.com/2017/10/16/the-connection-between-fairies-and-the-dead. Accessed 19 July 2023.

Fern, Ken. "Acacia melanoxylon." *Temperate Plants,* 7 Jan. 2024, https://temperate.theferns.info/plant/Acacia+melanoxylon. Accessed 27 Oct. 2023.

"Find America's Oldest Juniper Tree in the Northern California Mountains." *Active NorCal,* 2 Nov. 2023, https://www.activenorcal.com/find-americas-oldest-juniper-tree-in-the-northern-california-mountains. Accessed 13 Aug. 2023.

Giblin, Chad, and Gary Johnson. "Dutch elm disease-resistant elm trees." *University of Minnesota Extension*, https://extension.umn.edu/trees-and-shrubs/dutch-elm-disease-resistant-elm-trees. Accessed 18 Jul. 2023.

History.com Editors. "Dust Bowl: Causes, Definition & Years." *History,* https://www.history.com/topics/great-depression/dust-bowl. Accessed 18 Jul. 2023.

"Historically Significant Perfume Recipes." *Perfume Workshop,* https://www.perfumeworkshop.com/perfumeoil-historical.html. Accessed 6 Aug. 2023.

Howard, Janet L. "Sorghem halepense." *Fire Effects Information System,* 2004, https://www.fs.usda.gov/database/feis/plants/graminoid/sorhal/all.html. Accessed 10 Nov. 2023.

Hutcheson, Corey. "Blog Post 130—War Water." *New World Witchery—The Search for American Traditional Witchcraft*, https://www.facebook.com/WordPresscom, 7 June 2011, https://newworldwitchery.com/2011/06/07/blog-post-130-%E2%80%93-war-water/. Accessed 26 Feb. 2024.

Ioqayin. "Shapeshifting and a (WIP) Lycanthropic Ritual." *Tumblr,* 2015, https://ioqayin.tumblr.com/post/93666654796/shapeshifting-and-a-wip-lycanthropic-ritual. Accessed 3 Nov. 2023.

Kimmerer, Robin Wall. "The 'Honorable Harvest': Lessons from an Indigenous Tradition of Giving Thanks." *Yes! Magazine,* 26 Nov. 2016, https://www.yesmagazine.org/issue/good-health/2015/11/26/the-honorable-harvest-lessons-from-an-indigenous-tradition-of-giving-thanks. Accessed 20 Jan. 2024.

Meier, Allison. "The Transformative Influence of Alchemy on Art." *Hyperallergic,* 15 Nov. 2016, https://hyperallergic.com/327969/the-transformative-history-of-alchemy-and-art/. Accessed 20 Jan. 2024.

Meyer, Rachelle. "Albizia julibrissin." *Fire Effects Information System,* 2010, updates 30 Jan. 2018, https://www.fs.usda.gov/database/feis/plants/tree/albjul/all.html. Accessed 8 Nov. 2023.

Moss, Rebecca. "Rethinking the dreaded Siberian elm." *Santa Fe New Mexican,* https://www.santafenewmexican.com/news/local_news/rethinking-the-dreaded-siberian-elm/article_60654cca-f0a3-565a-8909-e36cd7e8d6a6.html. Accessed 18 Jul. 2023.

National Pesticide Information Center. "2, 4-D: General Fact Sheet." *Oregon State University Website,* Mar. 2009, http://npic.orst.edu/factsheets/24Dgen.html#wildlife. Accessed 20 Jan. 2024.

O'Driscoll, Dana. "Sacred Tree Profile: Black Locust's Medicine, Magic, Mythology and Meaning." *The Druids Garden,* 16 Apr. 2022. https://thedruidsgarden.com/2019/11/10/sacred-tree-profile-black-locusts-medicine-magic-mythology-and-meanings/. Accessed 28 Oct. 2023.

Osterloff, Emily. "What's so bad about the spotted lanternfly?" *Natural History Museum,* 15 Oct. 2021, https://www.nhm.ac.uk/discover/whats-so-bad-about-the-spotted-lanternfly.html. Accessed 30 Oct. 2023.

Pearlstine, Elise. "Enfleurage: Perfume Vocabulary and Fragrance Notes." *Bois de Jasmin: A Primer on Sensory Pursuits,* 13 Apr. 2011, https://boisdejasmin.com/2011/04/perfume-vocabulary-and-fragrance-notes-enfleurage.html. Accessed 6 Aug. 2023.

Plant Conservation Society. "Fact Sheet: Siberian Elm," *Plant Conservation Alliance's Alien Plant Working Group,* 28 Oct. 2005, https://www.invasive.org/alien/fact/pdf/ulpu1.pdf. Accessed 20 Jul. 2023.

Routhier, Ray. "Yarmouth braces for Herbie the tree's demise." *Press Herald,* 10 Aug. 2009, updated 5 Apr. 2016, https://www.pressherald.com/2009/08/10/yarmouth-braces-trees-demise/. Accessed 20 July 2023.

Rose, Melody. "Horseweed (Erigeron canadensis) Useful Plant, or Noxious Weed?" *Dave's Garden*, 3 Aug. 2019, https://davesgarden.com/guides/

articles/horseweed-erigeron-canadensis-useful-plant-or-noxious-weed. Accessed 5 Aug. 2023.

Ring, Jessica. "How to Use Different Base Alcohols in Botanical Perfumery." *Ring Botanicals*, 5 Mar. 2020, https://www.ringbotanicals.com/blogs/news/how-to-use-the-different-base-alcohols-in-botanical-perfumery. Accessed 6 Aug. 2023.

Sedbrook, Danielle. "2,4-D: The Most Dangerous Pesticide You've Never Heard Of." *NRDC*, 15 Mar. 2016, https://www.nrdc.org/stories/24-d-most-dangerous-pesticide-youve-never-heard. Accessed 6 Nov. 2023.

Sheff, Elaine. "Tending Mother Ocean: Herbs for the Lymph—Green Path Herb School." *Green Path Herb School*, Green Path Herb School, 28 Jan. 2016, https://www.greenpathherbschool.com/greenpathblog/tending-mother-ocean-herbs-for-the-lymph. Accessed 26 Feb. 2024.

"The Art of Enfleurage in Perfumery." *Wit & West Perfumes*, 19 April 2023, https://witandwest.com/blogs/wit-west-blog-field-notes/the-art-of-enfleurage-in-perfumery. Accessed 6 Aug. 2023.

The Witch is In. "Historical Witchcraft 101: Shapeshifting." *Tumblr*, 2 Jan. 2020, https://herecomesthewitch.tumblr.com/post/190017798129/historical-witchcraft-101-shapeshifting. Accessed 3 Nov. 2023.

Thompson, Chris. "The Ancestors and the Hollow Hills." *Story Archaeology*, 21 Sept. 2013, https://storyarchaeology.com/the-ancestors-and-the-hollow-hills/. Accessed 19 July 2023.

Tobin, Laura Giunta. "Beignet d'Acacia: Acacia Flower Fritters." *Your Guardian Chef*, 6 May 2018, update 21 Apr. 2023, https://yourguardianchef.com/beignet-dacacia-acacia-fritters-recipe-2/. Accessed 1 Sept. 2023.

United States Forest Service. "Four Threats." *US Forest Service Website*. 30 Oct. 2006, https://www.fs.usda.gov/projects-policies/four-threats/. Accessed 20 Jan. 2024.

"Wildcrafting, Wildtending, and Reciprocity." *Milk & Honey Herbs*, 17 Jul. 2018, https://www.milkandhoneyherbs.com/blog/2018/7/17/wildcrafting-wildtending-and-reciprocity. Accessed 11 Nov. 2023.

Wong, Mei. "Dandelion Cookies and Pickled Buds." *Medium*, 11 May 2017, https://medium.com/@3LittleBears/dandelion-flower-cookies-and-pickled-buds-2630d85b8765. Accessed 20 Jan. 2024.

Index

I

J

K

L

M

N

O

P

R

S

T

U

V

W

Z